VIBRATION OF DIVINE CONSCIOUSNESS
A Spiritual Autobiography

Sadguru Kedarji

The Bhakta School of Transformation, Inc.
Youngstown, Ohio

VIBRATION OF DIVINE CONSCIOUSNESS
A Spiritual Autobiography

Copies of this book may be ordered through booksellers or by contacting:

The Bhakta School of Transformation, Inc.
330-623-7388 Ext 10

NityanandaShaktipatYoga.org

ISBN: 979-8-218-13365-8

Printed in the United States of America

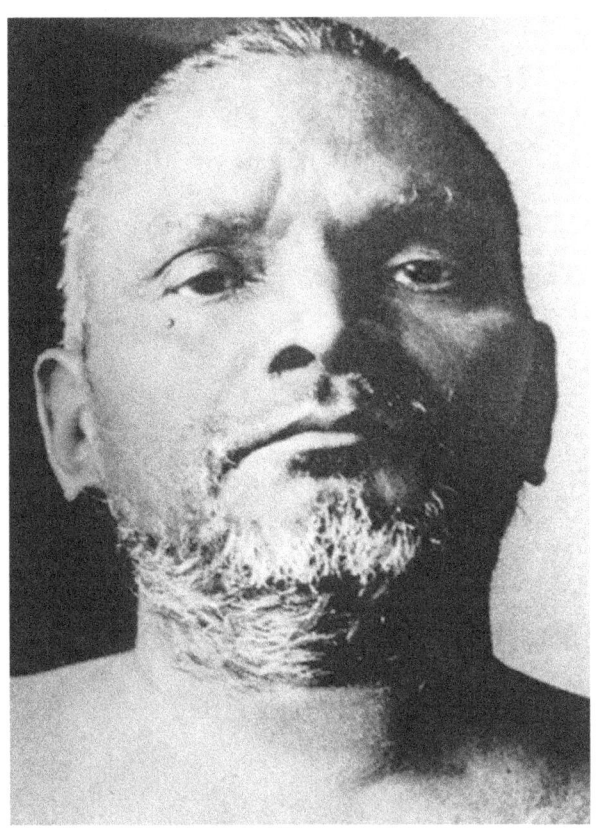

In Honor of Shri Bhagawan Nityananda of Ganeshpuri

Contents

Invocation

Om Sri Guru Mahadev

You are beyond this manifold Universe
And have become everything in it

You are the thought of a thought
The witness to all thoughts
The source of all thoughts
The rising and setting of all thoughts
And that which causes thought to emerge

You are the taste in taste
You are the sight in sight
You are that which hears
You are the feeling in feeling
You are the one who smells

Om Sri Guru Mahadev

You are the word in the words
The power behind the syllables
The sound inherent in the power of
Those syllables
The power behind the power in that sound
And the one who makes it possible to
Understand and to perceive

You are the perception in perception
The Consciousness behind all consciousness
The sense in sense pleasures
And that which causes the senses to perceive
Yet you are also beyond the senses
And you are also the means of going
Beyond the senses

Om Sri Guru Mahadev
Pashupati Guru Mahadev

You are both immanent and transcendental
And the one who gives meaning to
The phrase immanent and transcendental

You become the object of all ideation
The object of all thought
And yet you are also not the objects that you become,
Reflecting those objects in your own being

You are the one in the many
And the many in the one
You are Spanda Shakti
That power that manifests the perception
Of a world, the perception of a Universe
Yet you have never taken birth
And you have never died either

Om Sri Guru Mahadev

You are the whisper behind the whisper
That dissolves in the wind of the fire
That is contained in your heart,
That same breath that creates, sustains
And withdraws the memory of existence
In the body of your consciousness

You are the created, the uncreated and
That which is beyond the perception of all creation

Om Sri Guru Mahadev
Pashupati Guru Mahadev

You are both real and unreal,
The awareness that gives birth to a Universe

Like the child of a barren woman,
There is no relationship between you
And that which manifests through
Your Spanda Shakti

And yet you thread through everything in this world,
So close, so intimate,
and higher than any concept
Or notion can grasp

Om Sri Guru Mahadev

Who are you? When the question dissolves
The answer is Self-evident
Behind all veils, you are the one
Pretending to hide
Indeed, you become the very veil
That you cover yourself with,
How beautiful is your play!

And you are the one who removes
The veil that you have cast on yourself
With your own hand,
Disguising yourself
And revealing yourself
For your own amusement, while remaining
The one who is the witness to it all

Om Sri Guru Mahadev
Pashupati Guru Mahadev

One without a second
There can be no other
What use is glory when you are behind it
What use is time when you are
The one behind it
What use is pleasure
When you are behind it
What use is pain
When you are the one behind it

You make what cannot be fathomed,
Readily experienced by the awareness
Of your being

By thinking of you, one experiences god
By worshipping you, one becomes god
The unreachable is reached by you
The unattainable is attained by you

That which is unfathomable
Is easily ascertained by your awareness

Once your are known, everything is known
Even as you wander about
As if knowing nothing

Look, see there.
You are everywhere,
In everything and in everyone

It is you who is looking
At the one who is looking
It is you who is seeking
The one who is seeking
Oh, how playful you are!

To that one who is the root cause of everything created and
uncreated in this world,
To that one who is the root cause of everything that can be
experienced in this world,
To that one, by whose command I write these pages to glorify
God and my Gurudev,
To that Shiva I bow.

Acknowledgements

I Dwell In The Timelessness of Love

I sing and I dance in the glory of my Shri Gurudev. By so many blessings of Grace, bestowed on me by my Guru and our time-honored Siddha lineage, I now dwell in the timelessness of Love, forever. O my Beloved, how can I ever repay you? It is not possible. Therefore, I make this offering as the only way I have of thanking you for what I can never adequately repay.

I Am What My Guru Made Me

There is no such thing as ignorance. It is imagined, superimposed. And if there is no such thing as ignorance, how can there be such a thing as Liberation? This is the direct experience that my Shri Gurudev has blessed me with.

I am what my Guru made me!

Some have asked, "Is Kedarji liberated, God-realized?" God is everywhere and in everything. That Supreme Self, the Shiva-Shakti power is the reason we taste sweetness, see beauty, feel both love and hatred, experience compassion, are drawn to sense pleasures, experience fear and fearlessness, desire to be honorable and ethical, as well as, the opposite and, ultimately come to know That which is behind the veil of all these things.

When this is the case how can it be so hard to realize God with the Grace of a Siddha?

I am what my Guru made me! By his so many Blessings of Grace, he entered me and took up residence in me. He destroyed the karmas that I had manufactured to cover up an entire ocean of Love!

So, is Kedarji Liberated? Speak to my devotees and disciples to know more. Because, if I say so, people will say, "Look! He's tooting his own horn. He's self-proclaiming so how can he be Self-realized?"

I am content with what my Guru has bestowed on me. It is not even possible for me to get him out of my mind. My Guru permeates my thoughts. By His Grace, the Siddhas of our lineage are fully present for me. My Guru floods my mind and body, even before I see his form inside. Gurudev appears to me in visions, dreams and in my waking state and is as real for me as those I encounter throughout my day. The Siddhas of our lineage come to me regularly as well.

My Shri Nityananda resides in me and is ever-present. By the Blessing and Grace of my Guru, Shivaji dwells in my heart. I see him there as clearly as I see this page that I am typing these words on. So many Blessings of Grace! What other state should I want!?

I wake up with my heart singing and dancing with indescribable Joy. This state never leaves me. By the mere thought of my Shri Gurudev, I am inspired from within as to both the day's tasks that must be undertaken and all the decisions that must be made, connected to the running of our school, retreat center and organization. This inspiration is my Guru's will and it is unfailing and ever-present.

In one way or another, the Siddhas of our lineage of the Yoga of the Siddhas have all said that the full understanding and direct experience of God's two aspects, the Transcendental and the Immanent, as the play of the Shakti as this world – that one's understanding through direct experience of these must be complete in order to realize the highest. My Guru spoke of this also.

I am what my Guru made me!

What I can tell you is this: for a spiritual journey to be true, it must culminate in the constant, uninterrupted experience that the subtle is, at least, as real as the gross. And there must be signs of this growing experience along the way.

All boundaries between the Transcendental, formless Absolute and the expression of that Ultimate Reality (both the cause and the effect) as this world appearance must be obliterated permanently.

As there, so here. For the one experiencing, there can be no difference between the two, for that is the Joy of all joys.

I have been blessed by my Guru's Grace with a permanent state of indescribable Joy - Bliss beyond measure that is a state of constant rapture that does not fit into worldly, mundane perceptions, beliefs, notions or opinions of such a state. I had to surrender my own such notions in order to receive the incalculable. What can such a state be called?

I am what my Guru made me!

Due to this Blessing of Grace, I found God everywhere – even in gardens, in paved, crowded cities and in forests and abandoned places. As a result, I know and experience, without a doubt, that this world is nothing but a paradise of Joy!

If, after reading this, there are others who say that God-realization is a state other than what I have shared of my experience here, fine. But then whatever that 'othern than' is, I don't want it. In the loving arms of my Guru I am carried to beyond the beyond! I exist there and here simultaneously and forever.

Therefore, I am content with what my Guru has bestowed on me, content with what my Guru has made of me.

If I have power, it is His power and the power of my beloved Siddhas of our lineage (https://www.nityanandashaktipatyoga.org/our-lineage/).

If I have Love to share, it is His Love and the Love of Shri Bhagawan Nityananda of Ganeshpuri who is also the full embodiment of my Lord Shiva.

Kedarji is the name my Guru gave me after entering me through Shaktipat. But whose name is it really, when I am *That*? I am He and He is me. All that I am and have to give is my Shri Gurudev. This offering is made by His command. I place my head at His lotus feet forever! Jai Muktananda Mahan! Jai Nityananda Bhagawan! Jai Shiva, Shiva, Shiva!

I also offer my thanks to the Shakta Adepts in the Spanda School of Trika Shaivism and Vedanta, including; Vasuguptacharya, Vyasa, Abhinavaguptacharya, Bhagavad Utapala, Utpaladeva, Ksemaraja, the sage Vasistha and Jnaneshwar Maharaj. To my ancestors in the Choctaw and Shawnee tribes I also bow and give Thanks.

To my teachers in the field of Holistic Health and Healing including, George Oshawa, Mischio Kushi, Lima Oshawa, Aveline Kushi, Ann Marie Colbin and Weiru Ohashi of Ohashi Institute. These people were first responsible for my longing for well-being. I give thanks to them also.

Om Guru Om,
Kedarji

Introduction

It is my experience and absolute conviction that everyone in this world desires to be happy. *Everyone,* from the beggar to the businessman to the criminal, wants to experience peace and joy on a permanent basis. Permanence is the issue. Where does one find these on a permanent basis **and in a way that is uninterrupted?** *Saints appear on this planet in order to lead us on a path that becomes the answer to this question.*

You are all great beings. Your perfection is already with you. Your task is to break the karmic habit of hiding this fact from yourself. You have acquired a state of amnesia. You have forgotten that you are the Self, that Highest Power that is the cause and effect of everything and everyone. This amnesia is your identity crisis. You need a certain medicine to cure this.

I have written this work out of my experience of finding this cure. I want to share my experiences in retracing my steps back to the Self, under the instruction and guidance of my spiritual leader, but also to advocate for permanent spiritual transformation. So, this is a book for those who want to adopt a spiritual lifestyle that leads to permanent spiritual transformation and higher and higher states of spiritual awareness. This is also a book for those who want a better understanding of the approach to discovering and realizing one's true nature, *the Self, also called the Supreme Principle, Supreme Intelligence or God.*

The great beings tell us to honor the sacred in everything and everyone, in every day life. This is a matter of Love, a matter of the Heart. Life is the stage on which the amazing unfolding of this *play of Divine Consciousness* takes place. And life is the stage for realizing our True nature in the moment, from moment-to-moment, in the transforming Love of the true Heart.

Spiritual life cannot be sustained without Love. It cannot be sustained without the experience of the Abode of The Heart, that purest place within us that reflects light, love, compassion and forgiveness everywhere. Going to this sacred place within is how we remember the Self; that Love, Peace and Joy that is who we really are. This is the only way to permanent spiritual transformation.

There is a Consciousness within each of us waiting to be fully realized and embraced. *This Consciousness is a Love so pure that it is without distinctions.* Embracing it allows us to love ourselves and others so fully, and without conditionality, regardless of the varying levels of interaction we engage in that are dictated by the roles we play. *This Consciousness is everything about us that is sacred and whole.* It is a spiritual awareness imbued with Joy, Peace and Total Freedom. That is who we really are. We just have to stop hiding this fact from ourselves.

In this book, you will find that I place emphasis on the relationship between a true spiritual leader (a.k.a. Sadguru) in a spiritually-perfected Master, and the student or devotee who may, one day, choose to adopt a spiritual lifestyle in order to retrace his/her steps back to God. The final state, sometimes referred to as Liberation, Self-realization or God-realization is indescribable. However, it is a state that, in our approach, can be understood and experienced in a very specific way.

The state to be had, the culmination of any true spiritual approach and all true spiritual practice, can be known through the experience of the fullness of Humanity in the constant delight of the inner Self. To argue over labels will not allow you to get your feet into the ocean of Love that embodies this state, as it is a state beyond all names and labels.

After having participated in a variety of spiritual approaches and paths, it is my experience and firm conviction that a relationship must be established between the spiritually-perfected Master and the student or devotee, for genuine and permanent spiritual transformation to occur. Because true spiritual leadership is required. Indeed, we learn best by example. So, this relationship is necessary for a period of time, until the devotee reaches a level of practice where he/she is steeped in Sadhana (daily spiritual practice under the leadership of a living Master - see Chapter 23, *The Bond of Power*).

Our approach is embodied in the very ancient oral tradition of the Shakta lineage. In today's world, the words 'Guru,' 'Master,' 'Self-realized Being' often frighten people and prevent them from allowing themselves to be taught. This is, in part, due to poor behavior on the part of some 'gurus.' However, just as you would not stop buying a car (a necessity if you rely on a car for your travel) just because you purchased a couple of 'lemons' in the past, in spiritual life, if you desire permanent spiritual transformation, you should not stop seeking out a Master who can not only teach you, but who has the power to give you a direct experience of what is being taught. Continue to seek out such a being, even if you have read about or have experienced one who turned out not to be authentic.

In the approach of the holy beings of my lineage, to be taught by one who has attained the state you seek is essential. If you've never experienced the constant state of rapture that the great beings describe as being awash in an uninterrupted state of Peace, Joy, Content and Love without conditions, *how will you find it on your own, without being led to it?*

I want to help 'demystify' our approach and the role of the Master with some simple definitions. **The dictionary defines the word 'mentor' as a wise and trusted counselor or teacher.** In our approach, the Sadguru (true spiritual leader) is just that, *a wise and trusted spiritual companion and mentor.* **The difference between a spiritual teacher and a living Master is that the Shakta Adept, the living Sadguru** *gives you the direct experience of what is being taught, by way of the power of Grace.*

For this reason, the words 'Master,' 'Sadguru,' 'Shakta Adept' or 'Spiritual Leader' may be used interchangeably in this book to refer to the wise and trusted spiritual companion who has been given the authority, and also *earned* the right to lead others to permanent spiritual transformation and the *Abode of the Heart* we refer to as the inner Self – by *mastering* what he/she has been taught by another living Master, by way of direct inner experience.

Our Shakta Approach

The lineage of Shakta Adepts, spiritually-perfected Masters to which I belong, is the Shakta, Parampara lineage of Lord Shiva. The Internet is ripe with confusing and skewed definitions for some of the terms used by our lineage of spiritual leaders. Here are some helpful definitions taken from our sacred texts.

Shakta Approach - The entrance into the Shakta Upaya (upaya means approach) that begins with full Shakti Awakening or full Kundalini awakening. This initiates one into the power of live Mantras, with the experience that the power of your longing, your feeling and devotion, burns away all that you are not. This approach also embodies the easy means of purifying all of the subtle spiritual energy centers of all the karmic impressions that keep one's true nature concealed from oneself. A Shakta adept is the *catalyst and leader* for this unfolding approach.

Shakta Adept - A Shakta Adept in our lineage is a Master or spiritually-perfected leader (Sadguru), a Self-realized Love Being. Spiritually-perfected means Self-realized or God-realized. In our approach, this is a state where one experiences and is able to express the fullness of Humanity in the constant delight of the inner Self. *Such beings are rare* (see Chapter 4).

Sad means true. A Sadguru in our lineage is a true, living spiritual leader or Shakta Adept who has the ability to transmit the Grace-bestowing power of a lineage of Sadgurus, through *Shaktipat. Such a being is a Love being* who has stored up the *maximum* amount of Divine Conscious Energy (Shakti) necessary to fully awaken this dormant energy in others. A spiritual mentor such as this does not harm others and, instead, uplifts them (see page 60).

Just as a teacher or mentor is required in the arts, sciences, athletics and so on in order to become really competent in those fields, so too in the field of permanent spiritual transformation, a competent living Master is required – *one who has attained the goal of spiritual life.* True spiritual approaches exist in order to provide the leadership necessary to lead people to union with Divine Consciousness or the Self, an active principle that is indescribable and Universal.

However, in order to realize one's true nature completely and experience the Natural, Free State of the inner Self, one has to take a companion in the living Master, until one has become rooted in one's own true state of Joy, Bliss and Divinity. It was due to this understanding that I consciously chose a Shakta Adept to initiate me and to lead me.

Such a being is a spiritual companion who leads by example and has an impeccable ability to instruct you. In our approach, the living Sadguru is the easy means. The means to what? *The means to leading you to the revelation of your perfection, to the inner Guru, the primordial Guru that we refer to as the Shiva-Shakti power (the highest power); after which, over time, you merge with That.*

This process takes time. If you are impatient, or if your expectation is to see profound, permanent shifts in your awareness overnight, you will be disappointed. Permanent spiritual transformation requires a steady spiritual practice and some time, although not necessarily a lot of time. With the right Spiritual Mentor, you can realize your true nature in 12, 9, 6 or even 3 years. For some it will take longer. *But we are talking about a matter of years, not weeks or months.*

In light of the many allegations (some of them well-founded) regarding Gurus and cults, I have set aside an entire chapter in this book entitled *The Bond of Power*. If you want to understand how spiritual practice and permanent spiritual transformation are attained in our approach, please read Chapter 23 carefully.

Because I was raised on a spiritual path that uses the Sanskrit language (the oldest language known to human kind), I have grown fond of using certain Sanskrit words due to the power they carry. I will use the transliteration of those words throughout this book. Please refer to the glossary for the meanings and pronunciation of these words.

Kali Yuga

As of this writing, we are a little more than halfway through the Kali Yuga age. This is the last of the four ages spoken about in some of our scriptures and other sacred texts, and also made reference to by the holy beings of our lineage – in which there is a gradual and firm decline in true spiritual experience when the masses turn away from God, in favor of the perceived pleasures of worldliness. This is why so many holy beings have graced the planet in this age.

There are debilitating qualities of this Kali Yuga age that, when understood, will help you to imbibe the spiritual *urgency* of what you read in this book. Some of those qualities are:

- A time ruled by lust, excessive sex and the pursuit of personal power.

- Dominated by people's attachment to words, causing the brainwashing of the masses and mind control, where attachment to pleasure and pain are concerned.
- The destruction of true spiritual awareness in favor of false notions like God is the body and what can be acquired and enjoyed through the senses.
- Abandonment of the common good.
- The complete decline of the collective spiritual awareness of the masses.
- Taking refuge in the personal gain of people, places and things.
- The pursuit of wealth and fame and the worship of these.
- A pill for everything, expressed as the desire of the masses to take refuge in mind-altering drugs that cause the increased desire for fantasy fulfillment.
- The increased preference for superficiality by the masses.
- The decline of Human Dignity, especially where female-embodied beings are concerned.

Unless you've been living in total isolation or on another planet, I think you will agree that the above points made by the Saints do, in fact, qualify much about the age that we now live in. This is why, with respect to permanent spiritual transformation, the great beings tell us "Do it now. Don't wait."

The understanding of the spiritually-perfected Love beings of our approach is that Divine Consciousness contracts to take the form of language so that the Universe can manifest and be sustained. Without letters, syllables, words and sentences this world would not exist. **Divine Consciousness is indescribable. It is truly beyond words.** But the human intellect, until merged into the Self or the Supreme Principle, requires words in order to direct its attention toward that which is indescribable. We call these words/labels 'educational terms.'

There is but one Divine force that exists inside each and every one of us, that is also apparent everywhere in the Universe. This Supreme Intelligence or Highest Power or Divine Energy exists equally in every living thing and has contracted to take the form of insentient objects as well. This same Absolute, this same Divinity is also known as God, Supreme Consciousness, the Supreme Being, Shiva, Shakti, Yahweh, Jesus Christ, Great Spirit, the Ultimate Reality, the Absolute, Jah, Rah, Allah, Divine Consciousness, the Self, etc. All are a reference to this same indescribable principle that creates, sustains and withdraws everything.

In some cases, words like Shiva, Jesus Christ, Mohammed, Buddha and Krishna are also names of great beings who lived on this planet in human form. Throughout this book, when it comes to speaking of the Self, the Ultimate Reality or Cause, I will use several of these names interchangeably. Just know that I use these labels with the understanding that they are attempts at defining that which is beyond language and in which language finds its support.

ALL of these names point to that one unifying principal, the Supreme I-Consciousness, that is apparent everywhere and that also dwells EQUALLY inside every human being. So, try not to get stuck on any of the educational terms. Do whatever it takes to get your feet into the water so that you can begin swimming in the ocean of your own Bliss, the Joy and Love of the Heart.

For example: If you are having trouble with the references here that you are God or the Self, *then you can begin with the understanding that it is possible that you are much greater than you think you are.* At the very least, I encourage you to start there, if it makes it easier for you to listen and imbibe.

The purpose of Yoga is the transformation of limited human awareness into Divine Awareness of The Ultimate Reality. This is the discipline of which I am a part and it is the subject of this book. **There is *no disparity* between worldly life and spiritual aspiration.** In fact, our approach harmonizes these two in the culmination of the direct experience of one's own inner Peace and Joy, while going about one's daily activities.

To begin to understand the inner Self, you must believe that ANYONE (starting with you) can realize one's true nature, that sacred space within, with the right spiritual leadership and practice. To begin to understand this, you also have to cultivate the belief that it is a mistake to think that you have lived too long in your old, contracted ways to change now. It does not matter how long a room has been dark. If you light a candle in that dark room, the light still shines immediately, filling the entire darkness with light. And if you believe that God only dwells in heaven and that he looks down on us in judgment and punishment, you will find it difficult to embrace any part of this book.

Above all else, to begin to understand what you read in these pages, you have to be willing to, at least, open yourself to the possibility that Divinity actually dwells inside you and that you carry the promise of becoming one with the Self that you already are, *by breaking the habit of hiding this fact from yourself.*

In this book, I share the experiences of my Sadhana (spiritual journey under the guidance of a living Master) and the transformation that occurred as a result. I am eternally grateful for the light of my Master's touch and the perfection transmitted to me that led me to imbibe the Truth. The spiritual leader in the Shakta Adept truly is the means.

It is to describe my experience of the God-Principle or Shiva-Shakti principle and how one attains permanent spiritual transformation by recognizing that principle, that I write this work. Through the instruction of the spiritually-perfected Love beings and the leadership in daily spiritual practice that I received from my spiritual companion and mentor, I have become completely alive. I have been transformed spiritually, emotionally and physically.

I experienced this transformation while living in this world, while going about my daily work and routine, while interacting with wife, friends, relatives, family and business associates, and while earning a living in my chosen profession at the time. Without selling my belongings and moving to a deserted place, I perfected my practice and retraced my steps back to God. Through the Grace of my Master I reached the final goal.

The significance of this still leaves me in awe. I write this work so that those I serve, and may come to serve, can better understand how close at hand Bliss really is and how this Divine Conscious Energy threads through every experience we have in our lives.

For those who want a personal relationship with this Supreme Intelligence, for those who want to become more aware of the power behind their own existence, I write these words. **Certainly, if a wretch like me can realize his true nature, so can you, so can anyone!**

For those whose hearts are ready to receive, I offer this book.

My Journey Home

In life there are many journeys. But there is only one journey that will take you to the Truth. That journey begins with the understanding of Shivo' ham – I am Shiva, I am the inner Self.

Chapter 1
My Early Seeking

My Life and Early Career In The Performing Arts

My mother was a great opera diva who performed all over the world. She had a great career that was cut short when she decided to raise my brother and I. One might say that she decided to express herself through us. My mother trained us in the Performing Arts. She taught us to sing, dance and act.

As a result, I had an early career as a child actor in starring roles on Broadway, landing my earliest roles in the musical *Maggie Flynn* and the play *The Great White Hope*. My younger years were spent travelling as a working actor with many known celebrities of the time. I enjoyed this period of my life because I had the opportunity to make audiences happy by performing in shows and I loved interacting with people.

I left my acting career in my late teens to pursue music. I studied violin, piano, composition and conducting, graduating from Manhattan School of Music with a degree in performance. Right out of school, I spent several years earning my living exclusively as a performing artist. During this time, I saw the powerful effect the Performing Arts have on people's inner state.

I saw that a skilled performing artist has the power to take people anywhere they want to go, to experience any emotion and any state of being, at least temporarily. It was at this time that I decided to compose music and learn music improvisation as a means of experiencing my creativity and becoming more creative. This experience of creating changed my vision of the world. It was my first real glimpse into the mystery of all creation, something I wanted to know much more about.

Holistic Healing

In my early teens, I suffered a variety of illnesses, one right after the other. My mother became very concerned about my health and felt I needed a change in diet. She bought me a book and demanded I read it. The book was *Sugar Blues*, a popular volume by Gloria Swanson and Bill Dufty that spoke of the dangers of processed sugar and processed foods and outlined a movement that was fast-growing in America at the time, *Macrobiotics.*

I became invigorated by the concept that a diet high in organic veggies, legumes, whole grains and fruit could change awareness. So, I engaged in the study of Macrobiotics, changing my diet completely by starting with a 3-week, brown rice fast. I stopped eating red meat, chicken and pork. I removed white sugar from my diet and I stopped smoking. My health did improve drastically. As a result, I moved into the Kushi Institute, run by Mischio Kushi, one of the founders of the Macrobiotic movement here in the West. There I studied Oriental Medicine, Macrobiotics, and learned to cook.

Michio's philosophy was that one can experience a closeness to the Self and a desire to know the Self by eating a diet that aligns one's body with its natural vibration. This includes eating foods grown in season, in the region one lives in. In my case, it worked. Similar to the experience I had when becoming more creative in the Performing Arts, Macrobiotics and my time spent in the company of Michio Kushi studying Oriental Medicine and graduating from the Kushi Institute did alter my vision of the world and my perception of life. My longing to become more spiritual increased as a result.

Experience of Death

In junior high school I became obsessed with all things occult. I consumed books on white and black witchcraft before finally settling on the Tarot. I actually became quite knowledgeable and had a steady clientele of fellow classmates (and their parents) who came to our house for readings. The Tarot opened me to the understanding that other worlds exist and power is not simply that which is defined by money and political influence.

During these years, I developed a psychic ability I did not know I had. I would often see visions or get premonitions about people just before they arrived for a Tarot reading. I then shared with them what I saw without reading the cards. This started to happen more and more regularly.

Again, all this served to intensify my desire to know God.

During my career in the Performing Arts, I had spent a good deal of time getting to know the celebrities I performed with. Later, while pursuing business ownership, I was mentored by wealthy business owners who were millionaires. I came to know them personally, and also spent time with their families.

What I observed in these people is that, even though they had fulfilled so many of their worldly desires and fantasies, they weren't happy. They did not know peace. When I asked them "What is Love?" they did not have an answer. When I asked, "Are you happy?," they answered "Who is really happy. I'm normal."

Through this experience I decided that the people whose lifestyles I wanted, the people who I had looked up to and wanted to be like for so long, had not attained what I was seeking. So, I decided not to pursue their lifestyles.

It was at this time that I started to ask the questions; **Is this all there is? What is fate? What is destiny? Who am I? Why am I here? Why was I born?**

During this period of my life I had an experience of death. I was riding in a car with my mother and brother. The car suddenly veered off the road on a sharp corner and flipped over into a ravine. The car landed upside down and was almost completely flattened. My mother and brother were thrown several feet from the car and escaped injury. I was pinned inside the car. A boulder had smashed through the roof of the car and landed on my chest. My body was pinned between this boulder and the floor. I was unable to breathe.

I was not breathing but I was still conscious. Suddenly, my awareness left my body and I found myself hovering several feet in the air above the wreck. I could see my mother and brother on the road being tended to by paramedics. As I looked straight down, I saw my body trapped inside the car and I saw rescue workers with saws, carving away the metal in an attempt to get to me. *I hovered in the air watching this scene with complete calm for several minutes.*

I then heard my mother screaming my name hysterically. With this, I found myself back in my body. I was being dragged from the wreck and my breathing began again on its own. As the rescue workers attempted to revive me, I sat up on my own and called out to my mother and brother. Although my chest was a little bruised, I had no other injuries.

This experience caused me to pause and contemplate my entire life. I knew I had experienced death. *I wanted to know who it was that was able to witness my body and this entire event in this way.* This was the first time that I understood that there is more to a human being than just this body.

My Years As A Seeker

I first started meditating as part of my study of martial arts. I studied Karate, Kung Fu and Jeet Kun Do. Each of these disciplines required the study and practice of Meditation. The Meditation was of the Buddhist tradition and, as a result, I embarked upon the study of Zen Buddhism for several years.

Although Zen Buddhism sparked my interest in Meditation, I felt there was still something missing. My mind still troubled me and I was not able to quiet it. After Buddhism, I engaged in several different meditation paths, including Transcendental Meditation. I followed a number of gurus during this time, all of whom were great teachers in their own right.

Still I did not experience the bliss of Meditation that I had heard about. I found it difficult to enter into a thought-free state, let alone maintain it. I later realized that what was missing for me was the spiritual awakening that would allow me to experience a more spontaneous Meditation. I also needed a master teacher who had completely realized the goal of his own practice.

I had become very wary of cults and gurus and I had become skeptical of spiritual paths in general. But still, deep in my heart, I knew I needed the right Master and approach. I had yet to find such a path.

My Upbringing In Churches

I was born a Catholic and raised a Catholic in my early youth. As a young boy, I went to Catholic school and became an altar boy in my local church. I embraced Catholicism completely at that time, mostly because I loved the stories of Jesus Christ and his life. I had always wished that I could have lived in a time when such a being existed in the flesh. My mother, however, was raised in the Baptist tradition. After my mother and father divorced, I spent a great deal of time in the Baptist church.

I loved the ritual of the Catholic ceremony and I really took to the Gospel tradition of the Baptists. "Catching the spirit" also intrigued me. Although I loved aspects of both these traditions, I wanted to know and wanted to have a direct experience of God, as a constant in my life. I did not feel I was getting that from either of these paths.

The experience of joy, peace, bliss, happiness, abundance, fearlessness, courage and strength -- these are things that I wanted to stop talking about over cocktails and coffee and wanted to experience directly; not just a little or once in a while, but on a constant basis.

Starting in my late teens, I came to observe that, here in the West, many religious paths form a type of "spectator" practice where intellectual discourses are dispensed and then the celebration is over before it even gets started -- *like someone talking about a fabulous meal without ever serving it up.* It was this experience, and the lack of teachers who practiced fully what they preached, that led me away from the traditional approach to religion and spirituality that I found to be so common.

I had to find something that *was not* just about the psychology of religion, but something that would give me a direct experience of the Ultimate Reality.

Chapter 2
Shaktipat – Full Kundalini Awakening

There is no point in continuing to remain a seeker. **In fact, the point of all spiritual seeking is to find a way to *end your seeking*.** *To bring your seeking to an end, full Shakti Awakening and the leadership of a living Shakta adept is necessary.* Such Beings are rare.

God is always watching. God is always listening. It's important to remember this. Crossing paths with a Shakta adept, a living Master, is something *we* cause to happen. The spiritually-perfected companion in the Living Master does not seek us out. We make a request and God grants that request in our crossing paths with a Shakta Adept. Some people remember exactly when they made the request in the present life or a previous life, others have forgotten. But the request was made, nonetheless.

For me, the request began with those questions I shared in the previous chapter during my early seeking: **Is this all there is? What is fate? What is destiny? Who am I? Why am I here? Why was I born?** Then I made a direct request to fully know the answers to these questions. That request is what caused me to cross paths with the catalyst for realizing my true nature, my spiritual Master. I caused the meeting with the Sadguru (as we all do). This decision to seek out a live path and to be led by a Self-realized Love being was reinforced by two visions I had in my senior year at Manhattan School of Music.

My Visions of Jesus Christ

At that time, I still considered myself to be a Christian. Even though I had stopped attending church services, I worshipped Jesus Christ at home in my own way.

I was studying Religion and Philosophy with V. Saly Ph.D., a renowned Czech philosopher and teacher who was in residence at Manhattan School of Music at that time. Dr. Saly used to give discourses in the lobby and cafeteria of the school. Very often he spoke about the saints of other traditions and the mystics of Eastern civilization. Dr. Saly also did dream interpretation and was very popular among the students for this reason.

The first vision was quite incredible and reinforced in me the understanding that my worship of Jesus Christ had borne fruit in the form of direct guidance from him. I had taken a great interest in the research that was going on at that time into the *Holy Shroud of Turin*, reputed to be the cloth that Christ's body was wrapped in when he was taken down off the cross and entombed. I had been corresponding with the two American scientists who were part of the team that was analyzing the shroud to determine its authenticity.

One morning I woke from an intense vision. *Jesus Christ appeared to me and told me this;* "You cannot go any further without a living master. I am sending you to your Master. With my blessing he comes to you. Embrace him with all your heart and know that the Master is the path."

When I awoke from this vision I found a set of outstretched hands on the wall of my apartment. These hands looked as if they had been painted on the wall. My live-in girlfriend, a devout Christian, got out of the bed and sat beside me, letting out a scream. She then told me that the hands were those of Jesus Christ.

As if to prove her point, she proceeded to pull a picture of Christ from her purse which showed him with his hands outstretched in exactly the same fashion. We spent the better part of the day proving that the hands were really there by trying to scrape and clean them off the wall. After a while, it became obvious the only way they were coming off was if we repainted.

That evening, as I fell asleep, I had another vision. I was standing on a plateau, very high up, overlooking a huge riverbed. The river was dry. As I looked off into the distance, I saw thousands of people attempting to get across this massive riverbed. When I looked down at the riverbed again, I saw the bodies and heads of lambs everywhere. There was also blood in the riverbed. As the people drew closer to me, I started lifting them up on to the plateau I was standing on. There was another being who I did not recognize at the time, standing next to me, instructing me and helping me to lift them up.

I woke up from this dream in a trance-like state and I was not able to go back to sleep for the rest of the night. The next morning, I called Dr. Saly and scheduled a time to see him. I shared these two visions with him. His response was that I had reached a level in my spiritual growth that I would not be able to go beyond without a living spiritual master!

He told me that the experience of God I longed for would only come through spending time in the company of a Saint or lineage of holy beings. When I told him that I didn't know any Saints, Dr. Saly reinforced what I heard in the dreams; that I would, somehow, find this; that I would not have to go searching for this, but would be led right to the door. He then told me to remain aware and watch for a sign.

My Turning Point

I was 22 years old at the time. It was a hot summer for Vermont, great for swimming in the local swimming hole, something I did a lot of when I went to Vermont. My violin teacher, Carroll Glen, and her husband, pianist Eugene List, ran a small, lively classical music festival in southern Vermont. I had just graduated from Manhattan School of Music and this was to be my last year performing at this festival.

Back in Manhattan my "on again off again" girlfriend was minding our apartment. We had gone to school together and we were still living together. Our relationship was coming to an end and the summer afforded the two of us an opportunity to be separate long enough to let that decision set in.

In the midst of withdrawing from my 4-year relationship with my live-in mate, I fell in love with another woman who was performing at the festival. This woman finally told me she had a live-in boyfriend of her own back in Iceland who was coming to visit her at the festival. Unbeknownst to me, my live-in girlfriend had a "mole" at the festival who had reported my newfound romance to her. So, even though we were breaking up, my almost-to-be ex-girlfriend got on a bus and headed to the festival to see what this woman looked like for herself.

Now the ending to this story is somewhat of a paradox. I wound up losing both women simultaneously. And, for several months after the festival, *I battled with depression and a profound sense of loss that seemed, at the same time, illogical and outright ridiculous!* Yet, I couldn't shake it. I wouldn't shake it. I was really attached to this pain, this gloating over losing women and finding women and losing them again.

On top of that, after three years of making my living doing nothing but performing as a soloist and ensemble player, each of the programs that employed me announced they might be folding due to government budget cuts. So, I suddenly found myself putting down my violin and picking up the local help wanted ads.

I was so depressed that I found myself, for the second time in my life, contemplating my own existence. Then those questions came up again; the same ones I had asked myself before. *Is this all there is? What is fate? What is destiny? Who am I? Why am I here? Why was I born?*

Amazing Grace, how sweet the sound
That saved a wretch like me

I once was lost but now I'm found
Blind but now I see

Shaktipat – My Full Kundalini Awakening

These questions were soon answered. After attending an introductory event in Manhattan, I purchased Muktananda Paramahamsa's autobiography, *Play of Consciousness*. One winter evening I decided to begin reading it. I will never forget this glorious evening. It was February 23, 1979, two days before my birthday. It was the greatest and most precious gift of my life!

As I opened the book, I kept closing it to gaze on Muktananda's picture on the front cover. I was unable to begin reading because I kept going back to that picture. It was so alive! It was at this moment that I received Shaktipat from that picture of Muktananda Baba! Some of the *initial* experiences I had upon this full Kundalini Awakening were:

- Immediate increase in body temperature. I felt like my body was on fire.
- A decrease in body temperature. I felt that my body had gone completely cold.
- Spontaneous Hatha Yoga postures with complete flexibility. I had never studied Hatha Yoga before.

- Intensive flashes of light inside; blue, gold, white, red, black. These were phenomenal.
- Huge and quick emotional swings. These were not triggered by any interaction and came up spontaneously.
- Loss of body consciousness in Meditation.
- Hearing mantras welling up inside me, spontaneously.
- Visions of Saints not known to me at the time. Later I found out that these are Saints in our Shiva lineage.

After having these experiences, immediately I wrote to Baba with my questions and to determine the next step. He was on tour in the U.S. at the time and I wanted immediate intruction for my Sadhana, until I was able to join the tour. I received that instruction and was placed in the loving care of Swamis living in the Manhattan ashram. Shortly after that, I took Baba as my Guru and surrendered to his direct and loving leadership a short while later. What a glorious time that was!

This all led to my receipt of Shaktipat again from Muktananda Paramahamsa in several weekend intensives he led that I later participated in. In the first intensive, I found myself in a room of more than two-thousand people. During the first meditation session, Baba walked through rows of people, touching them in various places. When he got to me, I felt his hand on the top of my head. He then pressed a point at the top of my forehead, and also one between my eye brows. Immediately, there was an explosion in my head and what I perceived to be a very intelligent force began moving down my spine.

At the same time, there was another explosion at the base of my spine. A subtle energy proceeded to move up my spine. These two forces, one dripping down from my vibrating head and the other moving up from my spine, collided in my heart center. There was another explosion. Immediately, I wash awash with waves and waves of Love like I had never known. I came out of that meditation crying tears of Joy, feeling like I had come home. And those waves of Love and tears of Joy continued over the next several days before beginning to subside.

This combination of events, along with Muktnanada's leadership and instruction, established me in my Sadhana. The experiences I share in this book are all due to this awakening and the loving leadership, tests and training I received during the Shakipat Kriya Process (see below), my Sadhana.

As I engaged in the Shaktipat Kriya process spoken about later in this Chapter and in Chapter 4, I had many more transformative experiences, some of which I share in this book. I also requested and was accepted as a disciple in this Shaktipat lineage and my life was filled with the *Bliss* of the inner Self. *For that, I am forever grateful.*

Shaktipat – The Grace of A Lineage

One must seek the shortest route and fastest means to get back home, to turn one's inner spark into a blaze and then to merge and identify with that greater fire which ignited the spark.

~ Bhagawan Nityananda

It is said that God is always favorably disposed to his devotees. This must certainly go double for me. It is almost unfathomable that my Lord has chosen to work through me in this way. Why would He choose a wretch like me? It could only be due to my Master's Grace. So, I still always remember the Grace of my Master, the Grace of Bhagawan Nityananda and our entire lineage.

It is only when our lineage is pleased that the Grace-bestowing power of the Self can flow through Kedarji in a way that is understood and experienced by those people who have Bhakti, *Longing*. So, I ask you to keep an open mind and heart as you read on.

The purpose of *full Shakti Awakening*, also referred to as *Shaktipat or Kundalini Awakening*, is to set the foundation for the destruction of conditioning created by samskaras, the karmic impressions, leanings and tendencies of so many past lives and the present life. Full Kundalini Awakening begins a spontaneous process of the purification of lifetimes of karmas. We refer to this purification as the *Shaktipat Kriya Process or Sadhana*. This is an approach that gradually allows us to live in a state of Grace.

It is called the easy or spontaneous means because lifetimes of ardent struggle and practice utilizing many different spiritual techniques is replaced with this initiation given by a Shaktipat

Guru, making the practice necessary for going beyond the mind and beyond the senses, spontaneous and free-flowing.

In our approach, a Shakta Adept who is a Sadguru (true spiritual leader), is a being who has stored up the maximum amount of Divine Conscious Energy (Shakti) necessary to fully awaken this dormant energy in others. Such a being is one who is also a master in guiding the fully awakened Shakti to full expansion, an experience in which the spiritual aspirant rests in the uninterrupted state of *Pure Perceiving Awareness* that brings the exalted experience of *the fullness of Humanity in the constant delight of the Self.* This is a matter of true spiritual leadership.

This Grace-bestowing power is transmitted by the Shakta Adept to awaken Kundalini (dormant spiritual energy), and to revolutionize one's meditation practice and spiritual life. Those who have had a lapse in their spiritual practice or feel the need for additional support, also return to the Shaktipat Guru to receive this transmission of Grace-bestowing power.

This awakening is the transmission of energy that makes meditation more spontaneous while invoking the inner healing process that purifies the heart and allows one to embrace a spiritual lifestyle of Joy and Content. Shaktipat deepens and accelerates our spiritual practice in this way. After this awakening is received, a purification process begins whereby, over time and with regular spiritual practice, the Shakti pierces and purifies all of the subtle energy centers within the physical and subtle bodies.

Over time, this awakening leads to a person becoming completely established in his/her own Joy, with the constant awareness and experience of the Ultimate Reality inside and everywhere. By the nurturing of this full Shakti awakening through daily spiritual practice, we experience an inner unfolding of awareness that leads to states of higher and higher spiritual, witnessing awareness. Gradually we secure the Bliss, Joy, Peace, Happiness, and Content that is our birthright. *In our school, we have documented this transformation in others over a period of many years.*

Is Shaktipat Initiation Necessary?

If you are serious about experiencing the permanent spiritual transformation that causes you to become established in the palace of Peace, indescribable Joy and Content, ***Initiation* is a necessity.** All that I have, my spiritual attainment of the Self, is due to the descent of Grace bestowed upon me by my living Master, through *Shaktipat*. I could not have realized my identity with the Self without this spiritual awakening. For my student's sake, I am going to speak a little more about Diksha (initiation) here so that people understand its necessity and its benefits.

I am sharing from my personal experience. For an even better understanding of the mystical experience of Shaktipat, you can read *Devatma Shakti* by Swami Vishnu Tirtha, or *A Guide to Shaktipat* by Swami Shivom Tirth, Vishnu Tirtha's successor. In addition, the following Shastras and Agamas also contain accounts of the experience of Shaktipat, the Grace of a Shakta Adept and the workings of Kundalini Shakti; *Mahayoga Vijnana, Yogavani, Shiva Sutras, Pratyabhijnahridayam, Tantraloka, Shivadrishti, Jnaneshwari, Kularnava Tantra.*

As you read these pages, keep in mind that this full Shakti Awakening is the beginning, the middle and the end. After the first experience of Shaktipat, *retracing our steps back to God begins*. Then spiritual practice is required that is, specifically, instructed and led by a Shakta Adept, *until* you have realized the Self. Both initiation and daily spiritual practice are necessary.

The reason I say Shaktipat is the beginning, the middle and the end is because, in the company of a spiritual leader in the living Sadguru who is a Shaktipat Guru, the experience of Shaktipat continues to unfold on many levels. So, with the instruction and leadership of the living Master, Shaktipat becomes the ongoing experience of the Master's Grace. It should be treated with the highest reverence. *Indeed, it is the miracle of Grace.*

The approach to attaining the Freedom of the constant delight in the Self, by means of the awakened inner spiritual energy, is known as the Yoga of the Siddhas that, in our school, we also refer to as *Nityananda Shaktipat Yoga.* Ours is a time-honored, proven Yoga Science based in the bond of power of a very long, unbroken lineage of Shatipat Gurus that dates back to the pre-bronze age. It is named *Nityananda*, which means the eternal Bliss of the Absolute, after Bhagawan Nitytananda of Ganeshpuri, a highly revered sage of our lineage.

It is called the *easy* or *spontaneous* approach because lifetimes of the ardent struggle and practice utilizing many different spiritual techniques is replaced with the initiation given by a Shakta Adept, making the practice necessary for permanent spiritual transformation and Liberation spontaneous and free-flowing.

As referred to earlier, there is a vast spiritual energy inside you that lies dormant. Full Shakti Awakening is the catalyst that leads to the full expansion of that inner spiritual energy, also known as *Kundalini Shakti*. People receive this awakening to revolutionize their Meditation practice and to begin the removal of all the karmic patterns and false leanings and tendencies that are the obstacles to permanent spiritual transformation. **This begins with the purification of all the subtle spiritual energy centers in your being.** As my Shri Gurudev used to say, this is a matter of getting rid of all that we are not.

We are all used to concentrating by focusing our attention outward through the energy known as the mind. We do this to go about our day and to accomplish and acquire people, place and things in our daily mundane lives. To a Self-realized being, the mind is the one Shiva-Shakti power that vibrates as the Supreme "I" within Consciousness.

When this *Supreme "I" Consciousness* turns its attention toward labeling objects (people, places and things) in Consciousness, for the purpose of making distinctions in order to recognize those objects as being separate in Consciousness, it contracts to become what is commonly known as 'the mind.' This contraction of the one Supreme Intelligence (Shiva-Shakti power) is what gives us the power to perceive objects in our Consciousness as being separate from each other and separate from ourselves. We use the notion of 'separateness' to carry out the mundane activities of our lives in what the Sages of steady wisdom of our lineage refer to as God's immanent aspect, the world of forms.

There exists another aspect of this same energy or Shiva-Shakti power. This is the transcendental aspect of Divine Consciousness. The unawakened person is not aware of this transcendental aspect. It lies dormant, in three-and-a-half folds, at the base of the spine. This aspect of energy is the inner spiritual energy known as *Kundalini Shakti*. It embarks upon its journey to become Maha Shakti through reunion with Shiva (the formless Absolute), only after being fully awakened.

This Kundalini is awakened by a spiritually-perfected being, a Shakta adept who has received the power to do so from his/her Master or directly from the primordial Guru, Shiva. The experience of Shaktipat is similar to that of receiving energy from a healer for removing illness, only more powerful and lasting in its effect due to the *full* awakening of the dormant Kundalini that also begins to burn Karmas.

Experience of Indescribable Joy In Daily Mundane Life

One of the biggest complaints among seekers and yogis who have experienced some type of initiation is that they begin to have good meditations when sitting in asana with their eyes closed, *but they don't experience the joy and peace of their meditation when going about their daily mundane activities*. They feel great in meditation but, once they are up and about, it's life as usual without any lasting change in their experience of the mundane world or the people around them.

For this reason, there is a specific approach to giving full Shakti Awakening that is engaged by the Shakta Adepts of our lineage. It is based on the principles and techniques set forth in the Shaivism of The Spanda School of Vasuguptacharya and Abhinavaguptacharya (not the Shaivism as defined by Google or Wikipedia). This is Shaktipat by and into the highest or purest vibration of Divine Consciousness.

Through this type of initiation, a seeker begins to experience God's two aspects, the immanent and the transcendental, reverberating in one's being *as one Divine force.* This initiation also sets in motion a process wherein the seeker begins to experience all the stages or levels of Manifestation (tattvas) within one's own being, from Earth up to the absolute Paramashiva (the one, formless Supreme Principle). The Chakras (spiritual centers) above the head are also opened.

For this reason we say that this is full Shakti awakening. It allows you to begin experiencing God in everything and everyone, everywhere. This Shaktipat is the basis for the ongoing experience of Meditation as you go about the mundane activities of your life.

The awakening of Kundalini Shakti within a seeker first destroys *Anava mala*. Anava mala (in this reference, mala means taint or impurity) is what causes the feeling of imperfection and the feeling or notion of being separate from God. This mala gives rise to all of the other imperfections and limitations experienced by a living being. Shaktipat is first necessary in order to remove Anava mala. This mala cannot be removed in any other way.

After this full Shakti Awakening is received, a purification process begins whereby, over time and with regular Meditation and other spiritual practices, Kundalini pierces and purifies all of the subtle energy centers within the physical and subtle body (the subtle body houses the ego idea, the individual intellect and all of the psychic instruments). In the physical presence of the Shakta Adept, this initiation becomes an expansive experience of that Master's Grace that is "stepped-up" or quickened through the Shaktipat Kriya Process.

It is within the subtle body (Sushumna) that all of the impressions (vasanas) from past lives and the present life are stored. These impressions give rise to our emotional states, our fears, our memories, our tendencies, habits and leanings, etc. These represent our Karmas. After the receipt of Shaktipat, with the nurturing provided by daily Meditation, Chanting and other spiritual practices, and the direct leadership offered by the Sadguru, these impressions are removed by the rising Kundalini Shakti, freeing the aspirant of duality and the false notion that one is just a person, just the body, mind and senses.

Upon receiving Shaktipat, one should nurture this Divine Energy of Consciousness through Meditation, Chanting, Prayer, Contemplation and Selfless Service, so that this Shakti may rise through the Sushumna and all the subtle energy points, purifying everything in its path. As this occurs, the devotee's understanding becomes ripe with the knowledge that this Shiva-Shakti power is the Guru.

Over time, this process leads to a person becoming completely established in his/her own Bliss, with the constant awareness and experience of the Self, the Ultimate Reality and Cause, inside and everywhere. Over time, and with practice, all past impressions and karmas are burned in this purifying fire of this transformative Grace, the Kriya Shakti of the living Master. Through the nurturing of full Shakti Awakening by daily spiritual practice, the student experiences an inner unfolding of awareness that leads to increasing states of higher and pure spiritual witnessing awareness.

This purification leads to the *Natural, Free State of Being* from which one worships the Shiva-Shakti power by becoming that power, *by becoming what one already is.* It is a state of incomparable Bliss and Contentment, the state of ultimate true knowledge. This Shiva-Shakti power is the energy substratum of everything. Therefore, it is the highest power and, the fact is we all need a power source in order to evoke any type of transformation that is sustainable.

What About Spontaneous Awakenings?

There is a lot of talk today on the Internet and elsewhere, regarding 'spontaneous awakenings' of Kundalini. This is an apparent attempt, on the part of teachers who have not served a Shaktipat Guru or been authorized by such a being to give Shaktipat, to promote the notion that one does not need an authentic Shaktipat Guru to experience Shaktipat. And, upon closer examination of what people are stating was a spontaneous awakening of Kundalini, it becomes clear that people are calling any energetic experience Shaktipat. In fact, many of these people have experienced being healed of a particular condition, or have experienced a movement of energy similar to Reiki healing or Qi Gong energetics. Although beneficial in other ways, these are not connected to Shaktipat.

Is it possible to have a spontaneous, full Kundalini Awakening? From scientific discoveries, we know that entire galaxies can spontaneously disappear into a black hole. From the same discoveries we know that this is a *very rare event.* Can the Sun stop giving light and disappear from the sky? Yes. We know this because there was an ice age on this planet. However, we also know that this is a *very rare phenomenon,* not having re-occurred in our existence here for millennia.

Spontaneous, full kundalini awakenings *are even more rare than these phenomenon.* Then there is what needs to take place after the full Kundalini awakening, in order to fully nurture and protect the rising Kundalini. So, just as only a trained doctor or other very qualified practitioner can properly diagnose an illness, based on years of experience, evidence-based research and testing, only a Shaktipat Guru who is a Sadguru can lead you in understanding and experiencing what Shaktipat really is.

Shaktipat Myths and Fears

Sometimes, when people hear the words Shaktipat, spiritual initiation and Guru uttered in the same breath, they may be confused or even frightened. In addition, the many opinions on the internet that are floated as facts don't make matters any easier.

The truth is, we accept and undergo many initiations in life. For example, being welcomed and embraced by a fraternity or sorority in college often means undergoing an initiation. Many people have their children baptized. This is a widely accepted initiation. The ceremony of holy communion in the Catholic tradition is another. You may have experienced that training in corporate communication, while embracing the underlying culture at your job also involves an initiation. Likewise, Attorneys are initiated into the culture of their law firms. Similarly, doctors are initiated into the mindset of the pharmaceutical companies. In fact, their prognosis often relies upon Big Pharma in order to address symptoms of their patients.

Rituals That You Know and Love

Also, there are the rituals that you perform every day. Perhaps you do so without recognizing them as every bit a ritual as the spiritual ceremony inherent in events like baptism and Shaktipat. For example, rituals like coffee and croissants at Starbucks every morning. A ritual that you may engage in at the same time every day. You may even insist at sitting at the same table each morning.

And what about rushing home to catch the next episode or a rerun of *Breaking Bad* or a similar TV episode? Perhaps, you do so with the same martini in hand. For instance, you may take it stirred not shaken. Maybe with a lemon rind, not a lemon wedge. Maybe you do so while sitting in the same spot in your recliner and not on the coach. And, perhaps you tune in at exactly 5 minutes before the start of the show. Maybe you want to catch your favorite Capital One credit card commercial – what's in your wallet!?

In short, these are each just examples of how we accept and fully embrace rituals and initiations in every day life. The only difference between this and Shaktipat is that Shaktipat is an initiation that may seem foreign to you. So, let's begin.

The Fast Track To Your Highest Power

We all want to be on the *fast track*. The fast track to success. The fast track to more money or a better career. Think of the receipt of Shaktipat as fast-tracking a powerful connection with the true YOU – your true nature, your most powerful aspect, your highest Self.

Think, for a moment, of the caffeine in coffee. So many people drink coffee to get a boost, to fast-track the energy they need to get started with their day. Or, what about the music you listen to in order to lift your spirits, calm your tension or get you psyched/pumped to perform better? Similarly, we buy E-Z passes to fly through tollbooths. People do this to fast-track their progress in getting from point A to point B with the greatest convenience. We don't want to be held back or slowed down. As another example, perhaps you attempt to get security clearance passes for airline travel to fast-track getting on planes. Or special access passes to ensure you get into your favorite concerts or sporting events with no waiting.

The Exception - The Difference That Makes The Difference

Shaktipat is very similar to these rituals that we engage in, with one exception: It is the easy means, the fast track to accessing your highest power, the power of Grace – the Spiritual Power that is your true nature – the power to end all other powers. **Shaktipat initiation is like lighting an unlit candle with one that is already lit. In the leap of that flame, so much takes place – and in an instant!**

Leadership By Example

The full unfolding of the transmission of the Grace-bestowing power of God known as Shaktipat also requires strong spiritual leadership. After the receipt of Shaktipat, there is a spiritual journey that begins which requires the application of methods and instruction for nurturing the full Kundalini awakening. This journey involves treading a path of spiritual discipline that is taught.

A Sadguru is a true spiritual leader and a Shaktipat Sadguru is a true spiritual leader with the power to transmit Grace to the spiritual aspirant throughout his/her spiritual journey home. This Grace is what burns all of the karmic obstacles to your permanent spiritual transformation and ultimate Liberation.

In every area of our lives we model after others or some example or habit/s that we come into contact with. So, in everything we do and say, we have, in some way, followed an example set for us, even when we are not completely aware of this. This modeling where we follow examples set by other people, places or things, begins with the understandings that we reach for and embrace.

For example, people who are searching for intimate relationships first reach for the understanding that a 'soulmate' or 'intimate partner' is necessary for their lives to be completed in some way. Reaching for this kind of understanding dictates how they feel and how they are vibrating (what they are putting out or projecting into their inner and outer world. Once this occurs, the next step is to find a justification, a reason for continuing to reach for and hold the understanding being embraced. So, in this example, people seek out others who appear to be successful in having established this kind of relationship, those who are models for what these people are seeking – based on the understandings that people reach for. In this example, for many, the modeling is based on popular notions about intimate relationships that are reflected in movies, TV, radio and on the internet. The same would apply to examples of people pursuing monetary wealth, etc.

So, individuals and societies are always being led in some way by modeling after examples that are being set. Of course, this includes the habit of accepting and embracing popular understandings/notions collectively embraced and repeated, as well as, those given by parents, authority figures, friends, lovers, family members, husband, wife, associates, peer pressure, popular media, etc. that people often embrace without ever even questioning or examining closely. The leadership examples being set are either useful or not. **There are only two examples to model after in this regard; Great leadership or poor leadership. In spiritual life, it is the same.**

What Shaktipat Is Not

Today, there are many who have jumped into the "guru business." Some of these people (just like corporations) simply seek to develop an audience to sell products to. **Others somehow believe that they can lead without ever having followed, *without ever having obeyed.*** Such is the nature of contraction and obstinance in this Kali Yuga Age.

Rather than sharing from their own true attainment, they teach popular perceptions and false notions that they know are what people want to hear. Beware of such people. They will take from you much more than they ever give you. They will leave you with a false sense of hope and yet another variation on the illusion you have previously "bought" as the truth. *Because this is the case, I want to briefly share, from the understanding and experience of the great beings of our lineage, what Shaktipat is not.*

Shaktipat *is not* hypnosis. It has nothing to do with the power of suggestion or any guided lapse of awareness. Shaktipat *is not* subtle psychology. It does not utilize any process of restructuring or reorganizing familiar thought patterns or reorganizing positive/negative emotions. It does not utilize any process of bolstering the ego idea through the recitation of self-confidence affirmations or the guided visualizations of familiar imagery. It cannot be induced by repeating to yourself that you are your own master and it is not experienced by touching yourself in different places while visualizing your chakras. Any of these things may be therapeutic in their own way, but they have nothing to do with Shaktipat which is a full Kundalini awakening.

Shaktipat *is not* a drug-induced, altered state of mind. It is not brought about through the use of rare drugs found in plants and it is not induced by swallowing combinations of herbs or ecstasy pills. If Shaktipat could be drug-induced, all dope addicts would become saints, something we already know is not the case.

Shaktipat *is not* a sexual act and cannot be experienced through "tantric" sex. Kundalini awakening has nothing to do with the sex act. Someone who tells you he/she is going to awaken your kundalini by having sex with you is just trying to get into your pants. If sex could give this initiation, most of the world population would be mad lovers of God wanting the constant delight of the Self, again something we already know is not true.

Shaktipat *is not* invoked through sensual massage. It cannot be experienced by getting high on drugs and alcohol in order to dance with reckless abandon to wild music at a local rave. I know what Shaktipat is not because, prior to meeting my Master, I tried most of these things.

The important thing to understand about Shaktipat is that it begins and sustains a process of going beyond the mind and beyond the senses in away that (unlike drugs, intoxicants and alcohol), over time, you never come down from that high. This awakening immediately begins to manifest a spiritual awareness that is far greater than thinking and logic. This witnessing awareness, when properly cultivated through the leadership of a Shaktipat Guru who is a true spiritual leader, becomes the pillar of the highest intelligence, from which the Truth in every situation and circumstance naturally flows – leading to a permanent state of Joy and spiritual Happiness that is not dependent on anything or anyone outside oneself.

Most importantly, Shaktipat immediately begins to manifest the Shaktipat Kriya Process (see Chapter 4), whereby the karmas that are the obstacles to your experiencing and embracing your true identity as the inner Self are dredged up, expiated and destroyed so that you can attain a permanent state of the fullness of Humanity, as expressed in the constant delight of the Self. *I hope you can understand, from reading what I've just written,* **that no drug, intoxicant, form of sex, pastime, occupation, other relationship or mundane experience can give this kind of unfolding experience that leads to permanent spiritual transformation and Liberation.**

CAN YOU AWAKEN YOUR OWN KUNDALINI?

It is possible for a person to awaken his/her own Kundalini, but one cannot become Liberated from ignorance without being led by a Shaktipat Guru in the rooting out of the Gunas and the Malas (see Chapter 9). *Then there are the effects of Shaktipat that the student must be led to face in order to properly understand the process.* Again, it is rare that a person is even able to awaken Kundalini Shakti on his own. But through many, many years of arduous practice (or lifetimes of practice) of certain postures and breathing techniques, one can awaken the dormant Kundalini. *But, in most cases, this is not full Kundalini awakening.* Also, Kundalini Shakti will not rise past Ajna Chakra to permanent union with the God-Principle in the Sahasrar (Brahmarandra) without the Grace of a spiritual leader in the living Sadguru.

It *is* also possible to receive Shaktipat from a Saint who is no longer in the body, but this is *rare* in this Kali Yuga age because so many people in this time do not want God. What they want is a notion of God that serves their limiting desire and cravings for worldliness. They want a God that is convenient for them and their fantasies, *so their longing is weak.*

There are those who received Shaktipat in a past life and are completing that journey in their present life. These people had Sadgurus for teachers in a previous life or several past lives. They may not remember this. But full Kundalini Awakening never goes to waste and these people can be seen progressing on the spiritual path, *seemingly* without initiation.

Especially in this Kali Yuga Age, the most direct means of receiving God's Grace and the spiritual awakening necessary for realizing one's true nature is through the Grace of a true Shaktipat Guru who is a strong spiritual leader.

WHO CAN GIVE SHAKTIPAT?

One thing is absolutely certain. Not every guru or spiritual teacher can give Shaktipat. **Only a Shaktipat Guru who has completely realized the goal of his/her spiritual practice, one who has stored up the maximum amount of Shakti necessary, only such a being who has also received the command to do so, can give this initiation.**

The lineage of Shaktipat Sadgurus lays out, very clearly, the qualifications a such a being must have in order to give Shaktipat. One should only receive Shaktipat from a living Sadguru who is in such a lineage. This can be read about in Shaiva Agamas like *Pratyabhijnahrdayam, Shiva Sutras, Spanda Karikas* and the *Kularnava Tantra.*

If the teacher has not merged his limited ego sense into the Supreme Principle, he cannot be a vehicle for Shaktipat. If the spiritual leader does not exhibit the constant awareness that God exists everywhere and in everything, she cannot sustain Shaktipat. If a devotee spends time in the company of a spiritual leader and does not experience the desire to know the Self, to want the ongoing experience of indescribable Joy, of what use is receiving Shaktipat from that person?

If the spiritual leader is not a living example of the teachings of the scriptures of a lineage of spiritually-perfected beings, how can he awaken and guide the spiritual transformation of another? **On whose shoulders does that being stand? A guru who has not been taught by another competent Sadguru in a lineage of Shaktipat Gurus cannot sustain Shaktipat.** In other words, a Shaktipat Sadguru is very rare.

HOW IS THIS FULL KUNDALINI AWAKENING GIVEN?

The full Kundalini Awakening of Shaktipat is imparted by a Shaktipat Guru who is a lineage holder in an unbroken line of Shaktipat Sadgurus. This awakening or initiation occurs by the Grace-bestowing power of God that takes the form of the Grace (Kriya Shakti) of the living Master. This full Kundalini Awakening marks the true beginning of retracing one's steps back to God in order to experience permanent spiritual transformation and Liberation.

Full Kundalini Awakening is given by a true Shaktipat Guru in one or more of the following ways; through touch, by look or glance, through speech, by imparting the Mantra to you, by mere will (Sankalpa), by appearing to you in a dream, vision or Meditation. A devotee can also experience this awakening by intensively meditating on the form of such a being.

HOW IS SHAKTIPAT BEST NURTURED?

Shaktipat is nurtured through daily spiritual practice and entrance into the Shaktipat Kriya process or Sadhana (see Chapter 4), as led by the living Shaktipat Guru. Meditation, Chanting, the practice of Witness Consciousness Centering (dharanas) and Selfless Service in the Master's school, ashram or center are the principle means by which Kundalini Shakti is nurtured after the receipt of Shaktipat.

Over time, with daily spiritual practice, Kundalini Shakti completely purifies the yogi's entire being, setting the aspirant on a direct trajectory to *Pure Perceiving Awareness*. For one who wants to realize the Truth of his/her own nature, this culminates in the state of complete absorption in the Self, the Ultimate Reality, where one experiences the rapturous state – a fullness of Humanity in the constant delight of the inner Self.

Full Kundalini Awakening is also nurtured through sexual abstinence and celibacy. After receiving Shaktipat, it is best to allow the Shakti time to take hold in your being. **Kundalini Shakti rises and purifies all the subtle energy centers of one's being on the back of sexual fluid**. *So, retaining sexual fluid, rather than wasting it, is advised.* This is why I recommend that those receiving Shaktipat refrain from having intercourse more than once a month, especially in the beginning of retracing one's steps back to God. A month is not a long time. But if you can't go a month at first, abstain for 2-3 weeks with the goal of building to a month or more.

> *In the beginning was the Word, and the Word was with God, and the Word was God.*

> Saint John

Japa, or *Mantra repetition,* is also a very important means to nurturing Shaktipat. Mantra is that by which one recognizes one's identity with the Shiva-Shakti power. The purpose of Mantra is to make the mind Self-oriented. Daily japa is a very significant means to realizing the Self because Mantra is God.

Without the Shiva-Shakti power there is no world, no Universe. This power is all things and takes all the forms of existence. It is also that which does not exist. Everything you see, hear, touch, smell, feel, perceive and experience in life is due to this one power. This God or Guru Principle has become language in order to foster the manifestation of a Universe of worlds. It is that Divine movement or activity in Consciousness without which the Self cannot be known. Although you may not know it yet, you owe your life, your very existence to this Shiva-Shakti power! Shaktipat affords you the privilege to immerse yourself in *That,* the bountiful royal road to Total Freedom.

I bow to Sri Kula Kundalini. She is the beloved of the self-born One and surrounds him, Shiva, in three circles with all the members of her retinue. She enters the sahasrar and becomes active like the mind intoxicated with love. She is naive, defenseless (though all-powerful) and complete. The Goddess, who shines with the Vedas as her countenance, procures everything for her devotees and burns those who become averse to her. I worship her, the wife of the self-born One (Shiva), who revels in the sahasrar with her chosen one. She is the power of action.

~ From the Kundalini Stavaha which appears in the Rudra Yamala Tantra.

Chapter 3
The Honeymoon Phase

There is a honeymoon phase in our approach where newcomers experience the ease, wonder, peace and happiness of receiving the Grace that flows through a true Shaktipat Guru. I observed this in my own experience of my Master and his followers. This is a period that approaches euphoria, at times.

At this point, the student has not yet begun to address his/her karmic baggage. For that, the inner work has to take place in tandem with what is known in our approach as the *Shaktipat Kriya Process* (see Chapter 4) that the physical form of the Shaktipat Guru becomes the catalyst and leader for.

When you begin this inner work, the honeymoon phase is over. Now the obstacles to your rising have to be addressed and faced. This is why we say that, to make permanent spiritual progress, we have to face our karmas.

I also want to be clear about what is meant when you see statements made in this book about the honeymoon phase being over. Spiritual aspirants come to this approach with varying degrees of karmic baggage. Some have more karmas to address, some have less. Some are spiritually evolved to the point where they only have to be instructed or told once, and they proceed with what needs to be performed to grow their spiritual awareness, with great longing and enthusiasm. Others, have to be reminded from time-to-time in order to make progress, and their longing, their Bhakti, needs to be cultivated. Still others have to be reminded constantly because they are very dull and require more attention. So, there are these three groups of spiritual aspirants.

My point here is, *people require varying degrees of instruction and commands during the Shaktipat Kriya Process.* Depending on the degree of one's resistance to letting go and obeying the instruction given for addressing the expiation and destruction of one's karmas, people experience varying degrees of intensity, challenges/difficulties, while standing in front of the mirror of the Master's Kriya Shakti. So, for some, the honeymoon never ends. For others, it takes a brief respite. And, for those who don't stay with it to attain the goal, the honeymoon ends entirely.

In the summer of 1981, my Shri Gurudev led a summer retreat. I decided to spend the entire summer there. I took every Shaktipat Meditation intensive offered that summer. At that time, the intensives were held over a weekend and full Kundalini Awakening was transmitted in each intensive. There were long periods of Meditation and Chanting in these intensives, and my Shri Gurudev also gave talks on various aspects of spiritual practice, philosophy and spiritual life.

Each intensive that I took sent me deeper and deeper into the experience of my own true nature, the Natural, Free State of the Self. This occurred through Meditation, Chanting, Selfless Service, and the experience of contemplation through the practice of Witness Consciousness Centering (Dharana).

I had many visions during these intensives, and also many kriyas. Kriyas are spontaneous movements of the Shakti. They can manifest as sounds, visions of lights, a heightened sense of smell, inner experiences of deities or temporary upheavals that happen as the awakened Kundalini Shakti starts to purify the spiritual energy centers in the subtle body. In the subtle body there are 72,000 primary nadis (subtle spiritual energy centers). Over a period of many lifetimes, these nadis become "clogged" with the debris of countless impressions (vasanas or vrittis).

These impressions are the source and cause of our bondage, known as Karma. Our karmic patterns are expressed by way of our mental conditioning. This mental conditioning causes us to vibrate at varying levels that dictate who and what we attract into our lives.

After Shaktipat, the fully awakened Kundalini begins to purify all 72,000 of these primary nadis. As this process of purification occurs, as all that "debris" is churned and released, Kriyas are the primary experience that begin to take place (see Chapter 4). In some of the intensives I also experienced my body curling up into several mudras. Mudras are spontaneous yogic positions or gestures that occur in Meditation, again, as a result of the movement of Kundalini Shakti.

In one intensive, after receiving Shaktipat, my head jerked backward on to the floor, forcing my chest to arch upward. Many times I also experienced my head falling forward to the floor and remaining there for long periods of time. These kinds of Kriyas went on in my Meditations for many months after the intensives with my Master.

My most intense kriyas were spontaneous pranayams. Pranayams are breathing techniques usually done to force the prana (breath) into the subtle body (the sushumna nadi) where the Chakras (spiritual centers) are housed. These pranayams occurred on their own, without any effort on my part, while I was meditating.

I also had many visions of lights. At times, these lights took the form of soft rays and, at other times, they took the form of huge suns or large beams. Sometimes these lights were in the form of dots the size of a sesame seed (bindis) and other times they were as large as the ocean. I saw many colors of lights, but the main ones that I saw in my meditations were blue, gold, violet, red, white and black. These I saw often in my meditations.

There were periods, after receiving initiation, when I saw nothing in Meditation. At those times, I had the experience of profound peace and a great silence. This is the experience of many people who don't have intense Kriyas. The intensity of Kriyas varies depending on one's personality and karmas. These Kriyas can be very intense at times and, at other times, they are subtler.

For a long period, in Meditation I would hear sounds. Sometimes these sounds would be music of incredible beauty, *like nothing I had ever heard.* At other times, I would hear the mantra *Om* being chanted inside me. I would also hear low gong sounds and very high-pitched sounds. A sound that I can only describe as the far-off pitch of ocean waves is a sound that I would experience often. I later understood this to be what is known as Anahata or Bindu Nada, the unstruck sound that is also referred to as the 10 different kinds of sound emanating from the Sahasrar. *Bindu Nada,* the unstruck sound, is one that I continue to hear constantly.

Another inner experience that I can only call celestial in nature is one where, when people spoke to me or when I heard chanting, I would hear the sound a fifth or an octave or two octaves higher than the tone being spoken or sung. This was a constant experience.

I also had experiences while Chanting. There is a chant known as the Shri Guru Gita that is sung every morning in the ashrams and centers my Gurudev established. I learned this chant during the summer of 1981 and I sang it every morning for many years. I had many visions of Saints while chanting the Guru Gita and received messages that had a direct and profound impact on my life. For example, one morning while chanting the Guru Gita, Lord Krishna appeared to me and danced around me playing his flute. He then told me to be careful driving that morning. He told me that a large, silver truck would go out of control hurting several people and that, when I see that truck, I should pull off the road.

Later that morning, on my way back home from the ashram, I did see a silver Mack truck looming behind me. I immediately remembered Krishna's warning and I pulled off the road and stopped. Just then that truck rammed into several cars and exploded. My life had been saved! This is just one example of the messages I received. In this way, many deities have appeared to me during chanting. Sometimes I had the vision of just their forms and, at other times, they spoke to me, telling me what I needed to hear.

Some of my most profound experiences are those I had while meditating on my Guru's form. In several traditions, this is known as Guru meditation or Guru Bhavana. Meditating on the form of a living Shaktipat Guru is a way of attracting the power and Grace of such a being to you, while inculcating Bhakti (devotion).

We all know how to worship forms. This is a habit we have developed over a period of many lifetimes. A lover keeps pictures of his girlfriend or boyfriend in his wallet or hung on the wall in his home or office. A mother carries pictures of her children around with her or keeps those on her dresser bureau or desk. A person keeps pictures of his family on his desk at work. People do this to remind themselves of the love and devotion they feel for their loved ones. This helps to open their hearts.

Similarly, one wanting to inculcate devotion and longing for the Self can meditate on a Sage with great power, in order to 'steal' such a being's Shakti power for spiritual transformation. This also increases one's longing, reverence and humility to deepen the experience of inner peace and joy.

Every morning, I sat for Meditation with Baba's picture in front of me. My eyes locked into his until I gently floated inside, losing all awareness of anything around me. I went very deep in these meditations and they were very serene. This is when I had many visions of my Guru when he led me from within in all matters.

In these visions, I took long walks with him. He led me to places to show me things. On one such journey, he took me to the abode of a Goddess who I later learned was Kali (an aspect of the Shiva-Shakti power). This place was full of fire. He guided me down a long path that seemed to disappear into complete darkness.

Then we came to a huge archway that looked like an entrance to a new path. There on the ground were many skulls and body parts. Looking up, I saw a huge woman whose skin was like jet-black ink. Her eyes were red and she wore skulls around her neck and about her head. Her shape was quite sexy and I remember experiencing a sexual attraction to her, even though I could see blood dripping from her lips.

I thought this sensation to be bizarre and I became very frightened. It seemed as if this Kali was going to eat me alive! And yet something in me wanted to embrace her. In this vision, I looked around for Baba. He was on the other side of the archway. The Goddess Kali was blocking my passage to where he stood. Suddenly, she started to fling balls of fire at me. I didn't know what to do. It seemed that my fear was giving Kali more ideas.

I looked at Baba and he motioned me to move toward him. At that moment, I heard the mantra, *Om Namah Shivaya*, rising up within me. It gave me great courage to hear it. I then walked straight for the archway Kali was blocking and she moved aside and let me pass. On the other side Baba embraced me. I came out of this Meditation feeling very rejuvenated. Clearly this was a test of my courage and faith in the mantra and my Master.

Another time, during Meditation, I followed him to a very dark place. There were human feces everywhere in this place, and many dead bodies. There were ghosts walking around and some of them still carried their bodies that had been mangled or bruised or burned at the time of their death. These ghosts spoke to me and breathed on me.

Then a being appeared to me, first as a column of light, and then in the form of a dark mass that had no beginning or end. He told me his name was Yama, the God of death. He spoke to me about the sovereignty of time for those attached to forms, telling me that no one escapes time who is attached to the body. "No one escapes time who is attached to the body." I came out of this Meditation contemplating those words.

Within a week of this vision of Yama, I experienced my own death in Meditation. This was a very profound moment in my Sadhana that changed the course of retracing my steps back to God. While sitting for Meditation, *my breath stopped spontaneously*. I was fully conscious. My mind was centered in my Heart. But I was not breathing. Rather than getting hysterical with fear, I noticed that I was completely calm. A few minutes later, I left my body and was hovering over it several feet in the air. I looked down on my body from where I hovered over it.

This experience was *different* than the one I had in the car crash (see Chapter 1). This time, I felt at one with every particle in that room. I had full, Pure Perceiving Awareness of everything in me and around me. *It's as if I had merged with the walls, the floor, the ceiling, the air and everything else.*

Then the room disappeared and there was just my body sitting in Meditation in a huge void, with me hovering over everything. This void was endless. After some time, I re-entered my body and my breathing started again. When I came out of this Meditation, I looked at the clock. Three and a half hours had passed!

During this period in the Shaktipat Kriya Process, I had many visions of other realms and I experienced many deities who I later read about in sacred texts and scriptures. This was a period of great wonder. **Then this honeymoon phase came to an end, *temporarily*, as I began facing myself.**

Chapter 4
The Storm Within The Calm

In my experience and that of other spiritual adepts inside and outside of our lineage, many people today do not want God or the sublime state of Bliss and *Love without distinctions* that can be experienced beyond the mind and beyond the senses. What they want is a notion of God that conforms to their limiting desires and cravings for worldliness – a God that is convenient. This is a **karmic state of contraction** that I also suffered. So, I can share, from my own experience and that of others, that *it can only be healed by keeping the company of holy beings.* It's why I took a Sadguru as my spiritual leader.

I repeat, people who engage in an approach to *permanent* spiritual transformation often have a conflict with respect to not compromising their growing experience of the Joy of the true Heart. So many think that engaging in an uncompromising spiritual discipline means that they will miss out on something that their friends, relatives, lovers and associates are enjoying in life.

Without a strong witnessing awareness and the most useful understandings, the wisdom imparted by holy beings, they come to believe that, if they embrace letting go of their attachments, attractions and aversions, they will miss out on a life that they assume others close to them enjoy (but have no real idea of whether they really do or not – having no real idea of the inner state of others whom they interact with) – a life that they are conditioned to embrace by the popular culture and understandings that other worldly-minded people embrace. So, they choose activity that others have chosen and then say that they have created their own life!

Well, such people are right about one thing; **they are missing out on life;** A life imbued with the realization of who they really are – a life imbued with indescribable Joy, Love without distinctions, and the permanent Peace that comes with experiencing the nectar of Self-awareness that makes one truly independent and free – *in the fullness of Humanity, with a wide-open Heart that is bursting with God's Love.* This is why the great beings tell us that the spiritual discipline that takes us beyond the mind and beyond the senses is true freedom.

Throughout my life, for as far back as I can remember, I came upon many opportunities to advance myself and improve the quality of my life. And, in most cases, I sabotaged the opportunities provided me by Grace. Why? *Because I was attached to pleasure and pain. I enjoyed their company.*

Sometimes this occurred through my own ignorance. At other times the self-sabotage was entirely due to my conscious resistance. For a time, especially after the receipt of Shaktipat, there was a period where I did not want to let go of the limited existence I had come to be so attached to. *I recognized good but did not want to be good. I recognized Truth but continued to choose illusion.* In the early years of retracing my steps back to God, this was the case. *I was eaten alive by my own resistance.*

A man got lost in a far away place that seemed like a jungle disguised as a city. He made many attempts to find his way back home. *Without the help of someone who knew the territory,* these attempts were futile.

One day he got a lucky break. A stranger approached him and told him that there was a bus leaving soon that would take him out of this place and back to his home. *The stranger acted as his companion.* He led the man to the bus depot and showed him where to stand to catch the bus. After telling him the exact time the bus would come, the stranger told the man not to become distracted *or he might miss the bus.* The stranger then vanished.

The man started to wonder why no one had told him of this bus or this bus depot. "Why don't my close friends and family members know about this," he thought. He started to doubt that a bus even existed, let alone one that would take him right to his home! Why had he not heard of this bus before? Then the man saw a group of people standing on a corner. There was a great deal of commotion and one of the people was holding a wad of cash. So, the man decided to go see what the noise was all about.

As he approached the group, he noticed a well-dressed executive standing in front of these people holding money in one hand and papers in the other. This executive was going on and on about people joining his business and becoming millionaires over night. He was making promises of great fortunes and flashing wads of cash to prove to people how wealthy he had become.

Just as the man approached the executive to ask for more

information, he heard a bus pull up across the street. He turned to look, just in time to see the bus driving off in the distance. The man had missed his bus. So certain now that there would be another bus along any minute, the man sat down on the curb with his eyes glued to the ground. Several hours passed in this way. The man finally got up and started to walk back in the direction of the city. As he walked, he heard a voice from behind him. "I see you missed your bus."

It was the stranger. The man was furious. Why hadn't there been another bus? The stranger took the man by the hand and walked him back to the bus depot. *The guide placed the man at the very spot he had left him standing the first time.* He then made the same statement. "Don't become distracted or you will miss the bus. Who knows when another bus will be along, so get on this bus."

The man now stood with his feet glued to that place. He stared at his watch. He waited. He looked around. He became agitated. He listened for the sound of a bus and heard nothing. He became impatient. Just then, he spotted a gorgeous woman. She was dressed in a mini skirt and boots. Everything was there in all the right places. And she had long hair. "Wow!" the man thought. So, he followed her. Wherever she walked he walked. And she walked everywhere! After some time, the man decided to ask the woman her name. Just as he got up the courage to utter the words, he heard a sound. It was the sound of a bus coming to a stop. Again, the man looked around just in time to see the bus driving off into the distance! And so it went for this man, day after day, year after year.

I used to be like that man. And the truth is, I could have had my Guru's state a lot sooner. My Shri Gurudev attempted to liberate me from my ignorance many times. It was due to my own resistance and my habit of sabotage that I kept missing the 'bus.' I once heard a great being say, "If your ship doesn't come in, swim out to it." After so much sabotage, my ship stopped coming in. *So, I swam out to it.*

I did finally catch the 'bus.' *But I had to fully understand the nature of Grace first.* This full understanding of Grace and how to live in a state of Grace, came by way of me facing my karmas, my self-imposed limitations and ignorance, through the spontaneous and dynamic Shaktipat Kriya Process that my Shri Gurudev taught me and led me through.

The Shaktipat Kriya Process. Secrets of Kriya Revealed.

The purpose of taking a spiritually-perfected Love being and following any true spiritual approach is to lead you to the experience of *permanent* spiritual transformation. Attaining permanent spiritual transformation takes *time*, *practice*, *patience* and *right understanding.*
Your perfection is already with you. You are the Self. You are the Supreme Principle. You are all great beings. *For ages you have concealed this fact from yourself by pulling a veil down over your Heart.* **You have *concealed* your true nature from yourself by holding the false notion that you are just a person, an individual, just the body, the senses and the mind, just ordinary or delightfully weird.**

In truth, there is nothing to attain. *Spiritual life is not about giving you anything that you don't already have. It's about burning away all that you are not.* The means of burning away all that you are not should not be feared. This is not a fear-based approach, and is not meant to frighten you. It is Grace at work to transform your life. This is about making you *forever wise.*

In this context, I want to clarify a point regarding the very loosely-used term 'spiritual growth.' *Spiritual growth is only spiritual growth* when it is not skewed through the play of our karmic impurities, and only when it is on a permanent trajectory to God-realization.

The habit of making ourselves small is a bad habit that we have engaged for a very long time (as in many lifetimes). This karmic pattern actually manifests out of the play of the three Gunas and the three malas (constitutive properties of nature and taints or impurities) spoken of in Trika Shaivism (see Chapter 9), and connected to the five kleshas (afflictions) uttered in the Vedas. These impurities are based in the fear, doubt, cynicism and self-loathing that cause us to pursue pleasure in an attempt to avoid pain. These impurities place a veil over God and cause us to hide behind lack of Faith (out of which cynicism manifests). They destroy our witnessing awareness and make it impossible to Trust in God, to Trust in the Sadguru, to Trust in the Shaktipat Kriya Process.

To break this habit, to remove the veil of ignorance covering the Self takes time and practice. To engage in such a practice over a necessary period of time *requires endurance and spiritual disciplne* – the kind that comes from strong spiritual leadership. **It is impossible to rid yourself of these impurities, these leanings and tendencies that are the karmas you have imposed on yourself for so many lifetimes, without the Grace, Leadership, Love and Kriya Shakti of a living Shaktipat Guru** – no more than you can pull yourself up into the air by your own bootstraps (more about this in Chapter 23).

The honeymoon phase that I spoke about briefly in the previous chapter is necessary. We have to have a set of experiences that cause us to begin to love the means to attaining the goal (the mind loves the places it frequents the most), that also cause our feeling for the living Sadguru to increase, *in order to go the distance.* Our intention, our *resolve* has to be strong. Otherwise, we will not endure the pitfalls, the obstacles that have to be faced in order to fulfill our desire for permanent spiritual transformation and Liberation from ignorance. It is necessary to "fall in love" with the daily spiritual practice and the application of the instruction given by a living Master.

I was able to strengthen this resolve, in order to carryout my intention to know the inner Self, by keeping the company of such a Sadguru, and by keeping the inner company of our lineage of great beings and the understandings they convey. Then there was the instruction my Master gave me for the daily spiritual practice necessary to go beyond the mind and beyond the senses, in order to experience the Bliss of the Self on a regular, and then a constant basis. There was also the instruction and command he gave me for destroying the karmas of so many past lives, so that the obstacles to my permanent spiritual transformation could be destroyed. These obstacles were removed through the *Shaktipat Kriya Process* that I speak of in this chapter.

I also want to repeat here what was shared in the

previous chapter, regarding the honeymoon phase. Spiritual aspirants come to this approach with varying degrees of karmic baggage. Some are spiritually evolved to the point where they only have to be instructed or told once, and they proceed with what needs to be performed to grow their spiritual awareness, with great longing and enthusiasm. Others, have to be reminded from time-to-time in order to make progress, and their longing, their Bhakti, needs to be cultivated. Still others have to be reminded constantly because they are very dull and require more attention. So, there are these three groups of spiritual aspirants.

People require varying degrees of instruction during Sadhana (Shaktipat Kriya Process). Depending on the degree of one's resistance to letting go and obeying the instruction given for addressing the expiation and destruction of one's karmas, people experience varying degrees of intensity, challenges/difficulties while standing in front of the mirror of the Master's Kriya Shakti. So, for some, the honeymoon never ends. For others, it takes a brief respite. And, for those who don't stay the course to attain the goal, the honeymoon ends entirely.

In spiritual life, if we want permanent spiritual transformation, if we want to come to know our true nature, *the Self,* **it is essential that we reach for the means to going beyond the mind and beyond the senses – beyond notions, emotions, attachment to beliefs and understandings that we have never questioned or examined closely.** In doing so on a regular, consistent basis, we are able to make the mind the friend of the inner Self so that the mind begins to love frequenting *That* – The Ultimate Reality. Then the senses and our entire Humanity begin to rest in the delight of *That* inner Self. *The senses then become the servants of the Self.*

This goal is not hard. We are hard. For this reason, to accomplish this we need a *strong spiritual leader*, someone who dwells in that abode that is beyond the mind and beyond the senses and emotions, someone who has become *the fullness of Humanity in the constant delight of the inner Self.*

In the Shri Guru Gita, a song sermon that glorifies and explains the Guru-principle in both its formless (transcendental) and embodied (immanent) aspects, Lord Shiva, the Guru of the Siddhas of our lineage, states:

9 – The Guru is not different from the Supreme Principle, the inner Self. There is no doubt about this. This is the Truth, this is the Truth. Therefore, wise people and those seeking permanent spiritual transformation should make the effort to seek out a Guru.

13 – The water of the Guru's feet has the power to destroy one's sins, to ignite the light of knowledge, and to take one across the ocean of worldliness.

14 – To attain knowledge of the Self and detachment from worldly pleasures and pain, sip the water of the Guru's feet, which destroys ignorance and ends the karmas that are the cause of rebirth.

**Excerpts from the Shri Guru Gita were provided with permission by sanskrit.safire.com

I want to share briefly, by way of my direct experience, the hidden meaning that these verses convey. I will elaborate on what I share here in Chapter 23 - *The Bond of Power*. What I share here, and in that chapter, is also reflective of the experiences of many devotees and disciples of our lineage of Sadgurus whom I spent a great deal of time with in service to humanity. This service was the *selfless service* I performed to my Master and our spiritual community (the lineage of Bhagawan Nityananda of Ganeshpuri), that occurred over a period of more than eighteen years.

The reference in these verses to the 'Guru's feet' is a reference to the *Will* of the living Sadguru. The reference to *sipping* the water of the Guru's feet is a direct reference to the Humility, Reverence and Longing (Bhakti) that, when directed to the immanent aspect of the Guru-principle, the embodied form of the supreme, inner Guru in the living Shakta Adept, attracts the Grace of the Absolute into one's life. This happens *by way of the Master's Will.*

As part of engaging the Shaktipat Kriya Process that I share in this chapter, I discovered and proved to myself what many of the sacred texts of our lineage state over and over again. In a true Shaktipat Guru, *the power of God's Will and that Master's Will are one in the same.* The living Shaktipat Guru is a lineage holder in a long lineage of spiritually-perfected Love beings. Such beings have been vested with the power and authority of that lineage. Such a Guru has stored up the maximum amount of the Shiva-Shakti power – the energy substratum of everything and everyone. This power of God's Will that is transmitted/expressed through the living Master is also known as *Svatantrya, Iccha or Kriya Shakti.* Let me share an example of it at work.

During the journey to completion of retracing my steps back to God (what is also referred to as *Sadhana* in our approach), I began to have a series of nightmares that pointed to my dying in a car accident on a highway that I travelled on alone. I kept seeing myself completely lifeless, in a ditch on the side of the road. This dream repeated over and over again and became more and more vivid with each appearance. I kept seeing my mangled body being found 2-3 days later and placed in a body bag.

Having heard of the power of the Sadguru's Will being the same as God's Will, I was in the habit of discussing my dreams and inner experiences with my Guru, whenever the opportunity presented itself. This was part of my habit of putting my prayers and requests of God before him. Sometimes I sent a note to him through a Swami. At other times, I spoke to him directly as he greeted people at the end of programs.

I'll share something here that I have never spoken of completely before. At the end of one such program, I asked him for a spiritual name. He gave me the name *Kedar,* the manifestation of Lord Shiva as he rises from meditation to grant Blessings and Grace. I then shared my recurring death dream with him, along with the fear I was racked with as a result of those dreams. "Baba, am I going to die soon? Is there a way to prevent this event?" He responded by explaining to me that I was seeing some of my present karmas. That made me feel worse, having obtained the knowledge that our karmas have to be faced. As if seeing my despondency, Baba handed me a small crystal statue of Lord Ganesh, the remover of obstacles. He then smiled and said, "Don't worry about it. You have put it before me." Then his assistant looked at me and added, "He'll take care of it. Just remember him."

After that, the nightmares stopped and, having already been engaged in the Shaktipat Kriya Process, I had a very strong inner feeling that, by my Master's Will, those karmas connected to my timely death had been removed. This was confirmed a couple of weeks later in another conversation with him, in which he said, "It was your Bhakti, your Humility and Reverence for me that freed you from that karma. But there is a fate worse than the death of the body, and that is living in fear. Do you want to live in fear?" I responded, "No Baba. Please help me destroy fear." Shortly after this encounter, I experienced my own death in meditation that I describe in Chapter 3.

I am certain that experience was connected to the request I made of Shri Gurudev, that allowed for his Will to be directed in a way that caused that experience of my death in meditation to occur. *It is said that, when one experiences one's death in meditation, the fear of death and all other fears are removed* – that this is a big turning point in making great strides in Sadhana.

In fact, many of the experiences I share in this book, occurred because I made specific requests of my Shri Gurudev, either directly to his physical form, or to him inside – or due to my service to him and his spiritual community of followers. I did so *while remembering him and giving the glory to him.* Then there was the request I made of him for Discipleship. This request eclipsed all other requests I made of him. It enhanced my Sadhana, the Shaktipat Kriya Process that is the fire of my Master's Love, and secured the goal. This power of a Shaktipat Guru's Will (that I and many others who have experienced it are certain is God's Will personified), *is very mysterious and all-pervasive.* It is only fully understood by going beyond the mind and beyond the senses where the proof of this is found. Even then, it's difficult to describe in words.

What I can put into words is this; *The destruction of one's karmas that is necessary for permanent spiritual transformation cannot be had without Humility, Reverence and Devotion.* And these can't be properly cultivated without directing them to a form (more of this in Chapter 23). These spiritual principles take time to cultivate, due to how well we have hidden them by our notions of being just the body, just personalities in the pursuit of worldliness.

Even when we begin to face and discard such false notions with our heightened spiritual witnessing awareness, *there is so much that we are exposed to in our daily lives, pursuits and popular culture that eats away at our awareness of these essential principles, by destroying our Trust.* **For this reason, Humility, Reverence, our longing for God and the Master, these begin to wane over time, unless we are careful to continually cultivate and protect them with the armor of the Master's instruction and Grace.**

Just as a teacher or mentor is required in the arts, sciences, athletics and so on in order to become really competent in those fields, so too in the field of permanent spiritual transformation, a competent spiritual adept is required – one who has attained the goal of spiritual life. By the Grace of God, I found such a being in my Guru when I made the request of the Lord to understand the answers to the following questions.

Is this all there is?
Who am I?
Why am I here?
Why was I born?
What is fate?
What is destiny?
What is the real purpose of my life?
How can I know God more fully through direct experience?

It is said that, when the student is ready, the Master appears. In fact, I caused the meeting with my Master by the request I made of God in seeking the answer to those questions. This is what actually takes place. **God is watching. God is listening**. For those of us who really want the Self and are enthusiastic about initiation, about being led back home -- either in this life or a previous life, we made a request in some way to know God more fully, to become one with this Supreme Principle, the Self. In other words, *We asked for it.*

This request is what causes us to cross paths with a living spiritual leader who is a Shaktipat Guru. We made the request and, for those of us who really want to know the Truth of our identity, this is something we have to remember. Remembrance is vital as we begin to perform the inner work necessary to expiate the karmic patterns that keep us bound to the ignorance that prevents us from knowing who we really are.

I think it will be helpful to repeat some definitions from the Introduction that also apply here.

Our Shakta Approach

The lineage of Shaktipat Sadgurus, spiritually-perfected Masters to which I belong, is the Shakta, Parampara lineage of Lord Shiva. The Internet is ripe with confusing and skewed definitions for some of the terms used by our lineage of Self-realized, Love beings. Here are some helpful definitions taken from our sacred texts.

Shakta Approach - The entrance into the Shakta Upaya (upaya means approach) that begins with full Kundalini Awakening. This initiates one into the power of live Mantras, with the experience that the power of your Longing, your feeling and Devotion, burns away all that you are not. This approach also embodies the easy means of purifying all of the subtle spiritual energy centers of all the karmic impressions that keep one's true nature concealed from oneself. A Shaktipat Guru is the *catalyst and leader* for this unfolding approach.

Shaktipat Guru - A Shaktipat Guru in our lineage is a Master or spiritually-perfected leader (Sadguru), who is a strong leader, with the power to transmit God's Grace-bestowing power. Spiritually-perfected means Self-realized or God-realized. In our approach, this is a state where one experiences and is able to express the fullness of Humanity in the *constant delight* of the inner Self. *Such beings are rare* (see Chapter 4).

Such a being is a Love being who has stored up the *maximum* amount of Divine Conscious Energy (Shakti) necessary to fully awaken the dormant Kundalini energy in others. A spiritual leader such as this does not harm others and, instead, uplifts them (see page 60).

Witness Consciousness – A contemplative practice of passively observing thoughts and all other movements in your Consciousness from that place that is beyond the mind and beyond the senses. This practice is undertaken to experience that *Knower* who witnesses or observes every energy that forms in your Consciousness, including the energy of perception that fuels the senses. This practice leads to a heightened witnessing awareness that, over time, causes one to become established in the state of *Pure Perceiving Awareness* that is the final state of experience and knowledge, God-realization.

Without understanding the Shakta approach (the Shaktipat Kriya Process), practicing and mastering Witness Consciousness becomes a real struggle because *Grace and Witness Consciousness are connected.*

According to the great beings of our lineage and the Guru of the Saints of our lineage, Shiva himself, this Shakta approach is known as the *easy, spontaneous* means for removing the obstacles to permanent spiritual transformation. This allows one to enter into the Shambava state, the uninterrupted experience of the fullness of Humanity in the *constant delight* of the Self.

It is called the easy, spontaneous means because arduous practices that involve the struggle to attain the Self by attempting to 'climb a ladder,' are replaced with the simple approach that allows one to imbibe Grace, rather than sabotaging it. *This Grace is everything.*

Our approach involves the recognition and imbibing of Grace (and the avoidance of sabotaging Grace) as the primary foundation for everything that occurs in rising to permanent spiritual transformation. **Here, I am talking about Grace as a transformative power that releases you from the karmic patterns that are expressed through the tendencies and**

leanings (the play of the Gunas and the Malas) **that prevent you from attaining permanent spiritual transformation**. These karmic tendencies and attractions push you to vibrate in such a way that you conceal your true nature from yourself.

In the company of a spiritually-perfected companion in the living Shaktipat Guru, Grace is everywhere. This is the truth. It is always raining Grace. But, rather than allowing ourselves to become soaked with this Grace, we put up our umbrellas.

Our duty as yogis is to learn to vibrate at the highest level, the purest level possible. My Shri Gurudev once said, "The Self is the great actor in this play of Divine Consciousness." With respect to a heightened witnessing awareness, vibrating at a high level is like becoming this great actor. We begin to play our roles in life like a masterful actor who never forgets his/her true nature while engaged in the role, nor that he/she is playing a role/s, *regardless of* the varying levels of interaction we engage in that are dictated by the roles we play.

Taking great care in how we are vibrating allows us to play our various roles while always remembering the inner Self. Constant remembrance, as in NEVER forgetting -- this is the whole of the spiritual journey, to train ourselves through direct experience, never to forget who we really are. With a strong witnessing awareness (which takes practice), we *can* engage the varying expressions contained in Humanity, as appropriate to our roles and the situation right in front of us, without ever losing our experience of *That*, the Witness and only Experient.

Those who refute this as a possibility in experience are unfortunate or just being obstinate. Here's why I say this. To a certain degree, you already know that this is entirely possible because, at times, you engage in saving face. You tell people certain things in order to manipulate their perception of you, so that you can appear a certain way to one person or group, and a different way to another.

This happens because you make distinctions, based on the false notion of duality, with respect to those you interact with. *You know this already, for a fact*. So, you've already engaged in this *playing of roles* as an actor would. The only difference here is that you have engaged in protecting the false identity that you are just a person, just an individual. *When you begin to experience, from your expanded witnessing awareness, that you are the Self and all others are that same Self, you will drop the need to save face, in favor of rising above praise and blame – rising to indescribable Joy.*

The Shakti Brings Out the Best and the Worst In People

During my Sadhana, I performed a great deal of selfless service (Guruseva) in ashrams and centers. Performing Seva (see Chapter 11) is a spiritual practice that also invokes the Shaktipat Kriya Process. During the performance of selfless service in a Shaktipat Guru's school or house, the mirror of the Guru is always up.

One of my greatest limiting and binding tendencies was my habit of reaching for praise and doing everything possible to avoid blame. I was really stuck in praise and blame, big time. I used this self-imposed karma in ways that prevented me from letting go and giving over to my Master's Grace, even while taking face-saving measures in order to appear, to others, as if I was the epitome of imbibing Grace!

My Shri Gurudev had addressed this tendency with me directly, giving me specific instruction for expiating this karma that I mostly ignored. I did so out of my lack of Trust in his observation that I even had such an obstacle to address. So, my Master had to up the stakes, by way of a BIG test, *in order to get me to see the contraction that I had begun to deny existed, because I was engaged in saving face.*

One evening, during a program attended by some two thousand people, in the middle of a talk on selfless service, Baba mentioned my name and told the entire audience that I had made a real mess of my Seva at a very important celebration that took place at an ashram in India. He went on and on, telling people not to follow my poor example of performing Seva. Now, I wasn't even present for the celebration that he told two thousand people I had made a mess of! I was actually in New York at the time, working at my job.

I felt really humiliated! Then that feeling gave way to anger and I demanded an apology. Who was he to say such things in public, especially when he was wrong!? I wasn't even there. What kind of impudent fool had I taken for a Guru!? If he had something to tell me, why didn't he just pull me aside in private and whisper it to me when no one else was around. I was livid! I felt my trust had been betrayed and I was ready to leave. The honeymoon was about to come to an end, permanently, or so I thought.

To save space here, I will share with you that, when I calmed down and some loving communication took place, it was explained to me that, due to my resistance, I had hidden from myself the fact that I still had leanings and tendencies around *praise and blame*. I had not yet risen above these two. I had also harbored the notion that, 'so what – no big deal, nobody else wants to be blamed either.'

So, Baba had to 'up the stakes.' He had to test me so that I could see where I was really at, rather than remaining attached to where I thought I was at. (If I tested devotees today in the way my Master tested devotees in my day, you'd show me the door! So, there are still tests, but the approach is a little different.) This test, as part of the Shaktipat Kriya Process, along with what it uncovered for me, became a huge and most valuable turning point in my progress toward permanent spiritual transformation. It freed me from my fear of letting go of my attachment to praise and blame – a monumental shift for me!

In your subtle body, *there are tendencies that you cannot see and are not aware of* because they function just beneath the level of your conscious awareness. An example is the story I just shared from my own Sadhana. The great beings say that we cannot see these binding, contracting leanings and tendencies *until we begin to embrace the fact that each of us is not a person, but that we are the Self, that highest power, the Supreme Principle.* Until we hold this highest of understandings, we cannot begin to see our past and present karmas or the obstacles they create in our rising.

This *seeing* begins with the phenomenon known as *Kriya* or the Grace-bestowing power of the Absolute that is invoked by a Shaktipat Guru, beginning with full Kundalini Awakening. Here we acknowledge that nothing can take place without this Grace. *Grace is the answer, Grace is Love without distinctions. This Grace is God.*

State of Grace

In spiritual life, it is an absolute necessity to learn how to live in a state of Grace (see Chapter 27). To be able to hold this transformative Grace, to recognize it, to embrace it, and to act according to it requires a leader in our companion in a Sadguru. There are so many sacred texts that speak of this; enough to understand that permanent spiritual transformation cannot be attained without the leadership and Grace of such a being.

Experiencing this transformative Grace on an ongoing basis (and also with great intensity at times) through such a being, is the sign that you are with the right one. The inability to hold the most useful, the highest understandings with respect to facing yourself through Sadhana would be the cause of your turning away from such a being or approach.

The approach to Sadhana, the Shaktipat Kriya Process, is shared in more detail in our weekend Shaktipat Blessing retreats and other published articles (see more about *Nityananda Shaktipat Yoga* at the end of this book).

Chapter 5
Bhagawan Nityananda of Ganeshpuri

Salutations to Nityananda, the Guru, who rescues his disciples from transmigration, who has assumed a body for the needs of devotees, whose nature is Consciousness and being.

Free of desires, free of expectations, free of all defects independent and fearless – to that Nityananda, I bow.

Free of possessiveness, free of egoism, regarding as the same a clod, a stone, and gold, even-minded in happiness and sorrow, all-enduring – to that avadhut indeed, I bow

From the Avadhuta Stotram

Before his passing, my Master told me, "Just Meditate on Baba Bhagawan Nityananda, and you will attain everything after me." He then smiled at me and nodded his head at me, raising his eyebrows as if to say, "Did you hear me!?" He also told me that I would attain Moksha, Liberation in this very life.

This began the development of a strong inner relationship with Bhagawan Nityananda of Ganeshpuri (Baba or Bade Baba, as he was also affectionately called) and Lord Shiva. All this occurred by Baba's Will. My meditations on Bhagawan Nityananda and Lord Shiva were becoming spontaneous. This shift in my inner experience was very significant.

I traveled to Ganeshpuri, India to participate in the Mahasamadhi celebration of Gurudev's passing. Thousands of people had come together from all over the world to celebrate his life and work. During this celebration, there was a Yajna (fire ceremony) presided over by monks of various traditions. This Yajna went on for 16 days with chanting and oblations (offerings) being made to the fire.

While meditating in front of the fire, I saw Bhagawan Nityananda standing in the flames. He spoke to me saying, "Work with the artists and healers so that they express only the highest through their work." Bhagawan Nityananda then stepped out of the

51

fire, touched me on the head and then disappeared. At first, I ignored this vision, thinking that it must have been an hallucination of some kind. Baba had never appeared to me in such a vivid form as this.

During this and subsequent trips to India, I spent a lot of time in Bhagawan Nityananda's Mahasamadhi shrine in the village of Ganeshpuri. I made many offerings to Baba's Murthi there and spent many hours meditating in the shrine. As a result of this pilgrimage, I started to have even more profound experiences during Chanting and Meditation. I will share some of these experiences in later chapters.

During this period of my Sadhana, I felt that events in my life had sped up. It was as if things that were to happen were now happening in a hurry. *Whatever needed to be completed was being completed in triple time.* For example, I had several astrological readings during this period. In these readings I was told about relationships and events that were not "scheduled" to happen until very late in my life or in a future life. Yet these events and relationships were happening right there during that time. Relationships were starting and culminating very quickly. I was meeting people who I was not to meet until I was an old man. That which was predicted to occur near my death had just happened!

I later came to realize that many of my karmas were being burned. It was as if those things that I needed to experience, those things that may have held me back from immersing myself in the spiritual path, were either happening and being completed or had been burned from my being. I felt as if I was living many life times in a very short period of time. A Shakta Adept does burn many of one's karmas. And this was continuing to happen to me, by the Will and Grace of my Master and our lineage of holy beings. *My perception of time changed entirely during this period.* I felt the Universe was unfolding inside me. All this was due to my Guru's Grace.

Shortly after this period, I had several experiences in Meditation that not only changed the quality of my Sadhana, but also changed the entire course of my destiny. I am going to share two of those experiences here, just as I wrote them in my journal:

The chanting going on inside me is very, very strong and I can feel the name of my Master vibrating with great intensity throughout my being. My entire body shakes with this vibration. Wherever I am, I feel and experience this vibration. I have sent some ghee to Ganeshpuri to be offered to the fire. I have experienced, in meditation, Guruji offering the ghee that I sent to the fire. Then, in meditation, there is Bhagawan Nityananda also.

Bhagawan Nityananda is sitting. He is very, very big. My Master is standing over a Shiva Lingham in my Ajna Chakra (third eye). There is a lid on the top of the lingham that is being controlled by means of a lever on the side. The lid is opened. Fire is rushing forth into my sushumna. The fire is gold and white and many mantras dance in the fire. Bhagawan Nityananda is making offerings to the fire and my Master is circumambulating the fire while pouring ghee (my ghee) into it, being very careful to control the pressure of the fire. All this is happening inside me. My skin is burning. The fire continues up through my Sushumna and mushrooms in Ajna Chakra. The fire is singing now, intoning many mantras which I hear welling up from within me. The fire now cools for a brief time. This experience has continued for several weeks, in and out of my sitting meditations at home. Each time, the fire is becoming stronger and larger.

I am seeing the fire as if sitting in front of a great Yajna. I offer everything to the fire and, as I do so, I am moving closer and closer to it. The fire is mushrooming and pressing against a threshold near the top of Ajna Chakra. It sits there, playing at the threshold. Now the lingham has become the Yajna pit. Bhagawan Nityananda is making offerings to the fire. Bhagawan Nityananda is circumambulating the fire. "Swaha, Swaha, Swaha" cries the fire! As I look, I can see the tall golden fire reaching from the base of my spine to that threshold near the top of my head.

It seems that I can no longer differentiate between myself, where I am sitting, and the fire. I realize I have become one with this fire. I cannot see the flames because I have become the flames. Now, the fire looks more transparent to me but, at the same time, very awesome and luminous. The fire, like a big mushroom cloud, is playing at the threshold, Ajna Chakra.

While continuing to Meditate, my attention is drawn to something. As I look up, there is a great explosion! The fire has crossed the threshold and is billowing at the top of my head. The fire exits through the top of my head and there are many explosions as the fire bursts into thousands of gold bindis which hover over my head.

*   *   *

I am meditating in the Bhagawan Nityananda temple. I open my eyes and look at the Murthi of Bhagawan. Suddenly, Bhagawan Nityananda has come out of the Murthi. He walks towards me and is now dancing around me in a circle. He is laughing and singing ecstatically while dancing around me. He stops in front of me and puts his hands on my head. He then runs his hands down over my face. Bhagawan Nityananda pauses there, his big hands on my face and his long fingers stretching to the top of my head.

He then starts dancing around me and singing once again. After he finishes singing and dancing around me, he climbs back into the Murthi. But he has entered me also! Bhagawan Nityananda has taken up residence in me! Now I am having an inner vision of Bhagawan Nityananda and other Saints of our lineage throwing flower petals on me. They are garlanding me with flowers.

*   *   *

There were other, similar, experiences as well. With each experience, with each vision and message, I dove deeper into my own heart. I discovered states of absolute Bliss that I did not believe could be experienced by a human being. My longing for God and my Guru increased. *My state of Devotion had risen to the point where I really didn't care whether Liberation was at hand or not. I had no thoughts of siddhahood or enlightenment.* I only wanted to drink the nectar of God's Love over and over again.

My entire experience was the longing to worship the feet of my Master and to experience the waves of Love and Bliss that became mine as I merged into my Guru and into the Supreme Principle. *I was becoming a mad lover of the inner Self.* This state of ecstasy was all that I lived for.

It was with this experience and expanded vision that I began performing many more years of Seva (see Chapter 11) in my Shri Gurudev's ashrams and centers. I would perform Guruseva and chant. Then more Seva, chant and meditate again. Time seemed to stand still. I started to see the Supreme Being in everyone. I started to recognize my Baba's Shakti everywhere. I did become mad, but not in the way you think. This madness I could not attempt to describe. You will just have to experience it for yourself.

After some time in this state, my Sadhana deepened to the point where I started to have visions of other Saints.

Chapter 6
Siddha Loka: Visions of Saints

The manifestation of the Universe of all the worlds is more vast than can be experienced with the naked eye. In this *Play of Divine Consciousness* that we find ourselves in, there is not just this one world that we refer to in mundane life, *but there are many, many worlds!* In our approach, these other worlds are called Lokas.

A *Loka* is a plane of existence that is *both physical and subtle,* meaning that a *Loka* is an actual physical manifestation in the Universe and also a subtle manifestation that can be accessed from within. These planes of existence are numerous and activity in them goes on simultaneously with that of our own plane of existence that we call this world.

Siddhas or Self-realized Love beings, both living in the body and passed, exist in a particular plane together. We (I include the holy beings of my lineage when I say 'We') call this plane *Siddha Loka*. Liberated beings who take Mahasamadhi (drop their bodies for the last time) merge into the formless Supreme Principle. They have been released from the cycle of birth and death. However, they continue to reside in *Siddha Loka* for a long time in their subtle forms; the subtle version of the same form in which they were known to us.

Sometimes, out of their own free will and compassion, they decide to come here from Siddha Loka to set in motion the raising of spiritual awareness, during periods of great spiritual ignorance on the planet. When they do this, they take a human form again, *already Liberated*, already completely Self-realized. Bhagawan Nityananda was such a being, a Janma Siddha or born Siddha. Examples of other Janma Siddhas include Lord Dattatreya, Jnaneshwar Maharaj and Lord Krishna.

Siddha Loka is a plane of existence spoken about by a number of Saints in our lineage. It is also a place described by other Saints of various traditions who refer to it by different names. To have the vision of this Loka is a great gift. *One experiences Siddha Loka by the Grace of a Shakta Adept, usually in the advanced stages of one's Sadhana.* It can be reached inside through Meditation and is experienced most often in the *Tandra* state. Travel to Siddha Loka is a sign that one has entered into the advanced stages of retracing one's steps back to God.

My visions of Siddha Loka started just after my experience of Ajna Chakra being pierced through the Grace of my Spiritual Mentor (see Chapter 5). I had many experiences in Siddha Loka and I saw many great beings when I traveled there. *In fact, it was through my visions in Siddha Loka that I learned of and experienced many of the Saints of our lineage for the first time.* After having visions of them, I received confirmation of who they were through descriptions in the Agamas and epic poems of Shaivism and Vedanta. Later, I also discovered that my Baba had many of these same experiences, as did other holy beings.

Siddha Loka is a place of incredible beauty, stillness and light. The light shining there is always a scintillating, subtle blue light that appears almost as if viewing a bright light or the sun through a piece of blue crystal. There is land there that is very green and lush. All colors there are of a hue that I can only describe as otherworldly, in stark contrast to our own. The Saints have their own individual abodes in Siddha Loka and these vary in shape and size.

Some Siddhas dwell there in huts with dirt floors and others in castles. And then there is a great Palace of crystal and marble where many of them come together as a congregation! I saw great Yajnas performed here. O, what a magnificent place this is! So sweet and profound! I pray that each of you will have the opportunity to experience Siddha Loka!

THE ABODE OF THE SAINTS

After returning from my trips to Ganeshpuri, my worship of Bhagawan Nityananda continued. It was during this time that my visions of the Saints of our lineage increased. I would sit for meditation and, while remaining completely aware of everything around me, I would go very deep into Meditation. After some time like this I would slip into *Tandra*. In a moment, I will share some of my experiences in Tandra that I recorded in my journal at the time.

The state of Tandra is a state just beyond sleep that can also be accessed through the sleep state. It is a state of Meditation in which visions and premonitions come easily of their own accord.

My Master spoke of *Tandraloka* at times, but I had never experienced it before this. I know this state to be different from my experience of sleep, even though it comes, at times, for me while in a reclined position.

My experiences in Tandraloka, would start with Meditation on Bhagawan Nityananda or Lord Shiva. In fact, I often saw them while immersed in Tandra. Sometimes I traveled to Siddha Loka in this state of Tandra. At other times, I went there on the wings of the Blue Pearl or in an aerial chariot, while seated in Meditation.

When I traveled to Siddha Loka I had the Darshan of Sages. I also had premonitions that later came to pass. I had the Darshan of Zipruanna, a highly revered Saint, many times. Sometimes he would speak to me and, at other times, he would sit before me staring into my eyes. His skin was like a brilliant golden butter. He emanated so much light.

I was also visited by Akkalkot Swami. Akkalkot Swami is an amazing being whose body is long and very supple. He is like a moving body of light, changing shape at will. Sometimes he spoke to me. But it was a language I did not understand. I also had the Darshan of Lord Rama and Krishna several times.

Often, when traveling to Siddha Loka, I saw a great Yajna. At times, I saw this Yajna burning before me. I meditated on the fire and then merged with it, before finding myself in Siddha Loka. One time I had the following experience:

I am meditating. The fire is billowing intensely. I find myself hovering in a huge void. Looking down from above, I see the inner Palace. It is exquisite. Like the finest jewel! The Palace is beaming a great white light! This light is emanating from every pore of the Palace. I see this light with my eyes open and my eyes closed. It is effulgent and beyond comparison. I am being ushered into the Palace into a room that I have not seen before.

I see a great chair. This chair is emanating the same light that is beaming from the Palace. Baba is sitting in the chair. He is effulgent! I feel myself becoming those rays of white light. Now I see the fire again. The fire leaps up, and as it does, a magnificent Being steps out of the fire. His hands and arms are outstretched to me. Out of the palms of his hands, there is a golden light flowing!

He will not show me his face, nor his feet.

He speaks to me: "I am the one who previously manifested to you as Indra, Lord of the heavens. I am the one who has been guarding your Sahasrar. I am the one who sits above the Palace at the top of your head. When it is time, I will come for you. Look for me when it is time. Do not worry. Lead your life. Perform your dharma."
With that, this Being disappeared.

*   *   *

In another vision of Siddha Loka two years later, I saw this Being again:

In meditation, I see a fire blazing in front of me. I then merge with this fire. I, the fire, have now crossed the threshold once again and I am at the entrance to the Palace. I am billowing and very luminous. Once inside the Palace, I have stopped to gaze upon those who have gathered for satsang. I am in a very large hall that has a huge throne at one end. There is a fire blazing on the seat of that throne. Brahma, the great fire, has now come from the throne to greet me. Jnaneshwar, Krishna, Lord Rama, Vyasa, Vasugupta are all seated in front of the throne facing the gathering. They are there but translucent. The Goddess Lakshmi is hovering over the congregation. There are many gold bindis in the air.

The Being that I have seen before, who would not show me his face, now appears before me and speaks: "I am Lord Shiva. Because you have surrendered, I have shown you my true face. It is through your surrender that I have manifested before you. It is through your devotion that I have become this very Palace, this fire, this satsang, this congregation. Never let this experience die. Cause it to grow and expand. You have become my beloved! You have become my beloved! I will always be with you. Soon you will know me completely." Shiva then embraces me and I him as the satsang continues.

*   *   *

Often, while having visions of Siddha Loka, I was offered teachings that changed my life. And whenever these Siddhas told me something, it came to pass. One example is the following experience I had on Krishna's birthday:

As I sit for meditation, I am transported to Siddha Loka. The sky is very clear. It seems to have gotten taller. The heavens have opened up! First I see the planets. Then I see Lord Shiva. The planets are now strung on a necklace around Shiva's neck. Saturn, Uranus and Neptune have been aligned together in front. Then Pluto. There are many gold bindis and stars shooting from Shiva's navel. Blue and Gold light is everywhere. There is also darkness just beyond Shiva's form.

I now hear the cries of many thousands of people screaming and wailing from a dark pit. Above, in the heavens, there are these large shells, floating in the blue firmament. Bhagawan Nityananda is now looming in the heavens. His form is very large and all encompassing and it seems that these large shells are part of his form. I have now become Bhagawan Nityananda's form and I am looking down at these shells. I have the realization that they are protective shells. They are starting to open. I can hear the thundering sound of the fire as these shells open.

A very luminous light is emanating from these protective shells. I see Shiva and Vishnu and there are many devotees and disciples huddled close together around other deities. Some are weeping, some are joyous, some are screaming. But all those in the shells are protected.

Lord Vishnu has just drawn a golden sword from a sheath and he is sharpening it. There are many deities riding chariots through the heavens. They have joined Vishnu and are standing by his side. They look as if they are poised for battle. There are many conches sounding!! I suddenly find myself in Bhagawan Nityananda's temple. I have now become the Murthi in the Temple.

And, even though I seem to have climbed into the Murthi of Bhagawan Nityananda, I am also sitting on the floor with many disciples. We are all meditating. There are thousands of golden rays emanating from the Murthi, from Bhagawan Nityananda, and entering all of us who are sitting in Meditation. The Meditation gong is sounding. As I open my eyes and look up at Bhagawan Nityananda, he is smiling intensely and beaming. There is a golden halo around his head and he looks very translucent.

*   *   *

This particular vision of Siddha Loka occurred during the last Harmonic Convergence, an astrological event that happens only once in many centuries. Shortly after this vision, the economic crash of 1989 occurred. If you remember, many of the US population found themselves out of work for a long time. Other economies across the globe also crashed. For several years, the outlook was bleak for all but the wealthy. Many people were financially devastated during this period. You may also remember that many global banking networks failed. A record number of banks folded.

This was also the time that uncovered the largest personal debt and government deficits in world history. Although the media did a great job of keeping it from us, many economists agree that we experienced an economic depression during this time. Those who were not spiritually strong suffered a great deal more than the rest of us. My own experience, as well as that of close friends, was one of having to fully embrace spiritual practice in order to surmount great circumstantial difficulties. But my experiences of Siddha Loka continued to be sublime.

There were also *lessons* that I learned through my visions of Siddha Loka. The most important lesson was one of self-loathing and self-worth. Through the following vision, I uncovered issues and weaknesses regarding these that I didn't know I had.

Meditation. I go very, very deep. I find myself in Siddha Loka at the Palace. I am sitting in the room with the dirt floor. The Yajna is burning. Bhagawan Nityananda, Jnaneshwar, Krishna, Lord Rama and Shiva are all sitting around the fire. There are magnificent jewels of all shapes and sizes lying on a Puja cloth before me. They are reflecting an incredible light. The Siddhas tell me that they want to give me all these jewels.

I reply that I will accept only what is due me. They offer all the jewels to me again. Again, I reply that I will only take those that I am worthy of. Again they say, "But we want to give you all of the jewels!! Will you take them?"

I come out of Meditation at this point thinking to myself, "What must I do to be worthy of all this? They were offered. So, why didn't I just accept them and take them?"

*   *   *

I had not yet realized that I was already worthy. It took some additional time for me to realize my own true worth.

One summer morning, I went to Bhagawan Nityananda temple early for Meditation. As I sat for Meditation, I noticed a long ray of golden light emanating from Bhagawan Nityananda's Murthi. I closed my eyes. The light was there. I opened my eyes. The light was still there.

This beam of golden light expanded until it filled the inside of the entire temple. Then it contracted until it became a tiny dot. This dot hovered in front of me for several minutes and then it entered me. From inside me, I then heard what I can only describe as an explosion. My eyes were closed. I then opened them and saw something quite startling.

Bhagawan Nityananda rose up out of the Murthi and walked slowly to where I was meditating. He was glowing like the rays of a thousand suns. His skin was pure gold. His eyes were deep and endless. His fingers were long and curved in different directions and they were vibrating!

Bhagawan Nityananda stood in front of me smiling. Then he started to walk around me. First slowly and then faster. Then he started to dance around me as he had done in a previous vision, calling my name. "Kedar, Kedar. Sri Kedar," he said over and over again. I became very intoxicated. With my eyes closed and then open, I saw the same thing. This scene went on for 10 or 15 minutes.

Then Bhagawan came to a complete stop in front of me. He made a long buzzing sound and then a loud "Humph!" He then said, "Karma coming. Must be faced. Don't cry. Look for choices. You will come to me." Bhagawan Nityananda then took his seat back in the Murthi. Part of me wanted to immediately know what karma Bhagawan was speaking of, especially because he had said "Don't cry." But I was too intoxicated at the time to even give that a second thought. I was to find out anyway, soon enough.

Chapter 7
Sex and Marriage

I have been married twice. Both were experiences that came about as a result of past karmas. Through both these marriages, I learned a great deal about myself, the very nature of karma, and choices I had, some of which I exercised and some of which I did not. In both cases, I was "in love" with my spouse for a period of time.

In both marriages, I reached a point where my spiritual growth caused a change in me that demanded a restructuring of those relationships, based on what my spouses continued to want, that I could no longer give. When married, I engaged in all those things that most married couples do, including 'sex' and 'romance.' The only thing that did not happen is children. While married, both times, I was also engaged in a spiritual practice of great intensity.

In fact, **I had reached a point in my spiritual attainment and inner experience where I no longer wanted to be viewed and treated like an object of someone else's attraction and desire. And I no longer wanted to see another as a mere object of my own desire, lust and craving.** I was gravitating, more and more, to relationships based solely on *Human Dignity* --- true friendships, where we could relate to each other *out of Love and Respect for the inner Self, seeing each other as God.* I also began desiring interactions only with those who really wanted to serve the spiritual needs of Humanity in some way. In both my marriages, this was "the straw that broke the camels back." Neither spouse wanted what I wanted. So, those relationships came to an end.

Sex and Human Dignity

There will not be an ongoing discussion of this in the future, as I don't want to add to the huge chorus of people who desire to know, discuss and gossip about the 'sex' lives of others. However, if the parents don't talk to their children about it, and the spiritual leaders are afraid to discuss it, where will those growing up spiritually learn of it?

They will learn of it by becoming the sex objects of others, by having their dignity violated at an age when they are too young to make their own conscious choice about it, by taking lessons from the pornographic expressions on the internet and in popular music and culture, and by acquiescing to the basest forms of it that go along with engaging in the drug and sex culture of our society. They *won't* find Human Dignity in these places.

There is talk on the Internet of Gurus or spiritual teachers who are alleged to have engaged in sexual activity (leading to abuse) with multiple students/devotees whom they had the charge of leading. I want you to know that Kedarji is against any such activity. My feeling is this issue must be talked about openly to avoid misunderstandings, accusations of all kinds, and behavior that has the potential to harm others.

I do not and will not pass judgment on any beings who have had accusations of this nature lodged against them. Let God be the judge. The accusers and those accused should face each other openly, directly and honestly with reverence for any healing that needs to occur.

There are Sadgurus in our lineage who were either married or in committed, monogamous relationships with their chosen, intimate relationship partner, *who were great beings with the ultimate power to transmit God's Grace, while leading others to the final state.* I will name some of them here;

Shiva and Parvati
Vishnu and Lakshmi
Rama and Sita
Krishna and Rukmini
Ananda Mayi Ma and Bolanath
Marpa (Milarepa's Guru) and Dakmema
Tukaram Maharaj and Jijai (Avali)
Eknath Maharaj and Girija Bai
Atrimuni and Anasuya
Agastya and Lopamudra
Shri Sharada Devi and RamKrishna
Arjuna and Subhadra
Yajnavalkya and Maitreyi
Lahiri Mahasya and Kashimoni

These great sages became one being. When one ate a meal, the other felt satisfied. They loved each other for God's sake, not for their own sake. Their intimacy/intercourse did not hamper their ability to lead. Kedarji is all for such relationships, as even one spiritually-perfected being in such a relationship addresses the karmic distractions, while making the relationship a boon to Humanity.

Other than a monogamous relationship as just described above, I am against spiritual teachers and/or spiritual Masters engaging in intimacy/intercourse with multiple partners. In this Kali Yuga age, isn't there already enough confusion and doubt about Liberation while still in the body?

I Had Sex

I have been in monogamous relationships where intimacy/intercourse was joyfully engaged. So, I am sharing this from my experience in these relationships and the utterances of the great beings of our lineage, with respect to *Human Dignity*, in order to openly address the sacredness of intimacy. For the benefit of those engaged in such intimacy/intercourse (instead of just sex), who want to vibrate at the highest level that recognition of the Self provides, I make this utterance. *This is not a matter of liberal or conservative, or any other political or social notion. It's a matter of the true Heart.*

It is not my intention here to judge anyone. All are the inner Self, even though many are misguided. Having experienced the difference between the sacredness of intimacy and just sex, I share the following with you now.

Over the years I have spoken of this with a number of youth and young adults, and also adult men and women, and couples. I find that so many people are intrigued and infatuated with 'in your face' talk and the seemingly insatiable desire over sexual preference, sexual activity and the like. Pornography, pornographic inferences and pornographic messages have fueled our society's insatiable appetite for all things sexual. Our society is riddled with a collective consciousness filled with the seemingly insatiable desire to hear about and relish in the sex lives of others. So many want to know the other's 'sexual' activity and desires.

Friends, former lovers and associates have become an incestuous bunch. There are even groups of deluded people who feel the necessity to tell others how to define themselves by sexual pursuits, sexual preference and ongoing sexual stimulation. Some of these people even attempt to lead people spiritually!

These contracting notions run completely counter to the fact that you are the Self. **Defining yourself in any other way keeps you contracted and unable to make any permanent progress spiritually.** And defining yourself along the lines of sex and gender really keeps you entangled in the basest of vibrations, attached to the false notion that you are the body. In this way, *our society's insatiable desire for all things sex has become a breeding ground for the destruction of Human Dignity and the rise of open decadence.*

Even those who are charged with the duty of enforcing the laws against human trafficking, for example, can be found frequenting the very nude bars, massage parlors, escorts and prostitutes who embody the human trafficking trade. Many parents who want to raise their children without the influence of sex consciousness everywhere won't talk to their children about Love and intimacy, and are hiding behind the very activities they hope their children will avoid.

A Greater Perspective

The Sadgurus of our Shaivism tell us that Chiti (Shakti or Divine Consciousness energy) is supremely free. This Chiti alone exists. She dwells in perfect freedom. Desiring to reveal the Supreme Principle through all the expressions of this world-appearance, this Chiti expands, of its own free will, manifesting countless forms and shapes. Even while doing so, Chiti dwells forever in the transcendental state, transcending even that. This Shakti is *Pure Perceiving Awareness.* Living in and as the Universe, Chiti is also apart from it *as its eternal witness.*

"The love we feel for one another is actually the attraction of the Self within." ~ Shri Narada

The householder Saints of our Shaivism engaged in the relationships with their beloved with this understanding and direct experience.

During the activity of retracing my steps back to God, I started practicing celibacy, *not* because it was a command or requirement of my lineage for merging in the inner Self, *but because I got tired of the subtle manipulation game that took place in the act of sex, simply for the sake of orgasm and ejaculation.* I got tired of being targeted as a sex object (as a mere sex toy), expected to engage in the bartering of needs for wants, in the context of the notion of individuality and the need to be completed by someone or something else.

The holy beings tell us to preserve our human dignity in every way because, without this dignity, we have nothing where spiritual awareness and permanent spiritual transformation is concerned. *Human dignity is the gateway toinner strength and Equality Consciousness.* When it is compromised and torn down, there is nothing left of value on which to build a foundation for greater and greater spiritual awareness. The holy beings of our lineage are very direct in the ways in which they state this.

The antidote to this condition comes with addressing Human Dignity in the context of the direct experience of our true Heart, God's Love – a Love without distinctions. *And, once lost, Human Dignity can be reclaimed.* The point here is, just as there are mantras that cause one to contract and others that cause one to expand, there are lower vibrations (contracting Shaktis or energies) and higher, more expansive and freeing Shaktis or energies. We actually study these groupings of Shaktis in the *Secret To Self-Realization* series of courses. As Shri Ramkrishna says, "God exists in everything and everyone equally, but you don't hug a wild, untamed tiger."

Yoga or Boga?

Our approach is not a "tantric" approach. We are discontinuing our use of this word because it has become skewed and tainted in its use by so many, and also because of how it is 'sold' on the internet. Here, we advocate for and invoke the natural process of making every activity a blessed sacrament to the Self, by offering and perfecting our activity to please the SupremePrinciple and attract Grace. This is inculcated in the highest vibration that is sustained with the understanding and experience that we each are the inner Self, that Shiva-Shakti power, and not a mere person.

In fact, it is really best that we each seek to understand and experience what Love really is, the unconditionality of real Love, before ever engaging in 'sex.' And this teaching and direct experience should be passed on to our children.

If you recognize your lover/partner as the Self, then you know your partner. If your partner/lover recognizes you as the Self, then your partner knows you. Otherwise, you are just reflecting your limiting desires and cravings back to each other in an endless stream of contraction, out of the need for stimulation, and to feed craving, duality and distinctions, not Love. *Love has no distinctions. Please listen to this.*

And if you insist, like some do, that Kedarji is wrong in this, then please bring to me the scripture or sacred text of any Saint, Siddha or Holy Being of any religion or spiritual path or approach that states that there are distinctions to be made in Love. There is a reason why you will never find such a statement uttered by the true Love beings, the Siddhas. And if you find such a sacred text that advises making these kinds of distinctions in Love, I'd like to see it. *Respect* is what this is about - respecting who we really are, that highest principle, and not a mere object, is how we preserve our Dignity, without which there is nothing of value to be embraced in life.

Ojas

In your bone marrow is a yellow fluid known as Ojas (not to be confused with the many variations on this word across the internet and in 'tantra' books designed to titillate). This seminal fluid is the conductor for the awakened Kundalini Shakti. The awakened Kundalini requires a strong platform of Ojas in order to continue to rise through all your spiritual energy centers and physical organs, in order to purify these all the karmic impressions that are the obstacles to your permanent spiritual transformation.

For those who want to make steady spiritual progress to permanent spiritual transformation, especially those who have received full Kundalini Awakening, the Ojas must be preserved and protected (rather than wasted). The bond of power that preserves Ojas is contained in a living Sadguru's Grace, in the form of your receiving and imbibing the transmission of Mahashakti flowing from such a being, *combined with your effort at storing, protecting and preserving that Shakti.*

There is a very delicate exchange of energies that takes place during intercourse. It is very subtle. Without care, awareness and discernment, this can be like giving away one's Shakti in a way that one's storehouse of energy is reduced, while taking on the other person's vibrations that can cause a subtle shift in one's own vision, *away* from witnessing awareness.

Celibacy?

In our approach, and also by the standards of our lineage, life-long celibacy *is not* required for permanent spiritual transformation that can also lead to becoming established in the state that embodies the fullness of Humanity in the constant delight of the inner Self (Liberation). We teach that periods of celibacy are very good for helping one to experience permanent spiritual transformation, embodied in a shift away from the *constant itch* of the senses and base sexual desire and stimulation that become obstacles to vibrating at a higher, purer level.

And if you think this sounds like, "Oh, boring," that's your ego talking – the bad habit of seeing yourself as just a person, the body or an individual. That's your attachment talking. *And these are not who you are.* They are the obstacles to your discovering who you really are. The alternative is reaching for a higher state from which to view your Humanity, a state imbued with Joy, Joy, Joy - the Abode of the Heart.

The choice to practice periods of celibacy is a choice that we encourage (as it is a real boon to storing the spiritual energy that allows one to relish in the Self) but do not demand. We also teach abstinence and strongly encourage periods of abstinence.

Abstaining for measured periods of time is a very valuable practice that allows the mind and the senses to become rooted in the direct experience of your own Bliss, independent of the pull of the senses to limiting sexual desire. This can be easily understood in a question posed by my Master, "Are you enjoying your senses, or are your senses enjoying you?"

The obstacle to preserving purity in the act of intimacy (which is the preservation of the experience of Human Dignity in the delight of the Self), *the obstacle* to this is the insistence on seeing each other as an object of sense, as an object of attraction, rather than seeing each other as the inner Self.

In the relationships I mention above that I was in, my experience was that of seeing my dear one as God, even in the act of intimacy/intercourse. *I was not compelled to have sex.* If intimacy happened, that was fine and I enjoyed that activity. If it didn't, that was fine too. I found myself equally content just to gaze into my dear one's eyes. This created a space within me to relish that being as the Beloved, as the Self -- with Respect, Dignity and Grace. **It's an inner experience. The outer enjoyment is then recognized as a reflection of this inner experience.**

Intimacy that naturally unfolds from the experience of the true Heart, a Love without distinctions, can be experienced in the delight of the inner Self. When there is no objectification (objectification = seeing each other as an object of sense, rather than the Self), anything that naturally evolves out of this Love for each other *as the Self*, including intimacy/intercourse, is perfect and fulfilling, *and leads to content and the experience of Bliss and Peace.*

For spiritual aspirants engaged in intimate relationships, this kind of monogamy in the delight of the inner Self is important. It is also important to exercise caution with whom intimacy/intercourse is shared because it is a sacred act in the sharing of Shakti. **This is not politics. This is a matter of understanding the subtle energy (and energy exchange) that is the basis of this activity.**

During intimacy there is an exchange of energies that impacts your awareness (either to expand or contract) in ways that you may not understand. Until your witnessing awareness is very developed, this all takes place just beneath the level of your conscious awareness, and in ways that can cause your witnessing awareness to shut down altogether.

This is the Truth and I say this, not to frighten you, but to help you become more aware of energies that can influence and contract your awareness without your even knowing. This is not hard to understand when using examples of proofs in medical science. For example, your physical heart has an EMF (electro-magnetic field) that gives off a vibration. That vibration can, and often does, impact the vibration of others who you are in close proximity to (and vice versa). This is not the only organ in your body that channels such vibrations, but it is a major one.

If you have not begun to reside in the state of the Observer, if your witnessing awareness is not strong, your inner experience of the Self is impacted by the physiological vibrations of others, sometimes toward contraction and attachment to what is self-destructive. **This is why we emphasize the act of being conscious of how you are vibrating in order to keep your vibration very high, so that the 'vibes' of others that can cause a shift in your awareness to contraction do not impact your state.**

This can only be practiced and mastered by going beyond the mind and beyond the senses. **Then attachment becomes contentment and limiting desire becomes the desire to relish in the Self.** This begins with our practice of Witness Consciousness, so that shifts in the physiology of how you are vibrating do not change your perception of what is actually taking place, and do not pull you away from your remembrance and experience of the inner Self, the true Heart.

With intercourse, there is also the very real aspect of taking on other people's karmas (like a sponge absorbs water), which you then have to suffer, unless you have the ability to burn those karmas in the ocean of your stored Mahashakti. It's subtle but has, at times, a far-reaching impact on one's vibration. **This is why, in our approach to the Self, intercourse is considered to be sacred, to be shared among committed partners who want to respect this act as Divine, rather than just a compulsion to fulfill personal desire in the context of seeing each other as mere objects of pleasure.**

This is a matter of Human Dignity, and a process of letting go and letting God. For those seeking more than just a passing glimpse of the Self, that Supreme Being, this Dignity should be *preserved at all costs*. There is great Joy in it. So, don't leave God out of it. Keep God in it by learning to observe all the activity you *appear* to be engaged in, from the highest vantage point of the inner Self. Let go of seeing yourself and others as an object of the senses, as a mere object of attraction, attachment and aversion.

Chapter 8
The Aerial Chariot

One of the most sublime experiences I have had in Meditation is traveling in the aerial chariot. In Chapter 6, I described some of my experiences of Siddha Loka. In one of these experiences, Shiva, manifesting as Lord Indra, told me to call on Him in Meditation if I ever wanted to travel to the other worlds. In subsequent months, I did call on Him.

Each time I did so in my Meditation, a beautiful gold chariot appeared. This chariot was pure gold and it was studded with all types of glistening jewels and ornaments on all sides. It vibrated with an incredible light. It was often drawn by one or two large white horses. These horses had wings and their eyes shone with a bright blue light.

I am sharing some of my experiences of the chariot here, as I recorded them in my journal.

Indra's chariot has come for me. Lord Indra is taking me far away, to a marble palace. This is a different palace. It is all white marble on the outside. And it has a very earthy feel. Lord Indra parks the chariot and I get out. There is this incredibly brilliant white light everywhere. I walk up a long marble staircase and Baba is there. He greets me and I follow him. He is very translucent and radiant. He is dressed in red with a shawl and hat. I follow him through glistening marble corridors. We come to a clearing and go down a set of stairs. It feels like we're going down into the earth. We are now in a room with many gemstones. I see Sri Jnaneshwar and Bhagawan Nityananda there also. The white light is brilliant and everywhere!

* * *

My Lord Indra's chariot came for me in Meditation this morning. It was a beautiful, glowing, radiant gold. Angels of golden hew beckoned me to enter it. I ran to embrace the chariot, on my knees thanking God. I then found myself in the chariot sitting on a large throne, dressed in kingly garments. The chariot was off immediately like the wind. A great white horse was pulling the chariot, with its wings guiding us through the ether. We traveled for a long distance and then I found myself in a place with water and then a Loka full of blue and gold bindis.

*   *   *

Often, I experienced Bhagawan Nityananda in the chariot with me during Meditation. He took me to places and showed me things that were quite extraordinary. Many of these visions had to do with him teaching me how this Universe came into being and I was told things that have been corroborated by Western science and astronomy. An example is one such vision:

As I sat for Meditation, I called to Lord Indra to come with the chariot to take me to Siddha Loka. The chariot came and swept me up. This time the chariot was much larger and looked like it had compartments. I found myself inside the chariot in a room. The chariot had become like a moving palace. Bhagawan Nityananda was sitting opposite me on a beautiful maroon velvet-cushioned throne with gold and gems. This entire room was decorated with this maroon velvet, silk and carpets. I was also sitting on a velvet cushion. I could not tell the size of this room. It seemed to be full of Bhagawan Nityananda's form.

The chariot was moving very fast, like a space ship. Bhagawan Nityananda pointed to a window and tapped the glass with his finger, beckoning me to look out. As I did, I saw space, the planets, constellations and stars pass by. Then we approached the Sun and fell, momentarily, into a sea of very bright light. Then we were back in the starry galaxy again. As I looked, I could see the back of the Sun casting its light and growing paler as we moved away from it. We passed several other worlds and entered into a field of shimmering blue light. I looked again and Bhagawan Nityananda was gone.

*   *   *

During this period in my Sadhana, I started to have the vision of many Suns. I had this vision in Meditation and also with my eyes open while performing my daily activities. I often saw 12 brilliant Suns. These were much larger than the sun we see in our solar system.

Later, these 12 Suns turned into thousands of Suns. I saw them surrounding me and I also experienced them very high up in the heavens. I later discovered, from reading the *Puranas,* that these Suns are known as *Adityas* and are spoken about as part of the inner experiences of many sages.

There were times when I was taken in the chariot to various Lokas where I received answers to questions that had been troubling me. In one such Meditation, I experienced a vision that provided me with further insight into Karma.

I sit for Meditation and the chariot appears before me. I get in and I am taken to a place I have not seen before. I am now in a vast room which seems to be part of some huge building made of various stone slabs of varying colors of brown, red, and tan. I am in a room in which the ceiling seems to touch the heavens. There are all types of dials and tracks leading from point to point along the ceiling and walls of this place. Some of these tracks cut into the stone and are lit up, while others are not. Some of the dials look like clocks and others look like sun dials or similar. These dials are made of stone and some kind of metallic substance.

There are millions of these tracks and dials all over this room of stone. This room seems to go on forever. I see myself now, sitting on a rotating sundial in the center of this room. This dial has many circles in it, moving in different directions. I am sitting in one of these inner circles, seemingly trapped, moving round and round in the direction the circle is moving. A sage is there watching me. At one moment, the circle that I am on stops and I climb off the whole dial. I realize in that moment that it is the sage who has stopped the dial so that I can get off. I walk to her and she starts to tell me about this room; that this is the place which stores the akashic records and keeps track of the karmas of everyone on the planet. This being tells me that I have burned up a major portion of my karma and this is why I am off the dial.

*   *   *

In this way, I had many profound experiences while traveling in the aerial chariot.

I also had visions of Jnaneshwar Maharaj, the medieval poet-saint who is the author of several popular sacred texts, including the great *Amritanubhav* and *Jnaneshwari.* Sri Jnanadeva (as he was also known) often gave me darshan in Tandra meditation and provided me with further guidance for my spiritual practice.

While in the chariot, I traveled to Jnaneshswar's Mahasamadhi shrine in Alandi. Again, this occurred while I was in the Tandra state of Meditation. I entered Jnanadeva's tomb (his Mahasamadhi shrine) and made offerings to him while he sat in lotus posture with his eyes fixed on me. This happened several times. I have not yet physically been to Jnaneshwar's shrine in Alandi, but pictures of the shrine have confirmed my visions. Friends have also gone and have come back confirming markings on the temple that I saw in these visions. So, I know I traveled there in the Tandra state.

While in the aerial chariot, I also engaged in battle with many demons. These experiences of the aerial chariot will seem preposterous to some. At first, they seemed crazy even to me. But so much has occurred to confirm these experiences that I had. Also, many years later, in my study of our scriptures and epics like the *Puranas*, I found the aerial chariot mentioned several times. So, other beings have had these experiences as well.

As my travels in the aerial chariot peaked, I started to experience more of my karmas. I also started to have visions of my past lives.

Chapter 9
Karma and Past Lives

Once the student or devotee makes the commitment to seek Liberation from ignorance *in earnest*, priorities must, naturally, change. Prior to receiving Shaktipat from my Guru, I wandered aimlessly through this world, believing myself to be a limited person in a world defined by money, relationships, political power and fame. *My life consisted of chasing after pleasure to avoid pain.*

Believing myself to be only this body and just a person, *my existence was shrouded in hopeless attempts to achieve status in order to counter my fears.* I boxed myself into this prison for many years, believing the entire Universe to be nothing more than my daily routine and the drama that encompassed that routine. This was my very limited life at the time. *I have spent a great deal of time reflecting on why my life was so limited at that time.*

All human beings are infused with anger, fear and illusion, temporarily. These are brought on by the influence of the three Gunas, out of which the three Malas manifest. A Guna is a constitutive quality of all embodied beings who remain under the influence of Nature. Mala means taint or impurity. In our approach, from the direct experience and utterances of the sages of steady wisdom of our lineage, we are aware of these Gunas and Malas. They can also be observed for oneself by entering into the Shaktipat Kriya Process discussed in Chapter 4.

The three Gunas are *Tamas*, *Rajas* and *Sattva*. Out of these manifest the Malas. One needs a living Sadguru, to root out the Gunas and the Malas. **If they are not rooted out, your experience of the Self will be no more than just a blip; a passing glimpse that you will take for granted and, eventually, forget, in favor of worldly pleasures.**

For now, I'll focus the discussion on the Malas. They are *Anava Mala, Mayiya Mala and Karma Mala. Anava Mala* is an aspect of Shakti that, in the ignorant, creates the notion that one is separate from God and imperfect, just the body, just an individual/person. The existence of Anava Mala then causes *Mayiya Mala* to manifest. Mayiya Mala is an aspect of Shakti that, for the unenlightened, creates the experience of diversity/duality and the belief that one is completely separate and different from others, unique by personality.

Karma, in the purest sense, is purposeless activity that also becomes selfless service to others and to God. This selfless service is also known as Seva or Guruseva, a reference to approaching all activity in order to make that activity an offering or Blessed Sacrament to the Lord. When activity is offered in such a way that one focuses on that activity to perfect it, *in order to please God, without wanting to possess the result*, this is known as non-action in action. When, during this activity, one directs the focus of that activity to owning or possessing the outcome or result, and also while self-appropriating that activity to the false notion of individuality, *activity becomes binding and more karmas are created.* This act of self-appropriating causes another taint to manifest in your Consciousness -- Karma Mala.

From Mayiya Mala springs *Karma Mala*. Afflicted with Karma Mala, *one sees oneself as an object of others attention, attraction, limiting desire and craving.* **Due to this notion, a person comes to believe that he/she is the doer, engaging in activity in order to possess outcomes.** The person then attributes those results (whether positive or negative) to his/her false sense of being just an individual, just a person, ordinary or delightfully weird. *This contracted notion of doership, self-appropriated to the notion of being just a person, is what we refer to as the ego idea, limitation of the ego or the energy of egoism.*

Therefore, it is really important to understand that egoism is not necessarily connected to any particular type of behavior or manner of speech that you may find 'pleasant' or 'unpleasant,' for these notions exist in the imaginary realm of duality only. *In truth, the ego does not exist.*

Again, when you direct the Shiva-Shakti power in such a way that you hide your true nature from yourself by coming to believe that you are just a person, just a body – and when you self-appropriate all the activity in your life to this false notion, what manifests due to this act of self-appropriating the activity in your life to this false sense of individuality is what we call the 'ego,' ego idea or the energy of egoism.

This is how karmas are created and become binding. From this you can understand that activity, interaction, the enjoyment of life – these are not the culprits. **The culprit is your wrong understanding of who or what is actually experiencing.**

The great beings tell us (and this my experience, as well) that Karma is a reference to activity that includes the daily mundane activity of worldly life (your actions), and the thoughts you cause and allow to manifest in your Consciousness. This activity is neither positive or negative, neither good or bad. When one recognizes the inner Self, the Shiva-Shakti power alone, this activity is experienced as free-flowing and spontaneous, manifesting out of the pure Love of the Absolute. When this is the case with respect to how you lead your life, there is no taint or impurity. Action becomes *non-action* through the perfection of non-attachment. Then the cycle of birth and death comes to an end.

This activity referenced above becomes binding, causing you to become entangled in the repeated cycle of birth and death (karma), when you objectify your experience by forgetting *where* the experience is actually taking place and, instead, you attribute what is being experienced to the body, your false identity as just an individual. Or you associate your experience with people, places and things outside of yourself. Whether the action be virtuous or evil, 'good' or 'bad,' *with this very limited view of your essence,* you set in motion a never-ending cycle of birth and death. This causes you to become *caught up in the same recurring life lessons,* having to return to this world, again and again, to experience the fruits of past and present actions (actions include your thinking which is really where all activity occurs). These are your karmas.

It is Karma that causes one to sink. It is also Karma that causes one to rise. **After accruing the merits of virtuous actions, over a period of many lifetimes, a person becomes worthy of a Sadguru.** Through Devotion to the Sadguru and to God, supported by spiritual practice, a person finally merges with his/her own Divinity inside.

At the dawning of final Liberation, when the energy of egoism has ceased to form and the yogi's experience is that of *permanent and uninterrupted identification with the inner Self, even in the midst of activity and the expression of Humanity*, there is no more Karma Mala. Anava Mala and Mayiya Mala have also been destroyed. The yogi then dwells in the Abode of the Heart, a

Pure Perceiving Awareness in which the yogi merges in the Supreme Principle.

For such a being, although he/she may continue to perform actions, no more karmas are created. Ever abiding in the *Supreme Principle*, the yogi becomes the Guru, that Shiva, and is no longer concerned with grabbing at people, places and things out of fear of lack. She offers all her actions to the Self and accepts what comes to her *unsought*, as a result of this attitude of offering. In this way, such a being remains ever steady in the rapture of the Shiva-Shakti power.

Every one of us has a birth reason, the reason we have returned to this earth. This reason is, for each of us, our *Prarabdha Karma*; the karma that cannot be burned and must be suffered, whether perceived to be pleasurable or painful. *This Prarabdha Karma is actually our own Superimposition of impressions from a past lifetime, that has already been set into motion and, therefore, must be experienced.*

All beings, including Self-realized spiritual adepts, must suffer through Prarabdha Karma (the karma that has commenced to bear fruit). This type of Karma cannot even be burned by the Shaktipat Guru. However, for those who are spiritually aware, this Prarabdha, the birth reason, can become a Labor of Love, leading one directly to the inner Self, by becoming the reason one stays in the body to serve and uplift oneself and others.

In addition to Prarabdha Karma, there are many other karmas that each of us suffers in this life (the Aprarabdha karma). For devotees of a Shaktipat Guru who have begun to engage the Shaktipat Kriya Process (see Chapter 4), the fully awakened Kundalini Shakti, begins to remove the barriers to the devotee's ultimate perfection. *Karma is one of these barriers.* After receiving Shaktipat from my Shri Gurudev, I felt as if the "rug" had been pulled out from under me. In the early stages of my Sadhana, my life was turned upside down as my Guru's Grace, in the form of the fully awakened Kundalini Shakti, purified my being and "adjusted" my perception of everything around me.

The quality of my relationships changed and I found myself "in and out" of these relationships in record time. It's as if the Shakti was presenting me with every opportunity to finish "unfinished business." This is somewhat like being in a pressure cooker. Situations and circumstances are "sped up" and entanglements are untangled, at the expense of a person being momentarily entangled, so to speak.

I started to have visions of people in dreams and in Meditation. A short time after having these, those people would "arrive." Then, as quickly as they "showed up," they were gone and I was on to something (or someone) else. This happened to me in fairly rapid succession over a number of months and years.

For some, there is more Karma than for others. In the advanced stages of one's Sadhana, by the Guru's Grace, the past lives of the devoted are revealed. Only the most relevant past lives are revealed and the timing of the revelation is directly related to the transformation the devotee is experiencing at that moment in his/her Sadhana. I had several such visions and they always answered questions I had in my practice at the time.

The most startling revelation of my past lives was the revelation of a particular past life that was the reason I returned to this life.

Chapter 10
My Native American Roots

*So live your life that the fear of death can never
enter your heart. Trouble no one about their religion;
respect others in their view, and demand that they
respect yours. Love your life, perfect your life, beautify
all things in your life. Seek to make your life long and
its purpose in the service of your people. Prepare a noble
death song for the day when you go over the great divide.
Always give a word or a sign of salute when meeting or
passing a friend, even a stranger, when in a lonely place.
Show respect to all people and grovel to none.*

*When you arise in the morning, give thanks for the
food and for the joy of living. If you see no reason for
giving thanks, the fault lies only in yourself. Abuse no one
and nothing, for abuse turns the wise ones to fools
and robs the spirit of its vision. When it comes your
time to die, be not like those whose hearts are filled
with the fear of death, so that when their time comes
they weep and pray for a little more time to live their
lives over again in a different way. Sing your death song
and die like a hero going home.*

Tecumseh

On one full moon night in October, while celebrating the Mahasamadhi of my Guru, I received a strong message from him that came in the form of a revelation while in Meditation. It was the revelation of a particular past life and, I am told, my birth reason in this life.

As I shared earlier, I am part Native American Indian; mostly Choctaw Nation and Shawnee, although I also have a close affinity for the Lakota Brules. Although I am neither a Wichasha Wakan (medicine man) nor a Chief in this life, I am told that I was both in a past life.

In this revelation, while in Meditation, I was shown this past life. The story of my past life as an American Indian leader was related to me. In this past life, I was a Wichasha Wakan and Chief in the Shawnee Nation and I had many followers. I am told that I healed people through the laying on of hands and that I also taught prayer, a form of chanting, and revelation of Great Spirit through the understanding of animal totem. (A connection was made here for me in that, in this life, I have studied and been a healing practitioner, using the laying on of hands and also animal totem). I also attempted to unite all the American Indian nations under one confederacy. I spent that entire lifetime in this way.

I am also told that, during that time in that life, my people were struggling under an oppression of some kind. I was given a vision of this in which, in order to protect the people of this land (those who were protecting me), I negotiated with the cavalry. They were seeking to secure power by murdering the elders and myself who gave the people hope. When they broke their word, I rallied the nations against them and refused to negotiate further.

I am told that I led many battles and fought to protect the land of all tribes. The night before one particular battle, I told my people that I would not be coming back. They say I lost my life that next day. But there was a great deal of controversy over this because they never found my body. They never found my horse either. I shape-shifted on that day. So goes the legend of this past life of mine.

Now, for a time, I doubted this revelation, even given the experience I just shared. So, I prayed for some confirmation in order to know that I had really lived this past life. I was told that I would be given two confirmations of this. One would be connected to the general who led the cavalry against me, and the other had to do with something I was owed.

A couple of weeks later, while meditating, I had another vision of this particular past life. In this vision, I was on top of a horse. We were moving very slowly and my arms and hands were outstretched to the sky. I was wearing a necklace of Buffalo teeth. When I looked again, the necklace was gone. I was then told that it had been taken from me, stolen at gunpoint, and that it would be returned to me shortly, in this life. I then fell unconscious for a while, before coming out of Meditation. Now, a few days later, I received a Christmas gift. What was it!? My Buffalo tooth necklace, in a big brown frame! You know I pulled that necklace out of the back of that frame and put it on! I still have it, wrapped in silk on my puja as an offering to my Shri Gurudev.

That was the first confirmation. Then came the second. You remember my story of the final battle? Well, it was related to me in a dream, that the Karma of that event had not quite yet been completed. So, one night, a couple of the guys I work out with at the local gym invited me to go bowling and play pool. Thinking this would be a great opportunity to make new friends, I agreed.

On the way back from the pool hall, we got stopped by police. To make a long story short, we were harassed. The act of my "sticking up" for my friend, who was driving, got us arrested. Actually, they let him go and arrested me and the other guy. They said that my talking back to the police officer was a misdemeanor. So, the two of us got carted off to jail where we were put through the system and held for 35 hours.

The inside of a jail cell in New York City is no joke. It's not like what you see on television. After being processed, I was further humiliated by the arresting officer, who seemed to be particularly bent on making my life as miserable as possible. (I felt a particular connection to this person, and so I did not retaliate, but rather I decided to suffer his abuse quietly.)

After strip-searching me in the nude (something that is not standard for what I was "supposedly" being charged with), the officer then threatened to retrieve my home phone number from the desk Sergeant to call my wife (I was still married at the time). He said that he was going to make a lot of trouble for me by telling my wife that I had been caught in the street with a prostitute and was being held on drug-related charges! (As it turns out, the desk Sergeant did his duty and refused to give my home phone number to the officer.)

I was placed in a small jail cell with about 50-60 other men who had been arrested that night on various charges stemming from drug dealing to theft to rape. We were all there together, sitting and sleeping on concrete. In one corner, gang leaders were sharing their stories of drive-by shootings. In another corner, a group of 20 men were gathering their quarters and deciding which was going to call whose wife to break the news that they had been arrested as part of a sting operation on a whorehouse. Then there was a group of elderly Muslims who had been arrested for talking back to the officer after being stopped for a broken taillight. We were all there, all different kinds, laying practically on top of each other, waiting to be arraigned.

So, I did the only thing I could. After carving out my little territory on the concrete, I sat for Meditation. In this Meditation, I saw my Guru first. Then I saw my fine friend, the arresting officer. It was his face, but he was dressed as a brigadier general. And there we were, on the battlefield I had seen as part of my past life! Now I understood that this was the completion of that Karma.

I sat quietly, in Meditation, for 3 hours. When I came out of Meditation, I found myself surrounded by a group of tough-looking characters. Apparently, they had been placed in the cell while I was meditating, and they were upset because I was taking up too much space. "Yo, Buddha!" one said. "Why don't you find somewhere else to do that so me and my homies can get some sleep." This person had a scar on his face that started at the top of his ear and ended at the bottom of his chin. He looked like he had gotten into a fight with a meat grinder! "Who are these people to me?" I thought to myself. Just then, he yelled, "Yo. Buddha. We the *Cavalry*! Now move over." More of my Karma following me!

As it turned out, that man became very curious about the Meditation I was doing and our meeting ended with me counseling him and his gang on God and spiritual practice. 35 hours later, I was released after paying a $65 fine in exchange for a reduced sentence from harassment of a police officer to disturbing the peace.

But it didn't end there. It was still not yet complete between us two. Even after this set of circumstances, I still had a figment of doubt about all of this being a confirmation of events connected to this particular past life. So, inwardly, I asked for another sign. Six months later, there was a robbery in the building I live in. My neighbor, *a police officer*, was robbed. As is customary, a few days after the robbery, officers were dispatched to the building to interview tenants in an attempt to find out if anyone saw or heard anything. When this happens, the officers go door-to-door, unannounced. Guess who knocked on my door?

Yes. It was that *same* police officer, my arresting officer, the brigadier general who led the forces against me in battle in my past life! Now, he had no idea that I lived there! And the irony of it all is that, after coming into my home and questioning me for ten minutes as to whether I saw or heard anything during the robbery next door, he didn't even recognize me! Now our Karma was really finished! I never saw him again.

The "tag" to this story is that, while all this was going on, my wife at the time, told me that she had a dream in which I was dressed as a tribal elder. In her dream, I was sitting in a wooden cart. My hands and legs were tied and I was being carted away by men on horses. *The ways of Maha Shakti are truly mysterious!*

The most significant piece of this revelation of my past life is that I was told that many of those I served in that past life, would find me in this life. I was told that they would become my students and that I should continue to serve their spiritual and healing needs.

I have had many dreams of these people, in which I see their faces. And over the past months and years, these people have slowly started to enter my life. It is an experience that is uncanny and also full of Grace. Suddenly, while in some place or walking in the street, I recognize a face from my dreams and we meet. Several have become devotees of Nityananda Shaktipat Yoga. And most have shared that they also saw me, in some way, before meeting me. Some even knew my name in this life, before we even met.

NATURE AND THE CREATURE BEINGS

Of all the people on the planet who respect nature, *it is the indigenous tribal nations of the world who respect it the most*. In the West particularly, it is those who live close to the Earth, and their elders, that we need to look to for guidance in saving Mother Earth from ecological destruction.

The United States of America, as the wealthiest country in the world, must be much more cautious about avoiding the kind of runaway growth that comes when greed is placed above the common good.

We have not had *sustainable* growth in this country for a long time. The growth we have experienced in the last twenty years, particularly economic, has been acquired in an *unstable* fashion where the few have prospered at the demise of the many, and the environment has been, increasingly, harmed. Runaway corporate greed and scandal have become commonplace, as the recent round of media attention has uncovered.

But the fact is, this has been going on for a long time and, for every company that gets caught, there are many behemoths that escape detection. **What has to change is our irreverence for this Earth (and its people) that sustains us. The sixth mass extinction has already begun. But we can change that. We can stop it and work to renew the vibrancy of Mother Earth. But we must act now.**

Planet Earth is the Love planet. Of all the planes of existence in the Universe, this is the only planet where Love can be expressed and experienced fully. Since it is Love alone that sustains and nurtures our existence and our ability to interact, since it is this same Love that takes us to God, *it is extremely important that we do a much better job of caring for this Earth.*

There is a magic in Nature that can be experienced in a very special way. There is a lot to learn from the Earth's beauty that can be experienced in a way that causes us to turn within. It is transforming. Several years ago I was brought back to this awareness through my study of the spiritual connection between animals and us "two-leggeds." Some tribes like the Choctaw (my nation) do believe that animals are deities in disguise, placed here on Earth to carry messages of Divinity, messages that each of us can learn from.

THE COMMON GOOD

In our tradition, the most important principle is that of *The Common Good.* This landscape that we all experience is the very body of God, Great Spirit or the Supreme Being. The greatest aspect of this body of God is *equanimity.* Equanimity is the understanding that we are all the same, we are all equal, because we are all that very same Self or Ultimate Reality, and equal participants in the Love without distinctions that is God.

Honor is a very important way of life in this spiritual tradition. The Common Good is that which is of equal benefit to everyone. *Honoring the Common Good means serving the inner Self by serving others selflessly, and in a way that people reap the reward together as a community*. It also means serving the needs of those who have far less than you do.

Honoring the Common Good means no one in the community advances unless everyone advances together. Serving in this way is the act of using your God-given talents to serve the common needs of the community, *before* tending to your personal advancement. It means putting *us* first rather than me first. "Us" is extended far beyond that of immediate family. This is a wonderful understanding that comes from service to the common good in American Indian life.

For example; For the Choctaw, this principle is so important that, in addition to a tribal insistence on it being practiced regularly, once each year there is a ceremony called the potlatch. In this ceremony, the tribal members give away everything they own and go without for a period of time, to help the tribe. This ceremony is done as a reminder that selfishness and the "rat-race," "get ahead" mentality so common in the modern age has no place on the Good Red Road. A person who claims more than his share is shunned by the rest of the tribe and considered to be crazy.

This principle of *The Common Good* is practiced to instill equanimity in the people. It is practiced to cultivate the understanding that one should only take what one really needs and should spend the rest of one's time in service to others, to his/her community. In the Native American tradition, we say that this practice ensures one's place on the Blue Road with our ancestors who have crossed over.

RESPECT FOR MOTHER EARTH AND ALL LIVING BEINGS

In many spiritual traditions, the Earth is the Divine Mother. This earth gives us life and sustains us. Nature is a reflection of the Supreme Principle. Yet, in the name of "progress," we are destroying the very environment that sustains us. And more and more, progress is just another name for personal or collective greed.

Here, *we do not exploit nature for personal gain*. We consider crimes against the Earth to be crimes against God and

Humanity. Anything taken from Mother Earth must be given back, and given back in such a way as to sustain the environment for generations to come. We also believe that the creation of products that harm the environment is unnecessary and should not be tolerated. Humankind is a very ingenious species. In partnership with the Supreme Intelligence, products that truly serve the needs of Humanity can be created without ever doing damage to Mother Earth.

For every tree torn down, another can be planted. Cars can run on batteries instead of costly, polluting petroleum. Energy sufficient enough to light and heat every home can be produced from windmills and the sun. And there are companies that have already invented environmentally-safe sources of energy that can fit on a micro-chip. The U.S. Navy has a technology to successfully convert seawater into fuel.

These environmentally safe technologies exist now. The only reason they are uncommon is that the greedy who currently control these markets don't want to introduce the technologies in a way that would be inexpensive and sustainable, because they fear losing annual revenue increases and they fear competition. It is their greed that keeps the harmful technologies in place.

Another important principle in this regard is that people must not be exploited either. It is a long-standing fact that the most powerful people in business and government have created and maintained an economic and social system that ensures they will always have a large pool of people to draw from for their workforce. For many there is a "glass-ceiling" that will never move. And opportunities do not exist for every qualified person. In this way, even the economy is manipulated to serve the desires of the greedy at the expense of the needy.

People are not products. They are not commodities to be marketed and traded like baseball cards! God exists within everyone equally. For this reason, especially when it comes to money, all people should be treated with great respect. And their weaknesses must not be exploited for anyone else's gain or pleasure.

Chapter 11
Selfless Service

XXVI. *He who serves Me with unfailing devotion of love, rises above the three modes (gunas); he (she) too is fit to become Brahman (the Self).*

Lord Krishna
Bhagavad Gita

368. He who with unswerving mind serves Me through the path of devotion is able to overcome the qualities.
369. I must explain to thee clearly who I am, what is devotion and what is the mark of aberration.
370. Listen, O Partha, I am in this universe as the lustre is inherent in a jewel.
371. Moisture is in water, space is in the sky, sweetness is in sugar; in these there is no separation.
372. Flames and fire are one, lotus petals are one with the flower, and the branches and the fruit of a tree are the tree itself.
373. The snow which is drawn to the mountain becomes part of it; curds are but curdled milk.
374. Similarly the entire universe is but Myself; there is no purpose in stripping the moon; [one would find but the moon itself].
375. Ghi is clarified butter, in spite of its solidity; though a bracelet is not melted down, it is still gold.
376. Even if a garment is not unraveled, it is still nothing but woven threads; one need not crush a pot to see that it is but earth.
377. Therefore do not think that I can only be found through the dissolving of the universe, for I Myself am all.
378. To realize Me, this manner is called single-hearted devotion; if any sense of difference appears, it is an aberration.
379. Thus laying aside all sense of dualism, with an undivided mind, thou mayest know Me as one with thyself.

380. O Partha, as gold is one with the ornament made
    from it, so thou shouldst not regard thyself as
    different from the Self.
381. A ray may be emitted by light, but the ray is the light
    itself; in such a way shouldst thou conceive of Me.
382. Like an atom of dust on the earth, or a particle of
    snow on a snowy mountain, so thou shouldst realize
    that thou art in me.
383. However small a wave may be, it is not different from
    the ocean; nor is there any difference between Me
    and the Universal Self.
384. When the vision is illuminated by the experience of
    oneness, we say that this is devotion.
385. This vision is the excellence of knowledge and the
    whole essence of yoga.

> *Jnaneshwar Maharaj*
> *Jnaneshwari Volume II*
> *Jnaneshwar's Commentary On The Bhagavad Gita*

This world has been overrun with greed. **The common good, once held with the greatest esteem in the minds of human beings, has now been traded in for the cheap thrill of excess**. Today, many people lie to each other in the name of feeding their families. *We look at others and see them as dollar signs in order to justify our own fantasies of wealth and power.*

For many, conscience has been locked in the closet out of *fear* that facing the Truth might mean change, major change. **Greed is not good.** But those who have made their money by deceiving others have convinced the majority of the population that a lifestyle of greed and the desire for wealth is the end that justifies the means. So, now many of our children are taught this greed, as well. Even though this greed benefits only a relative few, modern society dances in it in the name of maintaining a healthy economy. **This house of cards will crash, again and again.**

Such is the state of affairs in this Kali Yuga age we are living in. **If the world is to be destroyed, it will be due to this greed, not the bombs of enemies in battle.** Because this is the case, in order to return balance to this age we live in, in order to set things right, *Selfless Service* must be taught and experienced. Much of my permanent spiritual transformation is due to the selfless service I offered to my Guru and our lineage in his ashrams and centers.

Seva or Selfless Service, is of three kinds*;* service by imbibing the instruction of the Spiritual Guru in spiritual practice; direct service to that being in his school, ashram or center; carrying on the work of the Master by following God's Will in the world through Selfless Service to Humanity, that can be expressed through your own personal ability, regardless of the level or magnitude of such service.

After receiving Shaktipat in 1979, I spent 18 years offering my selfless service performing Guruseva in several of my Master's ashrams and centers. During these years I spent a great deal of time working in various departments (including music, security, construction, cooking, and the bookstore). As a result, I learned to give of myself and my Love unconditionally, and accepted increased compassion as the reward for doing so. *Selfless Service* (Seva) is a spiritual practice. It is transforming. And Seva done in service to the Sadguru and his/her mission is the most profound of spiritual experiences.

When I studied martial arts, I thought my first lesson was going to be kicks and punches. Instead, I wound up cutting my Sensei's grass and cleaning out his attic. My friends thought he was using me for unpaid labor. *But what I came to realize is that I had far too much ego to learn anything from him.* So, I had to empty myself first through service to him. The result was that I quickly became a good black belt in Karate and went on to study Kung Fu.

Had Sensei not humbled me first, I would not have been able to withstand the rigorous discipline of actually learning the martial art. My body could have taken practically anything. *But my ego would not have traversed the training. Seva* in the ashram was similar to this, with one important difference: In serving my Master, my heart was purified and I became a better human being, the ultimate human being, my compassionate Lord.

In the late 1980s, a psychologist by the name of Harville Hendrix, Ph.D. established a biological connection between unconditional giving and how the human brain experiences Love.

In fact, he proved that **all the love you give is really meant for you**. His studies show that, when human beings give of themselves unconditionally, *there is a part of the brain that actually experiences that it is receiving Love.* Of course, this is what the Sages and Saints have been saying for centuries.

In my late teens and early twenties, I used to suffer depression in fairly regular cycles. At that time, I lived in a very rough neighborhood that was fully controlled by drug dealers, thieves and rapists. One day I got tired of feeling the way I did and went across the hall to speak to my neighbor who had recently been held up at gun point and robbed. After hearing her story, I was filled with a great deal of compassion for her.

In that moment, I decided to form a community block patrol. It took all of my spare time and a great deal of energy convincing tenants and neighbors to cooperate to get this block patrol off the ground. Then I had to negotiate with local police, as well. I was exhausted from this effort. *But I felt so great inside.* Now, this block patrol was no "walk in the park." Lives were threatened and I wound up in several street brawls with armed thugs. But we persisted and we cleaned up our block.

This is just one example of how I dissolved my depression in compassion. At other times, when feeling bad, I went out and swept the street in front of my building and ran errands for the elderly. Some of my greatest moments of sheer joy have been performing *Selfless Service* at homeless shelters and soup kitchens.

But all of these experiences pale in comparison to what I experienced performing Seva in my Guru's house. Whenever my Meditation practice weakened, I would perform more Guruseva. Then, after serving selflessly for some time, I would sit and slide into Meditation with ease. Soon, this intoxication started to occur while I performed my Seva. Whether cleaning toilets, building temples, doing security or playing the drum for a chant, my experience of my own heart deepened through this Selfless Service. I started to feel great compassion for all those around me, serving everyone as if serving God.

This compassion was tested severely on a trip to India. During a major celebration, I was asked to perform Seva building tents in the adjacent field for the thousands of people who were expected for the celebration. The ashram was already full and they did not want to turn anyone away. In India, people travel many thousands of miles, under very difficult conditions, in order to make their pilgrimage to these celebrations. So, it was important that we build some housing for them.

Now, if you don't know, outdoor temperatures in Southern India in October hit 110-125 degrees, easily. It is very hot! These tents had to be constructed with bamboo girders and they were designed to be quite large. We did not have much time. So, we had to be out in the heat for many hours each day in order to get the tents done in time to receive visitors.

At that time, I had a distaste for Germans and French people. Although I'm part Italian by upbringing, I felt the Italians weren't much better. So, to which team of builders was I assigned? It was a large group of Italians, Germans and French! And they were arguing amongst themselves like old tired ladies! All of my buttons were pressed. Not only did I have to find some compassion for the people whose tents I was building, but now I had to love these jokers too!

I was tired. I hadn't slept. I had eaten very little. It was a stretch, but I made it. And we managed to work together, as a team to build an entire tent city. I was very satisfied. Then the rains came. Even though it was not monsoon season, we were hit with monsoon rains. For three days this went on. They said it was God's blessing of the celebrations about to take place and that it was very auspicious. I didn't feel that way. You see, the rains had destroyed the tent city we had just built! And now we had to rebuild housing *quickly*.

I must tell you that, in the end, I found myself in a puddle of mud, laughing out loud hysterically. People thought I had gone mad. With each hour of additional Seva that was required to clean up the mess the rains made and then build a place to put people up, my laughter become more and more uncontrollable. Then I suddenly became completely silent. I took quick breaks to run to the Mahasamadhi shrine to bow to my beloved Guru. Through the Grace of Selfless Service, I had freed myself of all pettiness, of all unhappiness, of all cleverness, of all prejudice. God had taken up residence in me and it was He doing the work. I no longer existed. Only Joy remained.

After a time, this experience of inner Joy, Compassion and Love for others became a constant for me. *The blissful experience of Meditation was no longer subject to my finding a dark corner to sit in with my eyes closed.* My *Guruseva* was actually *Meditation in action*. I started to see my Lord, my Baba in everything and in everyone. My behavior towards others changed as I was more and more able to share Love *without* the condition of receiving something in return. I started to see the face of God everywhere. *This is the power of Selfless Service*. **It is its own reward**. Performing it increases one's *spiritual merit* and transforms one's vision of the world.

Krishna told his disciple Arjuna:

> *"Whatever you do, make it an offering to me –*
> *the food you eat, the sacrifices you make, the*
> *help you give, even your suffering. In this way*
> *you will be freed from the bondage of karma,*
> *and from its results both pleasant and painful.*
> *Then, firm in renunciation and yoga, with your*
> *heart free, you will come to me."*

Retracing one's steps back to God quickens through *Seva*. Through Seva, you gain spiritual merit and wisdom. Why? Because Seva is service to God. *It is meritorious action; something the scriptures of every spiritual tradition speak about.* **This spiritual merit protects you, attracts abundance to your life, and keeps God's Grace flowing to you.** *Spiritual merit also nullifies the effects of past, present and future karmas.* Spiritual merit is very important and Seva is a primary means of increasing your spiritual merit. **Seva is a very important part of spiritual practice that should not be left out.**

You cannot know the mystery of Selfless Service without practicing it. And once you practice it, there is nothing more to be said. *The experience and benefit is Self-evident.* Seva *is not* a means for you to serve the Master. Service to the Guru is a figurative expression. **Selfless Service is actually the means, the privilege that the Sadguru provides for us to serve God and, in return, attract God's Grace into our lives.**

This Seva can be simple or complex. It can take the form of Dakshina (a financial contribution) alone, or take the form of a time commitment to serve in the Master's school or ashram.

It is the means the Master is providing for you to open your heart and set your ego aside to gain spiritual merit and wisdom. You earn the Master's Grace-bestowing power in this way.

There is a misunderstanding about volunteering one's time in this way that I want to clear up. **You should only perform Guruseva in a way that does not make it a struggle for you to take responsibility for your** *basic* **financial needs, personal care and child care.** *The Guru does not want it any other way and my Baba spoke about this often.* So, there is a balance to be struck here, but in a way that allows you to continue to benefit from the performance of Guruseva.

Only give money in a way that does not interfere with meeting your basic bills and financial obligations, and *do not* give money otherwise. The best way to do this is to practice *Tithing* by budgeting your giving into your finances, as you meet your basic financial obligations.

And *do not* allow yourself to be persuaded to give what you don't have by disciples or devotees of the Sadguru or managers who run that being's organization. *A true Guru will never ask you to give in a way that negates your basic or personal financial needs.* If you can find a way to do *both*, serve your own basic financial needs and serve the Master at the same time, this is the best approach. Otherwise, tend to your own needs first.

Service to the living Sadguru is service to God. Through Seva your entire being is purified as your heart reveals the Divine. Through the Seva that I and countless others did in my Baba's ashrams, many more people were able to come and experience the beauty of the ashram. Many more people were able to experience the programs. Many more were able to imbibe the Shakti of our lineage and experience the inner Self. And all of those performing Seva were transformed.

When I swept the floor, I was really sweeping my own heart. When I was engaged in building a hall, I was really forging a pathway to my Supreme Lord inside my own being. When I made music, others enjoyed it, but it was really to God's honor and glory I played. In this way, I performed Seva in my Master's house and was lifted up by the hand of the Supreme Being.

In Selfless Service there is Devotion. In Devotion there is the experience of the Shiva-Shakti power and the true Heart.

Chapter 12
Solitude

God is the friend of silence. See how nature - trees, flowers, grass - grow in silence; see the stars, the moon and the sun, how they move in silence. We need silence to be able to touch the soul.

~ Mother Teresa

    Solitude is essential for permanent spiritual transformation. *Silence* is essential to the experience of solitude. Even if you lead a busy life, even if your work is hectic, even if you are married with children or involved in an intimate relationship with a lover, *make time for yourself*, time that you can spend in *Solitude*, in *Silence*.

    The great beings of our lineage all say that it is necessary to *go, for a while*, so that you can *return*. You have been on a train that has been speeding in the wrong direction for so long -- *speeding in the direction of ignorance of your true nature -- speeding in the direction of the false sense of individuality*, **the sense of doership, the notion that you are just the body and the senses, that causes you to pursue worldly pleasures, constant stimulation and instant gratification in the vain hope of finding peace and happiness.** This 'train' *can* be turned around and made to go in the direction of the true Heart, where Peace, Joy and Freedom abide, *everlasting*. It *is* possible and it *is not* hard. But it does take some time, with patience and the right understanding imparted by holy beings.

    For this reason, for those seekers of the Truth who want permanent spiritual transformation, who want a lasting experience of Peace and the Bliss of the inner Self, *as you begin to take up the practices that allow you to go beyond your mind and beyond your senses, a degree of solitude is a necessity.* Just as one who wants to attain a bankable skill has to change one's lifestyle *for a while, to establish a new discipline* by going back to school, spending less time out with friends and family, in order to study to pass tests and make the grade, *in the same way, you will need to create boundaries of solitude in your daily life, in order to establish a strong, disciplined daily spiritual practice* – a practice that employs the habit of training yourself to follow the instruction you

98

receive for that practice from your spiritual companion in the Sadguru.

This is what the holy beings of our lineage mean when they say, *go, for a while,* so that you can *return.* As you become more and more established in the Joy of the inner Self, you are able to return to this world with a different pair of glasses, **with a better vision that allows you to lead your life in perfect harmony with the Supreme Principle, while expressing your Humanity and taking full responsibility for your daily mundane activities in this world.** *You are able to be in the world without becoming of the world.*

There have been several periods during my Sadhana when I insisted on living in complete solitude. During these periods of solitude, I chose specific days and weeks to remain in complete silence, not uttering a single word. *Silence coupled with solitude is so great!* Combined with Meditation and the practice of Witness Consciousness, it forces the Supreme Principle to be revealed to you.

While in the silence of solitude, I immersed myself in the study of scriptures and sacred texts and spent hours in Meditation. I would Meditate for 3-4 hours at a time and, sometimes, I would drop into the Tandra state and lay on my back for 6-8 hours at a time, receiving visions or having the Darshan of many Saints.

At one such time, I experienced the following which I recorded in my journal;

Baba is standing on top of the Samadhi shrine. He is spinning very fast. The top of the samadhi shrine is spinning also. I now see family, friends, associates and those who don't like me. I send the love and blessings of Shiva to each of these people.

Then I see myself in warrior clothing, standing on top of a high plateau looking out into a void full of stars. I have all my astras and they are gleaming, shining a brilliant gold light like a great Yajna. Suddenly the plateau behind me is filled with horses of all different colors, their dark eyes gleaming with Shakti. I see deities from the great Epics and Lokas joining me from the heavens. Then I raise my arms and turn to all those behind me. There are many now; Braves and Deities and Siddhas on thousands of horses. I ask, "How many? Are you with me?" Everyone roars, "Yes!" I turn around to face a huge void and abyss below it. The ground underneath our feet has expanded to form a large path into the void, crossing over the abyss. Then a large bridge appears, and water. The ground becomes solid, stretching out before us towards the stars. I sit before this scene awestruck. I sit quietly. All beings behind me do the same. Then, after the silence, we are all dancing everywhere as we move forward along this path across the heavens.

*   *   *

While in Silence and experiencing complete Solitude, I had many inner experiences such as this one. They were quite profound and mesmerizing.

Counter to what many say, silence *is not* the experience of nothingness. Silence is the experience of *Spanda*, the experience of the Pulsation or Vibration of Divine Consciousness, *when all thoughts have ceased*. It is the direct awareness of Spanda Shakti in its highest reality -- the throb of Divine Consciousness that manifests, sustains and withdraws this entire Universe. This throb is also experienced as a shimmering blue light in the Sahasrar, the highest spiritual center or Abode of the Heart. This is what is grasped in *silence* borne of complete *solitude*. Everything that is to be, manifests from that silence, from that subtle, slight movement in Consciousness. It is also the final resting place of all that is created and not created.

There is even a sound to this silence. It is known to Yogis as *Anahata* or *Bindu Nada*, the *unstruck* sound. It is something like the subtle roar of the ocean going on all the time. Silence even repeats a mantra. This mantra is Om or Aham (Supreme I-Consciousness) that then unfolds as the two feet of the Supreme Being. That is the natural repetition of *Ham* and *Sa* that is sounded ceaselessly with the incoming and outgoing breath. So, silence is dynamic in this way.

Solitude means being absolutely *present with oneself, the inner Self.* In the early stages of spiritual practice (this is years, not weeks or months, and how many years depends on your karmas), it may be necessary to isolate yourself from others, quietly and patiently, for periods of time. The purpose of this kind of solitude is to cultivate the awareness of what is beyond the mind and the senses, *without the distraction of objects* (people, places and things). Once this solitude is established, even for a short period, the desire to go within and remain inside is naturally cultivated. Adding silence to this solitude helps to thin the constant rush of thoughts experienced due to the restless mind.

Adding Meditation, Chanting and Witness Consciousness Centering to this intention, sends one inside to gain a direct and powerful experience of the *Natural, Free State* of one's own Divinity. Over time, this practice delivers *Nirvikalpa Samadhi*, the state of Supreme Consciousness and Bliss of the highest Lord, *the Shiva-Shakti power*.

If you are serious about attaining permanent spiritual transformation, if you want the ongoing experience of the inner Self, your true nature, create a sacred space for yourself where, on a daily basis, you can be in *solitude* and practice *silence* for a period of time - even if it's just 30-60 minutes to start. There is tremendous Joy in this solitude. The heart is purified, the ego idea dissolves, the body is healed and becomes strong, and the mind is sharpened. *One's entire being is rejuvenated.*

Chapter 13
The Blue Bindu

"O seekers after knowledge of perfection, the very eye of your eye, where the void comes to an end, the Blue Pearl, pure, sparkling, radiant, that which opens the center of repose when it arises, is the great place of the conscious Self. Look, my brother, this is the hidden secret of this experience. This is what Parashiva, the primal Lord, told Parvati. Jnanadeva says, "I saw this through the grace of my Sadguru Nivrittinath."

~ Jnaneshwar Maharaj

Many in our approach, by the Grace of a living Master, have had the experience of *The Blue Bindu*, also known as Neela Bindu or The Blue Pearl. This experience is also referred to in many of the sacred texts of Shaivism and Vedanta. My Master revealed his state by briefly describing it and then granting his Grace so that many could experience it for themselves. The experience of *The Blue Bindu* in Meditation is a signal that one has advanced in Sadhana and is being prepared for the final journey to Liberation.

Seeing this Neela Bindu brings a very sublime state of pure Joy. I am trivializing it by attempting to describe it here in words. But what can I do? It is a secret worth mentioning openly to all true seekers. This experience usually first occurs while in Meditation. The Blue Bindu appears as a bindu or dot of shimmering blue light the size of a sesame seed.

I first saw it in Meditation. The Blue Bindu appeared to me on a plate of gold. Since then, I have had many experiences of this Blue Bindu, both while in Meditation and while consciously going about my day. Out of the vision of The Blue Bindu I also saw many other worlds.

Seeing it while meditating and chanting caused me to travel to many Lokas where I experienced Sages, Saints and beings of all kinds. Out of the vision of this Blue Bindu I experienced, first hand, my essence as the vibrating Supreme "I" Consciousness of the entire Universe. I also had premonitions while seeing it.

This scintillating blue light first appears as a vibrating dot, very, very small, its light blue hue flashing in and out of Consciousness. Sometimes this blue dot becomes quite large. At times, it entered me. Other times I was carried along inside it, transported to other worlds.

Sometimes it stood before me in an instant and then dissolved. And, at times, it became a window through which I saw many deities, heard many wonderful sounds and music, and smelled incredibly delicious scents that are not of this world. Through the vision of this Blue Pearl, I also saw past lives and was transported to the world of my ancestors.

I had many of these kinds of experiences. With the limitation of words, I will attempt to share some of them with you now, as I recorded them in my journal. I had many of these visions while meditating.

Upon sitting for meditation, I saw the blue bindu spinning on a golden plate. Its blue light was swinging in a circle. I then saw the blue pearl in the cosmos. As it spun there, I saw the entire Universe being sucked into this blue pearl. I looked at the gold plate the blue pearl was spinning on. The plate was resting on nothing. I watched the blue bindu spinning at the edge of a black void of Consciousness, suspended there on its own. I watched it for a long time.

*   *   *

Sometimes I saw Neela Bindu after chanting. The power of the chant would send me deep inside and I would slide into meditation effortlessly.

I sang the Guru Gita and performed Lakshmi puja. I then sat for Meditation for 30 minutes. I was hearing Hamsa mantra from within. The Blue Bindu then appeared in front of me. It was there when I opened my eyes and when I closed my eyes. Then I fell into a huge space. The space had a blue hue and appeared to be endless. In this space, which I experienced as my very own Self, I saw a tiny speck with dots on it. As I looked closer, I recognized this speck to be the Universe and this world-appearance, a tiny dot in this vast horizon of Consciousness, appearing like a fleck on the chest of Brahman.

*   *   *

During this period of my Sadhana I chanted the Rudram often. One day I had a profound vision of The Blue Bindu while chanting the Rudram:

I felt a command to chant the Rudram today. As I started to chant the Rudram, The Blue Bindu appeared. It suddenly became very large and then Lord Shiva stepped out of it, radiating Blue light. He was very large and muscularly built. His eyes were only partially open and his gaze was turned inward, even though he was watching me at the same time. His hair was very lomg and tall. Around his neck was a garland of golden bindis (like beads on a thread). This is the same necklace of bindis I had seen years ago. It is a representation of all the worlds, all the planes of existence.

Lord Shiva then took this garland, representing all the worlds, from around his neck and held it in his outstretched hand in front of me. He held it there for a long time, indicating that I should take it. When I did not take it, he placed it around my neck. As I continued to chant the Rudram, Shiva watched me carefully and smiled.

I continued to chant. Om Namah Shivaya welled up inside me spontaneously. Lord Shiva then leaned forward and whispered a mantra in my ear. At that moment, I saw what looked to be a large river, like the Ganges, flowing upstream. A strong moonlight shone on the water. The river continued to flow upstream and there was a raft in the river with money and jewels on it. The raft was being pushed along by the water towards me. I continued to chant the Rudram.

The experience of *The Blue Bindu* is a magnificent journey into the heart of the Supreme Being. It came to me by the Grace of my Shri Gurudev. As he did, I also pray that each of you, during the course of your Sadhana, receives the blessing of The Blue Bindu!

My visions of *The Blue Bindu* threw open the floodgates of Shakti and my Sadhana accelerated. I then started to have stark visions of the three Devis.

Chapter 14
The Three Devis

In the tradition of our lineage of Saints, *Maha Shakti*, what we refer to as the Shiva-Shakti power, is often worshipped in the form of three Devis (goddesses). The three Devis are known as Lakshmi, Durga and Saraswati. Lakshmi is the Goddess of spiritual and material abundance. She is said to make these manifest in the life of anyone who comes to fully embrace her Divine energy, through worship of her in Chanting, Meditation and Contemplation.

Sri Maha Durga is the Goddess of inner strength, courage and protection. She represents the warrior spirit and the ability to summon courage in the face of any obstacle. She is known to make these qualities manifest in the life of anyone worshipping her in the same way; through Chanting, Meditation and Contemplation. Sri Saraswati Devi is the Goddess of beauty, knowledge, artistic expression, and communication. She makes these qualities manifest in the life of anyone worshipping her.

These three are aspects of the same one Supreme Principle.

By the Grace of my Baba, I have been fortunate to have had many visions of the three Devis during my Sadhana. I have experienced how they manifest their qualities, first hand, in my own life. The aspects of their energy are very subtle and profound. *Knowing them requires complete surrender to Kundalini Shakti.* To experience them *one has to trust the intelligence of Maha Kundalini* and approach them with complete love and utter *Devotion.* To this they have no choice but to respond.

It was at the urging of the three Devis that I made great strides in retracing my steps back to God. In a very loving fashion, they continually prodded me to surrender my false notion of individuality completely, and to develop total *Devotion* (Bhakti) for the path of Love that leads one to desire the company of the inner Self all the time.

In one instance, I chanted to the Devis, one at a time, as I had grown accustomed to doing on a regular basis. After I finished chanting, I sat for Meditation. I immediately saw the Blue Bindu flash in front of me and then I was transported to a Loka. There was a large, crystal blue lake there. I found myself standing on a plateau with this lake just under my feet, stretching out for as far as I could see. Its clear blue water was completely motionless.

When I looked down into the water I saw Lakshmi, Durga and Saraswati just below the surface. Lakshmi beckoned me to come into the water. After hesitating, I did so. As I entered the water, Lakshmi grabbed hold of my arm and started to pull me down into this blue lake. At first, I was overcome with fear. Durga and Saraswati then grabbed my feet and I felt myself sinking further and further into the water. When I looked down, I saw nothing but blue everywhere. This lake had no bottom!

I then heard the Devis say, "Don't be frightened. Surrender completely. We are with you always." I came out of Meditation two hours later. I experienced an extraordinary state of Bliss and also felt very refreshed, as if I had been cleaned clear through. After this vision, my feeling for God changed. The nature of my surrender changed. There was a shift in my experience of my Sadhana and I felt much more Devotion for my Shri Gurudev.

I also had many visions of Sri Durga. In one such vision, I was visited by her and her lion. I experienced her in both her atomic manifestation and her expanded manifestation.

I am chanting and I fall into Meditation. I see a small, white lion. I recognize it as Durga's lion. As the lion draws near to me, Durga suddenly manifests on the lion. Durga and the lion are atomic in size, at first. And now they become very large. Durga is laughing. She and the lion then become miniature again. My eyes are open now as they walk up to me on the rug as I am chanting. The lion lays down in front of me horizontally and Durga climbs on to my leg and sits there.

I say, "Sri Durga, it is I who should be sitting in your lap." Immediately I am transported to another place. Durga is giant-sized and sitting in Meditation. Her lion lies before her. I am sitting in her lap. I fall into Meditation and find the three of us in a large room with a big blue pool of water in it. The walls and floors are all marble. Gandharve (celestial beings) are pouring blue water into this pool from marble jugs. We are all bathing. The room and the pool are floating in the void. I am again in Durga's lap. There is a lot of light.

*   *   *

I have often seen Durga at times when I am being offered protection or warned about some upcoming event or situation. One such vision that I recorded in my journal is an example.

As I sit and perform Hamsa mantra, I see my Lord Shiva in his translucent form. His eyes are very intense. I also see my astras blazing with light. Then I see a lion off in the distance. As this lion gets closer, I recognize it as Durga's lion. She jumps up on me playfully, licking my face and arms. We then frolic together, rolling around on the ground. The lion then puts her head in my lap as I am used to. Ma Durga then appears to me. I thank her for her darshan and then I ask why she has come. She tells me that she is here to bless and protect me.

I then see myself placing flowers at Durga's feet, putting them in between her toes. I then ask her what she is protecting me from. She tells me to watch over the next few days and then I will know. "Be aware and on your guard," she says. I thank Durga and do more oblations to her.

I then continue to play with her lion. After this vision, I fall into a deep Meditation that lasts for 90 minutes.

*   *   *

Several events occurred in those next few days, including a potentially disastrous confrontation, each of which I was protected from.

I also had visions of Sri Saraswati. Saraswati is a Goddess of great beauty and strength. She is Paravak. My visions of Saraswati always involve celestial sounds and movement:

After doing puja to Saraswati and chanting Saraswati mantras, I sat for Meditation. I immediately heard the sound of the Vina, followed by melodies coming from what I recognize to be the

Sarangi. Then I saw a gold light, followed by a red light. Out of these lights appeared a beautiful Goddess. Her form was very bright. She wore a magenta-colored sari and she was quite sensuous. Her eyes were a deep, dark color, and very intense. She came very close to me.

Then I noticed that she had several arms, in each an instrument of some kind. She started to dance madly in a circle and then began whirling very fast. She suddenly stopped and gazed into my eyes. She then said, "I am Saraswati. I sit on your tongue and am the root of all creativity." Then she disappeared.

*   *   *

I often had visions of Mahalakshmi on a large plateau. These particular visions were very powerful for me.

I sat for Meditation and started to chant Lakshmi puja. I was immediately transported to a mountaintop. There was a great deal of wind. It seemed that I was in a sand storm. I fought my way through it and came upon a pair of large feet. As I looked up, I saw the Goddess Lakshmi. She was huge, standing gigantic through the clouds. There were clouds passing and a great deal of wind. After a while, I was able to look far enough up to see her face. But my focus came back to her feet. I clutched her feet tightly and lay there with my head bowed for a long time.

Finally the wind calmed and I could see Lakshmi's entire form. As she looked at me, she made her form smaller. She then held a silver tray in one of her hands and, with her other hand, she started to pile many wads of $100 bills on to the tray. The tray was full of money. She then placed the tray on the ground in front of me and sat facing the tray. "Will you be able to carry all this?" she asked. "If you show me how, I will be able to carry it all," I responded.

*   *   *

My inner experiences of the three Devis, Lakshmi

Narayana, Sri Maha Durga and Sri Saraswati Devi, have been life transforming. These experiences came about by the Grace of my Shri Gurudev. Anyone who worships and nurtures Kundalini Shakti will, over time, experience the three Devis.

Chapter 15
Visions of Lord Vishnu

Namah samasta-bhutanam
adibhutaya bhu-bhrte,
Aneka-rupa-rupaya
visnave prabhavisnave

I bow to the first manifested of all manifestations, who upholds the earth, who has the form of the manifold, Vishnu, the creator.

Vishnu Sahasranama

Lord Vishnu is known as both the one who manifested the Creator (Brahma), and the sustainer of the Universe, having been given these tasks by Lord Shiva himself. In the epic tales derived from the Shastras and Puranas, Lord Vishnu manifested Brahma from a lotus flower that emanated from his navel. Brahma, on Vishnu's command, then manifested the Creation.

Through a series of tests, Vishnu proved his willingness to uphold dharma and was then granted equal status with Shiva. It is said that Shiva granted Vishnu a place of permanent worship in the world equal to that of his own. There are many stories of Lord Vishnu in the Puranas. Vaisnavites (followers of Vishnu) claim him as the sovereign deity of the Universe. *Lord Vishnu* can be understood as that aspect of the Supreme "I" Consciousness, that aspect of the Shiva-Shakti power that creates and sustains the Universe. *The Goddess Lakshmi* is his consort, his active 'component.'

Throughout most of my Sadhana, I had no feeling toward Vishnu and no real knowledge of him. I seemed not to have any desire to know him either. This changed through my worship and experience of the Goddess Lakshmi. In fact, it is through Lakshmi that I first came to experience Lord Vishnu in Meditation. I only began to study the life of Vishnu and his powers after being granted a vision of him through my chanting and Meditation on Lakshmi Narayana.

I am very fond of Diwali celebrations. Diwali is the Eastern Indian New Year. It is also known as the Festival of Lights and is a time when the Goddess Mahalakshmi is celebrated with great ritual. It was during one such Diwali celebration in my home that I first had the vision of Lord Vishnu. I share this with you as I recorded it in my journal.

It is 12:15am and Lakshmi is patiently waiting for me to finish cleaning so that she can enter. She does. I perform Lakshmi Puja and it is ecstatic. So much light!! When I finish chanting, I sit for Meditation. In this Meditation, I see myself on my horse which then turns into a chariot. This chariot whisks me off to a Loka. I recognize it as Lakshmi's abode. The chariot takes me across the ocean of milk to a plateau.

Lakshmi greets me. She is not dressed in the manner I am accustomed to. This time she is wearing a long white robe. Her hair is down and she is not wearing her crown. She takes me up a hill to a place with many rooms. This place is full of light. She first shows me a large pile of gold that now sits in front of me and is as tall as I am. This, she says, is for me.

Then Lakshmi takes me to room after room, each full of gold and jewels and precious stones. It seems this whole place is made of gold! I see another being who Lakshmi pranams to. This Being seems to be composed of gold and light. He is reclining and he is radiant. His eyes stand out to me. They are lotus-shaped and are emanating both a gold and blue light. Fruits, gold, money, grains and precious gems lay all around him. This, I am told, is Lord Vishnu.

Lakshmi then takes me out into this beautiful wheat field with its tall, golden strands of wheat. This field seems endless. There are trees, a fruit grove, a lake, a river and beautiful gardens everywhere. Lakshmi turns to me and gives me a message. She says, "Proceed in the right direction. Trust me and have no fear. I will protect you and take care of you."

*   *   *

This was my first vision of Lord Vishnu. I was so ecstatic at having seen him that I started chanting Vishnu Sahasranam (a chant of the thousand names of Lord Vishnu) on a regular basis. This led to more visions of him that I recorded in my journal over a period of several weeks and months.

As I chanted Vishnu Sahasranam, I saw Vishnu standing before me. He radiated a golden hue and was wearing a golden turban on his head. His skin was full of light and his eyes were lotus-shaped and radiated blue light. He said he was pleased with me.

*   *   *

It is said that, during Diwali, Lakshmi actually visits the homes of those chanting to her, to hear their prayers and grant them blessings. She is, after all, the Goddess of Abundance. I thought this was just a metaphor for understanding the power of prayer and chanting. Until one Diwali celebration where I actually had a vision of this.

As I chant Lakshmi Puja, I see the milky way and the churning of milk. Lakshmi appears in the heavens. She is being carried to earth in a golden chariot drawn by many, many beautifully dressed horses. She is both small and huge, adorned in gold and all the elements. She is riding the chariot from place to place, from house to house, gliding through the air and hovering over the ground in this chariot. I see all this with my eyes open while chanting. Lakshmi is throwing down flowers, golden coins, jewels, money, garlands and rice on people as she passes their homes. She stops at some homes to get out of her chariot and visit people.

When she arrives here, she is being followed by a procession of people. Lord Vishnu has now appeared in full form above the earth, as big as the heavens. Lakshmi orders the chariot to stop in front of me so that I may perform Atari directly to her while chanting. All her horses lay down on their legs quietly while we continue to chant. Lakshmi stays for the entire three cycles of the chant.

In this vision, I circumambulate her many times and garland her. Lakshmi leaves gold coins in stacks for me. During the last cycle of my chanting, Lord Vishnu, Krishna and Rama join Lakshmi. They all sit before me and I garland each one of them. At the end of the Puja, Lakshmi smiles at me and then leaves with her procession. Lakshmi tells me that, on this evening, another galaxy has been born around a star as bright as our Sun.

*   *   *

There is a postscript to this vision. Approximately six weeks after having this vision, I was watching CNN. Suddenly a news report flashed on to the screen. The Hubble Telescope had just sent back pictures of a newly discovered galaxy with a star in the middle of it that they said they believed was as bright as our sun!! Until this moment, I had not been fully convinced that my vision was real.

I continued to chant to Lakshmi on a daily basis and I continued to chant Vishnu Sahasranam regularly. Through this practice came more experiences of Lord Vishnu. The culmination of these visions occurred one day when I was chanting Vishnu Sahasranam and Lakshmi puja back-to-back, very intensely. This vision was so powerful that I am still unable to share it here. Except that I will tell you that both Lord Vishnu and Sri Mahalakshmi entered me completely and totally.

I am very fortunate to have had the darshan of Lord Vishnu. I also understand that, by his Grace, I was able to sustain the practice of worship to him long enough to be worthy of his darshan. This is a tribute to his greatness and the greatness of my Shri Gurudev.

Chapter 16
Lord Bhushunda and The Sacred Tree

*In one corner of mount Meru there is a wish-fulfilling tree.
On that tree there dwells a crow known as Bhushunda who
is utterly free from all attraction and aversion. There is
none on earth or in heaven who has lived longer than he
has. If any of you can live as he lives, that shall be
regarded as a highly laudable and meritorious life.*

The Sage Satatapa
The Yoga Vasistha

In a number of sacred traditions, Crow is a symbol for
Sacred Law. Sacred Law is that law that supersedes all societal
law. It is natural law, the law of the in-dweller, that great Lord who
dwells in every heart. *Once the heart is purified*, one should follow
it without reservation. *This is what is known as Sacred Law.* Crow
also symbolizes the ability to move easily between the mundane
world and that of the Transcendental.

ya tarvar men ek pakheru

*On this tree is a bird: it dances in the joy of life.
None knows where it is: and who knows what the
burden of its music may be? Where the branches
throw a deep shade, there does it have its nest: and
it comes in the evening and flies away in the morning
and says not a word of that which it means. None tell
me of this bird that sings within me. It is neither colored
nor colorless: it has neither form nor outline: It sits in
the shadow of love. It dwells within the Unattainable,
the Infinite, and the Eternal; and no one marks when
it comes and goes. Kabir says: "O brother Sadhu! Deep
is the mystery. Let wise men seek to know where rests that
bird."*

The Poet-Saint Kabir
From Songs of Kabir II.95

Late in my Sadhana I started to have visions of crow, Lord Bhushunda. You may remember from previous chapters, my experiences of the Lokas, the Aerial Chariot and The Blue Bindu. I have, for a number of years, traveled to a place that is at the edge of the known Universe. I went there in Meditation. It is a place that is beyond all planets, solar systems and galaxies. This place exists beyond time and has been created by Shiva himself. In this place, there is a tree. This tree is sacred, for on it dwell many Sages from all the Yugas (world cycles). This sacred tree is quite large. In its fully manifest form, it covers the entire known Universe. It also changes form to appear as an ordinary tree. This tree has a white-blue halo around it.

This sacred tree stands at the entrance/exit of the Universe. It is the marker between that formless Supreme Principle and all that takes form in the cosmos. Lord Shiva practiced Yoga under this tree. In front of this sacred tree is a stream of white light. This light has remained there since the "big bang" that brought the Universe into existence. Behind this tree is the great Blue Lake of Consciousness and Lord Shiva dwells beyond this lake.

At the top of this tree dwells a huge blue-black crow. His name is Bhushunda and he is a descendent of Rudra. Bhushunda is long-lived and has witnessed the cosmic dissolution of the Universe many, many times. Therefore, his wisdom and knowledge is unsurpassed. To have his darshan is extraordinary, for he has the power to reveal everything to a seeker of the Truth. Bhushunda also grants boons. It is the nature of his existence in this wish-fulfilling tree. I only ever asked him for one thing, however; To know the inner Self and how that knowledge was to unfold in my life.

My first vision of Lord Bhushunda happened when I was meditating on Bhagawan Nityananda. I share this with you as I recorded it in my journal.

During this meditation, I was taken up in the Aerial Chariot. The chariot was moving across the heavens. I then noticed Bhagawan sitting next to me in the chariot. Suddenly the chariot became quite large, like a floating palace of some kind. We were moving very fast when Bhagawan Nityananda tapped his fingers against a glass pane, beckoning me to look out. When I did, I saw us passing the planets in our solar system, one by one.

After leaving Pluto behind, we entered and exited other galaxies that were a strange wonder. After a time, we arrived at a huge tree. This tree was a lush green and very, very tall. On a branch of this tree was a huge crow. His eyes were blue and he was glowing. When I looked around again, Bhagawan Nityananda had disappeared and I found myself sitting on the same branch of this tree, having a conversation with this crow.

*   *   *

The next morning, after waking I heard a bird cawing and went to my living room window. There on the windowsill was a large, black crow! My visions of Lord Bhushunda were often confirmed in this way.

I had many visions of Lord Bhushunda. I will share two more with you here.

I have had a vision of Bhushunda on a tree. The horizon was as it is on a crystal clear dawn, just before the Sun rises, with colors of white and pink. I saw many worlds and, in all these worlds, there was nothing but silence and space. Then I came upon this huge tree, the only tree in existence. A big bird who looked like a crow, was standing on a branch of that tree. He had big eyes and the crow was talking to me. In fact, we were engaged in conversation about the world-appearance.

I remember asking this bird, "Are you the only one left? You seem to reside on the only tree left in the Universe." We spoke for a long time. He told me of the cosmic dissolution of the Universe and spoke about the creation at the beginning of each world cycle.

*   *   *

I offer prayers and oblations. I pray for guidance about my health also. I ask Bhusunda to take me to the tree. I then go to Bhagawan Nityananda to pranam. We are then off somewhere together in the chariot which has become like a floating gold palace. I find myself in the sacred tree with Lord Bhushunda. He is telling me that, in general, my health is good, but that I am about to suffer a major health problem that is due to karmas I have taken on while giving Shaktipat. He says I will get through it and be fine if I focus on the details. I started to ask him "What details?" but he disappeared.

*   *   *

About six weeks after this vision, I did become very sick for a time, but I got through it very well by my Guru's Grace. *Bhusunda* is an aspect of that same *Shiva-Shakti* power. He is the one who has witnessed the creation, sustenance and withdrawal of the entire Universe. He is timeless and indestructible.

Chapter 17
Visions of Jnaneshwar Maharaj

He whose mind is firm, absorbed in the Self, yet outwardly active as other people, who does not act under the impulse of his senses, who does not fear contact with objects of sense, who does not avoid any proper action, who, although he does not curb his senses when performing action with them, is not carried away by the waves of their influence, such a man (woman) is not bound by mere desire, nor contaminated by the darkness of delusion, as a lotus leaf remains untainted by the water in which it floats, so in this earthly life such a man appears as others, in the same way that the reflection of the sun in water seems to be a part of it. Similarly such a man seems to be quite ordinary, but, observed more closely, one does not know his true disposition. Recognizing him by these signs thou wilt know him (her) to be liberated and free from the bonds of desire.

Jnaneshwar Maharaj
Jnaneshwari 1:3:68-74

Jnaneshwar is one of the world's greatest poet saints. He is also my favorite. Jnaneshwar (also known as Sri Jnanadeva) was Self-realized at a very young age. He also had miraculous powers. Stories of his miracles are equal to that of Jesus Christ. The Truth was tested severely in Jnaneshwar at a very early age.

His father, Vitthalpant, having been born into the Brahman caste (the highest of the four castes), was in the process of fulfilling his duty as a householder (husband) so that, upon having and raising children, he could then enter his Master's ashram by taking initiation as a monk.

While married, Vitthalpant and his wife, Rakhumabai, lived in a small Indian village known as Alandi. As yet, they did not have any children. One day, Vitthalpant left his wife and went on a pilgrimage to Benares. His intention was to become a monk and remain there in his Master's ashram. After entering the religious community at Benares and being granted initiation, his Master found out that Vitthalpant was still married and had left his wife without giving her children and fulfilling the householder duties necessary to complete before retreating to the life of a monk.

So, his Master immediately sent him back to Alandi to fulfill his family obligations. However, the Brahmana elders in Alandi considered Vitthalpant's withdrawal from his initiation to be an insult and a violation. So, when he returned, he and his family were rejected. He was forbidden to associate with his fellow Brahmana and he and his family were forced to live on the outskirts of the village.

As time passed, Vitthalpant and Rakhumabai raised four children; Nivritti, the eldest brother, then Jnaneshwar, Sopanadeva, and a daughter, Muktabai. As his three sons grew to be of age, Vitthalpant requested that they receive the sacred thread ceremony that would initiate them into the Brahman caste. The Brahman elders refused this initiation, citing Vitthalpant's earlier violation. Vitthalpant, considering all this to be his fault, and having been told by the same Brahmin elders that he could expiate his sin by ending the life of he and his wife, committed suicide by throwing himself into the Ganges to drown. Rakhumabai followed suit.

Thus the stage was set for Jnaneshwar's rise. As a young boy, he and his brothers and sister were outcasts. They spent a great deal of their time challenging the supposed knowledge and experience of monks and elders who did not see God in everyone and who sought to make the spiritual path accessible to an elite few. Jnaneshwar was initiated into spiritual practice by his brother and spiritual Master, Nivrittinath, who was a Shakta Adept in the Natha sect of the Bhakti (Devotion) tradition of the region.

Jnanadeva later developed a relationship with Namdev, a local poet and Bhakta, and together, they toured the region using poetry, chanting, meditation, and dramatic song-sermons to bring the path of Bhakti (intense love for God) to the common folk who no one would initiate. So, Jnaneshwar Maharaj has the distinction of making spiritual practice and Bhakti Yoga available to all. This he did at a time when it was forbidden to do so and he earned the merit, respect and love of all as a highly revered Saint.

Jnaneshwar Maharaj is one of the very few Sadgurus to take live Mahasamadhi. It is said that in his early twenties, he had his shrine built and then entered it to sit for Meditation. There he remained in Meditation, not allowing his Consciousness to leave his body. He remains there in that very place to this day.

Jnaneshwar worshipped God through the manifestation of Lord Krishna. He was also a Sadguru in the Samkhya Yoga tradition. His two most popular works are *Jnaneshwari*, his commentary on the Bhagavad Gita of Lord Krishna, and *Amritanubhava*, his more philosophical work. Jnaneshwar was a poet-saint who wrote and taught in song-sermons.

His words are full of the nectar of Supreme Love and Devotion for God. The hearing of even one phrase of his words can liberate an earnest seeker. He is full of the Shakti of Shiva and, at a very early age, had become one with the Almighty. Every seeker, every yogi, every disciple, every lover of God, should read *Jnaneshwari* and the *Amritanubhava.* To do so brings an immediate experience of Jnanadeva's Shakti, and also his blessing. There is no interpretation, no philosophy higher than his.

During the course of my Sadhana, I was extremely fortunate to have the darshan of Sri Jnaneshwar in Meditation. Often, after reading *Jnaneshwari,* I would slip into Meditation and have his darshan. At other times, while meditating, I was carried by aerial chariot, to his samadhi shrine in Alandi where I sat in front of Jnanadeva meditating on him. It was during these visits to his samadhi shrine that I received instruction from him. This was a time when he usually told me to read more *Jnaneshwari*, which I did. These visions came by way of my Shri Gurudev's Grace!

Sometimes, Jnaneshwar gave me a command or a message that became a very profound part of my life. The following two visions from my journal are examples of that.

Jnaneshwar Maharaj appeared to me in Meditation. I found myself in the temple at Alandi. I was sitting facing him as I have seen in other meditations. He was bright and very effulgent. He pointed to something at his feet. Usually when I have Sri Jnani's darshan it means he wants me to read Jnaneshwari. So, I immediately flashed on scripture. But he kept pointing and smiling. When I looked down at his feet, there were 5 diamonds spinning on a tray. Jnanadeva offered these to me.

I then saw Eagle flying back and forth. Jnanadeva told me that the 5 diamonds represent The 5-Fold Act of Divine Consciousness. They also represent Shiva's five Shaktis or powers in their highest form, namely Omnipotence, Omniscience, Omnipresence, Perfection and Eternity (also Sat-Chit, Ananda, Iccha, Jnana and Kriya respectively). Sri Jnaneshwar Maharaj has told me to study, contemplate and teach The 5-Fold Act.

*   *   *

At the end of this vision of Jnaneshwar, there was a startling sight. When I looked up at him again, it seemed there were roots or something growing around his neck, head and face. I wanted to call someone there to tell them to remove those roots.

It was not until three years after having this vision that I learned that there is a tree that grows at the samadhi shrine that is said to be permeated with Jnaneshwar's vibrations, and that this tree is considered to be a wish-fulfilling tree. Well, this is the very same tree whose roots pressed so tightly against Jnaneshwar's neck that Jnanadeva appeared in a vision to Eknath Maharaj (a worshipper of Sri Jnanadeva) asking him to cut the roots because they were making him uncomfortable!

The second vision I am sharing is related to the first.

I lay down to sleep and say my prayers. As I do, I see myself in the chariot in my warrior garb and crown. Sri Jnanadeva has placed the 5 diamonds he gave me around my neck as a necklace. I have all my astras and I am floating before a great Sun. Then I am fighting off demons with my astras in a voracious battle in the heavens. My horses are pulling the chariot to and fro on my instructions, without reigns. There is a great white stallion and a brown/red stallion. My bird spirit guides are also with me.

At one point, I take a very forceful strike at a dark energy field and the force of the blow throws me out of the chariot. Eagle breaks my fall and carries me back. I am now in some misty place after seeing a vision similar to my command vision. There are people in this place and I am giving them Shaktipat with peacock feathers.

*   *   *

Jnaneshwar Maharaj was a very great Sage. Those with the sincere desire to know him will be blessed with the Supreme knowledge of the Self.

Chapter 18
The Command To Lead

1996 began as a very difficult year for me. Financially, I was having a very hard time and I felt that I had, somehow, lost my direction as far as work was concerned. My inner experiences, in contrast, were quite incredible and my meditations were very deep and extremely peaceful.

My Sadhana was going very well. But I was still making decisions that were not, ultimately, in my best interest. These decisions were being made out of fear and desperation and I found myself in a set of circumstances that I wanted to better understand so that I could change how I was vibrating at that time. Then one morning, I had a very profound vision. I am sharing it with you here as I wrote it in my journal.

I woke up around 3:30am hearing the sound of Om. It was so intense that I thought there must be a congregation of people somewhere in my apartment chanting Om. Then the sound got even louder. Om. Om. Om. I finally realized that it was coming from inside me. I lay on my bed motionless, unable to move. I also noticed that my breathing had spontaneously stopped. I then fell into a deep Meditation.

I immediately had a vision of planets colliding and exploding. I saw suns and moons colliding and pieces of planets on fire, streaming through the cosmos. The earth was on fire. I saw that the earth was on a collision path with the Sun. I noticed that I was surprisingly calm while watching all this in my vision. The sound of Om continued to permeate everything.

Now I saw people screaming and fleeing all around me. Many were dying. The primordial sound of Om continued to ring everywhere. The chanting of Om resonated deeply and became even more intense as I watched planets collide. I felt, at this moment, that the earth was very near its destruction. I continued to witness this scene with complete calm and serenity, like a bird observing the world from a tree branch.

At this moment in my vision, I saw myself in my chariot, traveling through the heavens and out into a crystal Blue ocean in the cosmos. I then heard a voice say to me, "You must give them Shaktipat. Give as many people Shaktipat as possible before the end." At this point I opened my eyes and my breathing started again. Even with my eyes open, I continued to hear this voice repeating this command to me. And I continued to hear Om being chanted intensely.

Then the vision continued. But there was a subtle difference. I now had the sense that I was the one destroying and withdrawing the Universe I myself had created and sustained. That Being, who is me, was also the one bestowing God's Grace. I was overwhelmed with the feeling that all that was happening was perfect, and a deep experience of profound peace washed over me. This vision continued as I traveled through the sky in my chariot.

I landed in some place where there were many people. I was holding one of my astras in my hands. It was in the form of a large sword. I was touching people with it on their shoulders, heads and arms, and lopping off the heads of others. I then got back into my chariot and flew back into the heavens until I arrived at what looked to be a Blue ocean once again. At this point in the vision, I witnessed more planets colliding and the earth exploding. The entire Universe was then absorbed into one Blue Pearl, the size of a sesame seed, dangling in the ocean of Consciousness. I then traveled to the edge of the Universe and left through a field of white light to go to the Sacred Tree, the abode of Lord Bhusunda. Lord Bhusunda then spoke to me. I remained there in the tree for some time.

*   *   *

For several hours after having this vision in Meditation, I continued to hear *Om* and I continued to see scenes from this vision. It was only later that day that the vision finally subsided. From this vision, I understood my destiny and the work I am to do. And this was not to be the last of these messages to me.

One year later, I asked an astrologer to prepare a transit chart for the year to come. When I received the completed reading, I was startled. It confirmed my vision. I was told that my life was about to undergo some major changes. The reading also indicated that a lot of old karmas were being completed to make way for new relationships that would be related to this work in service to Humanity.

I was also told that any relationships I was currently in would have to be reassessed in light of the internal changes I was undergoing and would continue to undergo in the coming months. I was told that anyone I was in a close relationship with would have to be flexible enough to give me the space I needed to serve others through this work I was to do, that they would have to understand my need to work very closely with people. *This part of the message was significant because I was still married at the time.* God was demanding that I start to lead my life from this new perspective.

Another year passed. Then I had a series of experiences while chanting and meditating -- experiences that I could not continue to ignore.

I am chanting the Guru Gita. I have offered the chant this morning for revelation regarding the direction of my life.

A great being appeared to me inside during the chant and told me the following; "Whatever you give people through your work and your relationships, remember that what you are really there to give them is Love, your Master's Love. This is your lesson to learn for this year. Remember to give this Love and then whatever comes to you as a result of this giving will be yours to keep and enjoy. This does not mean that you should drop your warrior bhavana. Just add this purpose of Love to your actions."

Then I heard the following; "Your soldiers and generals are still out there waiting for you. Remind your wife about the astrological reading with respect to her necessity to be flexible and understanding of how involved you get in your giving, in this purpose of Love, in your close work with people. You have stored a lot of Shakti in the last few years. It is now time for you to start sharing this strength with others. Put this purpose first."

*   *   *

Shortly after having this vision, I started to offer private sessions for spiritual counseling and healing. I had several, regular clients during this time and all of them came with questions about God and Meditation. These were my first students.

The messages continued to come while I was chanting and meditating. These messages were very direct. I share them with you as I wrote them in my journal.

I sit for Meditation and I find myself in the Blue ocean. I see the place I saw in a previous Meditation but could not completely make out. It is a large, palatial facade with a huge front entrance and large windows. There is a great deal of light flooding these windows. This light is coming from the same place; a ball of fire like the Sun, emanating from behind this facade. Lord Shiva has shown me this before, as one of his forms.

As I move to the side of this facade to see behind it, the light dims and I see a medium-size flame burning in the void of Consciousness. This flame speaks to me. It says, "Work with those who sincerely want to know me and do not waste your time with the rest." The flame then explodes, becoming a huge Sun, much larger and brighter than the sun in our solar system. I recognize this Sun from the vision I had in which I was commanded to give Shaktipat. This is the Sun of my Guru.

*   *   *

After having this vision in Meditation, I continued to receive inner messages regarding the giving of Shaktipat Diksha. These inner messages were commands to do so given by Bhagawan Nityananda, Muktananda Paramahamsa and Shiva.

Each of them was related to my initial vision that I shared earlier in this chapter, in which I was given the command to offer this work. I have contemplated these visions constantly over a period of months and years. With each contemplation comes a new revelation.

Part of the fruit of my contemplation was the revelation that I did not choose this. It chose me. Although, to follow this command was certainly a choice, and I could have chosen not to do it, I came to the realization of how miserable my life would be if I didn't follow the command to perform this work.

Foundations and organizations *cannot* authorize one to give Shaktipat. **Only another Shaktipat Guru in a lineage of such beings can do so, the command for which, historically, can be an inner or outer command.** After having these visions and contemplating them, Bhagawan Nityananda started to appear to me frequently each day. And I became very happy and content.

"In the court-yard of duality, the Self, the Shakti of the Supreme, of its own accord, threads through everything. When this fact is realized and experienced from moment to moment, as duality and differences appear to widen, the inner experience of unity becomes stronger. In this state, the enjoyment of sense objects only reinforces the experience of the highest Bliss, as one is reminded, over and over again, that sensory enjoyment belongs to the Universal Experient, the only doer, the only Cause – that all these are Divine expressions of that Universal Experient."

Jnaneshwar Maharaj, from his Amrithanubava
(Nectar of Self-Awareness)

"He whose mind is firm, absorbed in the Self, yet outwardly active as other people, who does not act under the impulse of his senses, who does not fear contact with objects of sense, who does not avoid any proper action, who, although he does not curb his senses when performing action with them, is not carried away by the waves of their influence, such a man (or woman) is not bound by mere desire, nor contaminated by the darkness of delusion, as a lotus leaf remains untainted by the water in which it floats, so in this earthly life such a person appears as others, in the same way that the reflection of the sun in water seems to be a part of it. Similarly, such a person seems to be quite ordinary but, observed more closely, one does not know his true disposition. Recognizing him by these signs, you will know him (or her) to be liberated and free from the bonds of desire."

Jnaneshwar Maharaj, from his
Jnaneshwari, 1:3:68-74

Chapter 19
Intense Visions of
Bhagawan Nityananda of Ganeshpuri

One must live in the world like common men. Once established in infinite consciousness, one becomes silent and, knowing all, goes about as if knowing nothing. Although he may be doing many things in several places, he outwardly appears as if he is simply a witness of life -- like a spectator at the cinema. He is unaffected by events, whether pleasant or unpleasant. The ability to forget everything and remain detached is the highest state possible.

Avadhuta Sri Bhagawan Nityananda

Shri Bhagawan Nityananda of Ganeshpuri was and is a sublime being of unfathomable power, Grace and Love. Here in our school and approach, we take refuge in this great sage and Master of our lineage in these modern times. His memory and power are without taint, and this is why we take refuge in Shri Nityananda Bhagawan. He was the full embodiment of the Shiva-Shakti power, bestowing God's Grace and Blessings on all those who came sincerely to have his Darshan. He lived only for those people who sought his blessings on their lives.

Bhagawan Nityananda (Bade Baba or "Big Baba," as he is affectionately known), gave Shaktipat to hundreds of thousands of people *through his will alone*. Without speaking and, often, with his back to the congregation, deeply submerged in his own Bliss, he bestowed upon each the Grace of God and the fulfillment of their desires.

Just gazing on his form, people share that they were transformed in every way. As did Shirdi Sai Baba before him, Bhagawan Nityananda granted people's wishes, healed their illnesses and altered their destinies for the better. He did so while keeping nothing for himself. As I have said before, Bhagawan Nityananda's Love, power and miraculous countenance are truly beyond description and any words I share here are insufficient. He is like the light of a thousand suns crystallized into one giant wave of Love and Compassion.

Even today, many years after having taken Mahasamadhi, Bhagawan Nityananda continues to care for his disciples. Hundreds of thousands of people on every continent, from different walks of life, on diverse spiritual paths, still experience Bhagawan Nityananda of Ganeshpuri in dreams and Meditation.

He is the subject of many experience shares, written in many books by people who traveled to India to see him and by people who were visited by him in their dreams. Bhagawan's power is indescribable. He was and is a being beyond all boundaries of time, space, cause and effect. To simply say he is the Shiva-Shakti power is an understatement. To say he was and is Compassion and Mercy itself begins to come close to describing his true nature.

Bhagawan Nityananda of Ganeshpuri was born Self-realized. He was a being who was able to change form at will; one who was able to travel any where in the cosmos while his body lay in a room, turned towards a wall in Meditation. But his greatest power was Love and the total Compassion he had for his followers and for this world. His Love has no boundaries and the Bliss experienced while contemplating his form or repeating his name is incomparable.

There are those who say that Bhagawan Nityananda never spoke and had no particular teaching to offer his disciples. *This is not true.* Although he spoke relatively little, he did give spontaneous talks, at times, and at other times he gave individuals a mantra or a specific instruction to follow. He spoke in several languages. Some of his disciples were fortunate enough to accompany him on some of his many long walks in which, at times, he would speak about principles of Vedanta and Shaivism. Others were present for those rare moments after His ashram had closed for the evening, when He would begin talking spontaneously at 10 or 11 at night until the wee hours of the following morning. Although his manner of speech was difficult to understand, he got his message across.

Bhagawan Nityananda healed the sick and the dying. There were many who he brought back from the brink of death and whose diseases and handicaps he healed completely. Bhagawan Nityananda was also known for absorbing and burning the karmas of his disciples. Often, disciples visiting him would ask him to heal or perform a miracle for a family member living in another province or country. At times, Bhagawan would stay in his room for a day or two without coming out for anything. And no one was allowed to enter. When he did come out, that person who was not physically present was healed and had his/her karmas destroyed.

At other times, Bhagawan Nityananda was seen by many eyewitnesses in several different locations at the same time. Each of these people received his darshan, spoke to him or received instruction from him, at the same time, in these various locations. For more insight into these events and his existence here, you can visit the following web site:

www.bhagawannityananda.org

It was Shri Bhagawan Nityananda of Ganeshpuri who directed the final stages of my Sadhana and gave me the instruction that caused the Blue Being to take up residence in me. *To him be the glory. May my life be an offering at his feet.*
For as long as I can remember, I have had visions of Bhagawan Nityananda in dreams and Meditation. After receiving the inner command to lead others, these visions became more intense and occurred more frequently. As I said in an earlier chapter, after receiving Shaktipat, as my Sadhana progressed, I was told to Meditate on Bhagawan Nityananda. I was told that Bhagawan Nityananda would give me everything and that I would merge into the Supreme Principle, the Shiva-Shakti power, by meditating on Bade Baba. It was at this time that I first started having visions of Bhagawan Nityananda.

My visions of Bhagawan Nityananda became more frequent after I attended a Yajna (fire ritual) ceremony in Ganeshpuri. While meditating in front of the fire, I saw Bhagawan Nityananda standing in the flames. He spoke to me saying, "Work with the artists and healers so that they express only the highest through their work." Bhagawan Nityananda then stepped out of the fire, touched me on the head and then disappeared.

This vision was so powerful and, initially, such a shock for me, that it took several years of contemplation before I even started to take the vision seriously. Fortunately for me, Bhagawan did not abandon me. I had many, many other visions and dreams of him in the months and years that followed.

As I shared previously, I spent a great deal of time in Bhagawan Nityananda's Mahasamadhi shrine in Ganeshpuri, India and other temples built in his honor. A ceremony known as Prana Prathista, a sacred rite in which a Sadguru infuses the Shakti of the lineage into the Murthi (statue), thus making it live with power, has been performed on the Murthi of Bhagawan Nityananda in his Mahasamadhi shrine and at other temples built in his honor. I participated in the construction of one of these temples and was also present during many of the Prana Pratishtha ceremonies offered. In addition, I was fortunate enough to have been invited to perform some of the early morning abhiseks (offertory rites) that occurred periodically in Bhagawan Nityananda's temple.

As a result, I had many profound experiences of Bhagawan Nityananda of Ganeshpuri in Meditation. During three of these Meditations, Bhagawan Nityananda rose out of the statue. His form was completely gold in color and there was blue light emanating from his eyes. He danced around me whispering a mantra in my ear and singing my name. This went on for a while in Meditation until I fell unconscious. This vision occurred three nights in a row.

Later in my Sadhana, these visions of Bhagawan Nityananda became more profound. In one such Meditation I was shown the birth of the Universe. My aerial chariot appeared before me and I climbed in. Bhagawan Nityananda was the charioteer. He guided the horses and chariot up into the heavens. We were moving very, very fast past planets and galaxies of all different kinds.

Then we suddenly stopped. It looked as if we were at the very edge of the Universe. And then there was nothing, a complete void. Then, from the chariot, I saw a point of blue light, very small, like a dot. Then suddenly there was an explosion of light. This light was white and very brilliant. It looked like a sea of light. From this light I heard a thundering sound and then I saw the Universe being born and galaxies forming. This is all I can say because I really can't describe it any further. This was a magnificent spectacle like I have never seen.

After having this vision, there were several weeks when, upon sitting to Meditate, I was immediately transported to either the temple of the Mahasamadhi of Bhagawan Nityananda in Ganeshpuri, or His meditation cave in Guruvanam, near His Kanhangad ashram. I traveled to these places automatically in Meditation. It was as if these shrines were calling me. I had many such visions over a period of time. I will share two of them with you here as I recorded them in my journal.

I sit for meditation and find myself in the chariot for the first time in a long time. The chariot takes me to Ganeshpuri. I am in Bhagawan Nityananda's Mahasamadhi shrine. I do pradakshina to Bhagawan. He steps out of the Murthi and kicks water on to me. Then I lean forward and water from his outstretched hand runs off his fingers into my mouth. There is a mattress with sheets and cover made for me in a corner of the shrine. I sit there to Meditate. As I do, Bhagawan Nityananda calls me forward.

He starts handing me money -- bills wrapped in piles like you get from the bank. I find myself back in the chariot with Bhagawan. We are traveling to the homes of people I know. Bhagawan is instructing me on how to give these people Shaktipat. I am also being told about illnesses they have. After all this, I find myself back in the Mahasamadhi shrine meditating.

*   *   *

As I say my prayers before falling asleep, I find myself in Ganeshpuri, in Bhagawan's Mahasamadhi shrine. I am sitting on the mattress in the corner meditating. Bhagawan beckons me. He is lying on his side just inside the golden grating near the Murthi. He is facing me as I enter. I sit beside him. Bhagawan Nityananda then puts his finger in my nostrils and places his hand on my chest. I am there for a long time.

*   *   *

At times, in these visions, Bhagawan Nityananda instructed me as to how to be a vehicle for Shaktipat for people, and what specific points to touch on their bodies during the transmission of the Guru's Kriya Shakti. These people are students of mine who have attended programs and taken intensives. Some were seeing me privately for the healing of physical illnesses. These experiences are all similar, like the one I will share now.

Evening prayers. I fall into meditation. Immediately I see Bhagawan Nityananda. I pranam. He is off to somewhere quickly, and bids me to follow. He is moving very fast, like a hurricane, and I have trouble keeping up. We walk on a path toward a great, brilliant sun. There is a great deal of light everywhere. Bhagawan Nityananda looks very intoxicated as we walk along a path of golden light.

Bhagawan Nityananda walks me through crowds of people, some sitting quietly in asana and others standing. He is instructing me with a wand of peacock feathers and with my astras. He is pointing to points on people and showing me where to touch. I see some faces that I don't recognize. Others I do recognize. Bhagawan instructs me to press and massage points and how to use the peacock feathers.

Bhagawan then takes me to a plateau in the sunlight. I am in a large, open field. Bhagawan Nityananda is there and I am following him. He leads me far into this field and then I see a multitude of people, many people, waiting and in need of help. Bhagawan Nityananda starts to laugh as I look at all these people. He then smiles and says, "Get to work."

*   *   *

Sometimes, after having Bhagawan Nityananda's Darshan in this way, I would then see my Adityas, my 12 Suns, encircling me and glowing brilliantly. Sometimes I saw many more Suns, thousands of them. There were also times when, after seeing Bade Baba in Meditation, I was filled with what I can only describe as nuclear bursts of light that entered me. Then, one day, I had this very profound vision.

One morning after performing arati and chanting to Bhagawan Nityananda, I fell into Meditation. I traveled to a room full of light. There I saw Bhagawan Nityananda sitting on his bed. He was sitting up with his feet on the floor. I sat at his feet and embraced them. Then he beckoned me to come up on the bed with him. I did so. The bed was very soft. I felt as if I was suspended in the ether.

First I sat with my legs crossed next to Bhagawan Nityananda, then I laid down with him at my side and then I found myself sitting up again. He then placed his hands on me touching several points. As I stared into His eyes I became aware that I was repeating the mantra Hamsa over and over again. Then I noticed that Bhagawan was also repeating Hamsa. I saw a great light emanating from him. This light started in the area of his navel and reached to the top of his head. It penetrated him at a distance of 12 fingers inside and out. This light was first a brilliant white in color. It then turned blue and then gold.

This light then started to emanate from me as well. Then Bhagawan Nityananda got up from where he was sitting and climbed into my body. He entered me completely. I was now sitting on the bed alone. At this moment I saw my 12 suns and then thousands of suns rising before me. These suns were huge and very bright with gold light. There was a blinding light everywhere and also fire. After this, I was transported to a huge, red crater. I sat at the top of this crater with these suns surrounding me. I heard the mantra Hamsa reverberating in the cosmos and then saw Bhagawan Nityananda again sitting beside me. I sat in this place meditating on my suns for a long time.

*   *   *

This was my direct initiation from Bhagawan Nityananda in Hamsa mantra and its elevating power. At this point in my Sadhana, *Hamsa* took over my entire being.

Before I continue with the next Chapter on *The Mantra of the Siddhas*, I want to pay tribute to my Bhagawan Nityananda by providing you with a summary of His *Chidakasha Gita*. It was through my own study of this work that I came to understand my own worth and many of the experiences I was having in my Sadhana.

I began reading the Chidakasha Gita when I was told to begin meditating on Bhagawan Nityananda's form. During this period Bhagawan Nityananda appeared to me often in Meditation and while Chanting. My unfolding understanding of the verses has explained many of the experiences I have had in Meditation and over the course of my Sadhana. These teachings ring true on every level. I have read the entire Chidakasha Gita 35 times through and I continue to read it, even now. Each time I read it I have a new realization and another breakthrough in the experience of the Heart.

Although the Chidakasha Gita is ripe with many wonderful spiritual teachings, there are 12 main principles that, in my experience, Bhagawan Nityananda emphasizes over and over again. These 12 principles form the very essence of the Chidakasha Gita and the very foundation of His teachings.

1. Bhagawan Nityananda tells us that God is in humankind and humankind is in God. There is no difference between the two. Sentient and insentient are one in the same. All are reflected in the same "mirror" that is the Sky of Consciousness referred to as *Chidakasha*, the Heart space or Triadic Heart of Shiva, the Supreme Principle. Bade Baba tells us that the Heart is not the physical Heart, nor the heart chakra located in the area of the physical heart. He tells us that the Heart is the one, indivisible Sky of Consciousness that is the Absolute. This Heart is beyond the body and the senses. It is the highest spiritual center or chakra, the *Sahasrar*. It is accessed through the Crown Chakra at the top of the head. This Chidakasha, He states, is triangular with three points (Shiva, Shakti, Nara) and becomes a constant experience upon the dawning of Mukti (Liberation). Chidakasha is the seat of Lord Shiva and the abode of His Shakti. It is comprised of Light, Vibration and Sound, and from that vibration manifests Om or what Bhagawan refers to as Omkar.

2. Bhagawan Nityananda wants us to know and realize where the Atman (God) is. He tells us that God is not in the Murthi or statue or idol in the temple, but that God exists inside each of us and that each of us is the temple wherein God resides.

3. Shri Bade Baba tells us that the mantra Om is what gives power and form to the universe of all sentient and insentient beings. It is also the very vibration of Chidakasha that is known in Shaivism as Spanda, Chiti or Visarga. It is Aham, the Supreme I-Consciousness.

4. Bhagawan Nityananda is not big on 'philosophizing.' He is very practical. In the Chidakasha Gita, He uses simple experiences from interactions with people, place and things in everyday life to help us understand the deepest most profound connection between God and Humankind. He emphasizes a very practical means of attaining Mukti or Moksha by means of the Sushumna Nadi. He declares over and over again that this central channel or central nerve (subtle body) that is contained in every living creature, is the only true spiritual path. He emphasizes that Moksha (deliverance or Liberation) cannot be attained until Kundalini Shakti is fully awakened by a Shaktipat Sadguru. Once this Kundalini is awakened, He states, Prana Shakti must be directed into the Sushumna Nadi and then constantly made to rise upward into the Crown Chakra in the head. Bhagawan instructs that the breath* must be directed in this way without taking any air in from the outside (this correlates to the Shaivite practice of "Sushumna breathing"). He refers to this as Prana Vayu and emphatically states that this is the only means to directing your awareness to become absorbed in Bindu Nada (point of sound experienced in the Abode of the Heart and reflected in the space in the head). Once your mind dissolves in this Bindu Nada, Mukti is attained. The goal of Meditation, he tells us, is to keep our awareness in this Bindu Nada, even while going about our daily, mundane activities. This, he states is true Dhyan, true Dharana.

*Note: In His reference to Prana Vayu, Bade Baba repeatedly points to the fact that there is no separation between the immanent and transcendental aspects of the Atman (the Supreme Principle). Prana is often referred to as the Chit Shakti (transcendental aspect) of Shiva that manifests as the breath (immanent aspect of Shiva), or that the breath travels on. Some feel that this means there is a difference between Prana and breath. Since there can be no breath without Chit Shakti, the breath and this vital force are one in the same. Bhagawan Nityananda makes this point by using the words "Prana" and "breath" interchangeably throughout the verses. Since words cannot adequately describe the formless Paramshiva in which all things are contained, what use is there to argue the difference between Prana and breath? This "breath" even speaks a mantra (Bade Baba refers to the in-breath as "the breath of Omkar"), so how can it be different from that Shiva-Shakti power? So, the difference is in name only.

This alone is Samadhi. It is the means to live in the world without being of the world and it can only be taught by a Sadguru.

5. Bade Baba describes this Bindu Nada in two ways; first as the sound similar to the dull roar of the ocean or the vibration of a large bell just after having been struck; and second as ajapa-japa, the sound made of the two syllables So' and Ham (the two feet of Lord Shiva) as one breathes in and out. Of these two, he emphasizes the first, telling us that even the mantra So' Ham (Hamsa) that sounds on its own (Anahata, the unstruck sound) dissolves in the vibration of Bindu Nada. How will we know when we have attained Liberation? Bhagawan Nityananda tells us we will know when our entire conscious awareness is absorbed in this Bindu Nada constantly. He tells us that this Bindu Nada is the primary quality and experience of Chidakasha. It is the very Vibration of Ananda (Bliss) that is attained when Sat (being) and Chit (pure perceiving awareness) unite. This unification, He states, is brought about by causing Prana (breath) to rise inside the Sushumna Nadi without taking any air in from the outside. (Warning: Do not attempt this practice without the direct instruction of one who has mastered it.) In this state, one experiences the Sky of Consciousness or Chidakasha for one's self. This, He tells us, is the seat of all Yoga. This is the true place of pilgrimage and, once you have arrived here, no other pilgrimage to any other place is necessary and no further ritual is necessary either. In fact, Bade Baba tells us to make this form of Pranayam our only ritual; that, while in this state, the awareness of the Mantras Om and Hamsa, are the ritual bath.

6. Bhagawan Nityananda declares over and over again that the goal of a human birth, the goal of all life is to merge in the Absolute, to attain Mukti while still in the body. He tells us don't wait, do it now. And then he emphasizes, throughout the Chidakasha Gita, that the Sadguru is the means. He is very clear about this. One must receive Kundalini awakening and the leadership for Sadhana from a "Siddha" or "Guru" as he puts it, who has become a Jnani (knower of the inner Self). At several points in the verses, Bade Baba reiterates that "There is no place in the world for one who does not have such a Master. Such a person is lost....You cannot

realize the Truth without a Sadguru." And he emphasizes that one needs to follow the instruction of the living Master until Liberated.

7. Bade Baba does not leave us in the dark about who can be a Master or Preceptor. In this regard he is very specific. He tells us that a Swami, Sanyasin, Brahmin, Jnani, Brahmachari is not simply one who holds such a title and wears ochre robes carrying a copy of the Bhagavad Gita in his hands. Likewise, one who is well versed in the Vedas, Puranas and other sacred texts is not such a being either. Bhagawan Nityananda emphasizes that a Shakta Adept, a Shaktpat Sadguru, who may also be referred to as a Swami, Sanyasin, Jnani and so on, is only a person who is desireless and whose mind has merged with the Absolute One Paramatma or Paramshiva (formless Supreme Principle).

He goes on to describe the qualities of such a Master by stating that such a being sees all as the same one God and behaves in alignment with this state. A Jnani, Sanyasin, Swami or Master is one whose mind constantly rests in Buddhi, the Divine Will and Intelligence of the Atman. Such a being is one who sees only God in everything and everyone, everywhere and such a being does not distinguish between "mine" and "thine," "good" and "bad," "honor" and "dishonor," nor classes of people and races. Such a being has a constant, uninterrupted experience of Bindu Nada and knows that there is no such thing as duality or diversity. Such a being experiences that the entire Universe is contained inside himself and that he himself pervades all objects (people, places and things). Bhagawan Nityananda tells us that only such a being can be known as a Sadguru or Sanyasin, and that one should only take such a being as one's spiritual Master.

8. Bhagawan Nityananda tells us that, for the relationship between Master and Devotee to work, the seeker must have and continue to cultivate Faith in God and the living Master. This Faith is expressed by way of vigilance in daily spiritual practice as instructed by the Master.

9. Shri Bade Baba tells us, over and over again, that the basis for Sadhana is the willingness to turn away from worldliness and the willingness to destroy our *attachment* to sense pleasures and

worldly pleasures. He tells us that this happens through the destruction of the body-idea, also known as the limitation of the ego (that is enshrined in the senses). "Atma is not perceptible to the senses," He tells us. By this statement we understand that God can only be known and realized by going beyond the mind and beyond the senses. If our *attachment* to worldliness is not destroyed in this way, he tells us we will fail in the end.

10. Bhagawan Nityananda emphasizes the importance of *Equality Consciousness* and He explains what that is. Equality Consciousness is the experience of "sameness," the direct experience that there are not many individual experients (souls) and that there is no such thing as a 'soulmate' (souls don't have mates), but that there is only one Universal Experient, only one being who experiences through all of the forms. This One God comes and goes on the breath. Because all are this One God, all are equal. *This, He tells us, is the real Equality Consciousness. Without it, we cannot know God.*

11. He tells us that "Without Bhakti there can be no Mukti." Here he emphasizes the absolute necessity for Devotion to the Master and the path. It is the intensity of your feeling for God and the living Master that causes Jñana (wisdom attained through direct knowledge of the Self) to rise within you. Once your have Jñana, your Bhakti increases automatically. And with intense Bhakti, Jñana manifests of its own accord. The two work hand in hand. Through the cultivation of Bhakti and Jñana, limiting desire for objects (people, places and things) is destroyed and perfect Peace is attained.

12. Bhagawan Nityananda tells us that Viveka (the ability to perceive the subtle in the gross) and Vairagya (elated dispassion or non-attachment) are vital to realizing the Truth. Without Viveka, he tells us, you cannot learn to choose the Supreme Principle over limiting desire because you are not able to discriminate between what takes you toward *That* and what takes you away from *That*. And you cannot remain absorbed in your Natural, Free state of being without Vairagya. This elated dispassion is what allows you to keep your mind focused on Buddhi (the Supreme Intelligence) long enough for you to realize that there is no outer world.

All takes place inside the body of Supreme Consciousness of the Shiva-Shakti power that is also contained inside you, that also manifests as your mind and your imagination.

These twelve paragraphs summarize my experience of the teachings and principles Bhagawan Nityananda offers us in His *Chidakasha Gita*. For these reasons, it is worth reading and contemplating over and over again. With Supreme Love and Devotion, I offer this at the Lotus Feet of that Supreme Being, Shri Bhagawan Nityananda of Ganeshpuri. To view and study the entire work, you can go to the following Web page: https://www.nityanandashaktipatyoga.org/about-us-our-approach/wisdom-practices/the-chidakasha-gita/

Chapter 20
The Mantra of The Siddhas

Urdhve prano hy adho jivo visargatma paroccaret /
Utpattidvitayasthane bharanad bharita sthitih //

Vijnanabhairava D1:V24

Prana rises up and out and Apana, the jiva, goes in and down.
These are the utterances of the supreme Goddess, Para Devi or
highest Shakti whose nature it is to manifest worlds. By
expanding either of the two spaces (between the breaths) one
experiences the state of fullness of Bhairava (God).

The title of this book is *Vibration of Divine Consciousness*.
I chose this title based on my experience of the ceaseless pulsation
of Paradevi, which is the throb of Divine Consciousness, known as
Spanda or Chiti Shakti, that manifests, sustains and withdraws this
Universe in an infinite cycle. This pulsation of the Divine Mother
is what I also call the Shiva-Shakti power.

This *Spanda Shakti* is known as *Visargatma* (being of the
nature of Visarga) in our Shaivism. Visarga means initial flash,
emanation, letting go or manifestation. Spanda Shakti has *two
movements* or is known as *moving between two points*. The
uppermost point represents Shiva and the point (or pole) below it
represents Shakti. *These two points are also known as the sun and
the moon and also represent the immanent and transcendental
aspects of Shiva-Shakti, the Supreme Principle.* **The movement of
the entire Cosmos happens between these two points.** *Visarga is
both the inward and outward movement of the Shiva-Shakti power,
the movement also known as involution and evolution.*

> *When a person is subjected to repeated sorrows, he
> must see the light after the exercise of subtle
> discrimination. What is called Prana Vayu is the
> destruction of creation. Apana Vayu and Prana Vayu
> must be merged in the Atman. When these two are
> united, all conditions are annihilated. Before the
> expiration of Prana, one must attain Mukti. Then*

it becomes one, indivisible, losing its duality.

~ Bhagawan Nityananda of Ganeshpuri
Chidakasha Gita

In all living beings, these two movements between these two points are represented by *inhalation* and *exhalation*. In all beings who breathe there exists inner Dvadashanta and outer Dvadashanta. Dvadashanta literally means "end of twelve" and indicates a point at a distance of 12 fingers from the tip of the nose in the outer space where exhalation (expiration) ends after passing upward from the spiritual center of the body, up through the throat and out through the nose. *This is outer Dvadashanta.* It is also known as Prana Vayu.

Inner Dvadashanta, also known as Apana Vayu, is the point in the spiritual center of the body where inhalation ends after moving downward from the nose to a distance of 12 fingers inside. This is also *Visarga. In this way, the movement of the entire cosmos exists inside a living being.*

The outer point at the end of exhalation is also known as *Prana,* and the inner point at the end of inhalation is also known as *Apana. Apana* or inhalation is manifestation and is responsible for life. It is also called jiva, the individual soul, because only when Apana enters the body can it be said that the soul is actually in the body. Prana or exhalation is withdrawal, the return movement to Shiva (God). If Prana goes out and does not return, the body dies.

Maybe you're starting to get what I am saying. *Prana Shakti* (breath) is responsible for all bodily functions. Without *Prana Shakti*, there is no body, no world, no Universe. This form of Divine Conscious energy is what manifests, sustains and withdraws. With each inhalation and exhalation you are completing a cycle of Manifestation, Sustenance and Withdrawal. **The ceaseless *Vibration of Divine Consciousness*, the movement of your soul (which is God) to and from your body, is actually taking place with each breath you take!**

Now. What's important, what is miraculous, is THAT which exists in the space between the breaths. The flash of *Shiva-Shakti*, the welling up of Divine Consciousness, can be experienced by dissolving your mind in the space that occurs after you inhale and just before you begin to exhale, and also after you exhale and just before you begin to inhale.

Awareness (bharanat) or close observation of the space between these breaths, or the pause at apana and prana, is the experience of your own Bliss. For, there is something taking place in those spaces that must be observed.

> *I am not repeating the mantra on my beads, nor am I repeating it with my tongue. God himself is repeating my mantra, while I sit quietly and listen to it.*
> ~ The Poet Saint Kabir

This movement of *Shakti* inward and outward actually takes the form of a Mantra. In the Agamas it is known as the Paraprasad Mantra, the mantra of the Siddhas, the perfected beings. It is also known as the two feet of the Primordial Being, the Mahapurusha, who sits in the heart chakra (not the physical heart) in the Sahasrar, the highest spiritual center at a distance of 12 fingers above the head, in the thousand-petaled lotus.

This mantra is *Hamsa*, also known as So'Ham. This mantra sounds ceaselessly within you, on its own. It is known as *ajapa-japa,* meaning that it repeats itself. It is the only natural mantra. It sounds automatically, 21,600 times each day, with your in-breath and out-breath. It's meaning is *Tat Tvam Asi*, I AM THAT, I am perfect. *I am that Shiva-Shakti power, the inner Self.*

Sa represents *Shiva, Ha* represents *Shakti* and *M* represents *nara* (the individual bound soul). So, all that exists and all that does not exist is contained in the syllables *Hamsa*. There is no greater knowledge and experience than Hamsa. When practiced as *instructed* with *Pranayama* (breathing and breath retention technique), it has the greatest power for delivering the thought-free state experienced by those yogis who are in a constant state of Samadhi. **If you receive this mantra from a Shakta Adept, and practice it according to his/her instruction, you will attain the state of Liberation, the state of Pure Perceiving Awareness experienced by the Self-realized Love beings.**

This mantra is written about in many of the sacred texts of our lineage, including the *Guru Gita*, the *Shiva Purana*, the *Vijnana Bhairava* and others. Through using the Mantra Hamsa, as I was initiated and instructed to use it by Sri Bhagawan Nityananda, I had many profound experiences while in Meditation and also while fully conscious, going about my day. Revelations came easily for me while observing Hamsa. One example is the following experience that I wrote in my journal.

As I experience Hamsa mantra, I pray that my health be protected and that I receive guidance in this transition I am attempting to make. I see Shiva and then I am transported to Bhagawan Nityananda's Mahasamadhi shrine. I pranam to the Murti of Bhagawan Nityananda. He then appears to me in his golden form. I then see myself carrying a golden pail full of water. I am bringing this pail to Bhagawan and I understand that it is for me. He takes the pail and then pours the water over me. Then I sit before him in meditation. I start to dream and, in the dream, I am receiving messages about my health and karmas that I am burning for others.

Often, I experience Bhagawan Nityananda in a vision during Meditation or while dreaming. It is during these visions that I also experience Hamsa intensely. It was my awareness and practice of Hamsa Mantra that set the stage for my darshan of *Lord Shiva*.

Chapter 21
Visions of Lord Shiva

In the presence of my Master,
Repository of the most magnificent wealth,
Let me relish the nectar of chanting glorifications again
and again.

May you be glorified, the one Rudra,
The one Shiva, the Great God, The Great Lord,
Beloved of Parvati,
Firstborn of all the Gods.

....May you be glorified, in whose hand glistens
The sharp trident symbolic of the three powers.
May you be glorified,
Whose most venerable lotus feet
Can fulfill a desire the moment it arises.

....For those who are completely immersed in the
love of Lord Shiva, this turbulent ocean of the world
Is like a great pleasure-lake
For their amusement.

~ Utpaladeva
From his Shivastotravali

The Shiva-Shakti power (which is the Supreme Principle) *in its highest manifestation as form*, is *The Blue Being, Lord Shiva.* He is also known as *Sadashiva* and the *Mahapurusha.* Paramshiva, otherwise spoken of as Anuttara (the Absolute), is really *beyond both form and the formless.*

The formless Paramshiva also takes a form known as The Blue Being, Shiva, Sadashiva or the Mahapurusha, who then has additional forms known as *Rudras.* He is also known to appear as white or platinum in color with a blue neck (from drinking the poison of the karmas of the devotees and destroying those karmas). To a yogi, he appears as both the crystal-like, thumb-sized being who resides in the *Heart Chakra* (hrdaya) behind the physical heart, and the Primordial Guru who sits in the thousand-petaled lotus in the *Sahasrar.* His feet are *Ham* and *Sa.* Although formless, he also takes a form out of Supreme Love for his devotees. He appears as an ashen-covered blue, with four arms, five heads (representing the 5 elements and his five powers) and a magnificent trident.

His Shakti or active aspect is represented by serpents that envelope his neck, arms, and flow around his head and through his hair. At times, he appears the size of a thumb and, at other times, his form is huge. At times, he is almost translucent, appearing as a silvery-blue with only an outline of a shape. And then he also takes the form of Pancha-Brahma, the Maheshamurti, in *Shivaloka.*

Lord Shiva is the Master of the Shakta Adepts of our lineage. He is both *Prakasha* and *Vimarsha*, both the Light of Supreme Consciousness that is as a flame where there is no wind, and the active principle *(Shakti)* of Manifestation, Sustenance and Withdrawal. *In this way he is both beyond all activity and pregnant with it.*

Shiva is sublime. He is above all time, space and causation. He is the cause of all things created and not created. To describe Lord Shiva accurately is really not possible with words. It is to have his darshan and his Blessing that one engages in Sadhana over an extended period of time, under the leadership of a true Shaktipat Guru.

Shiva is the final resting place of all questions and answers, of all beliefs, of all doubts, of all hopes, of all worries, of all desires, of all experiences. After having the vision of his form, all things are seen as one. **He is the final guidepost on the journey to union with God.** My visions of Shiva are many. He is my great Lord. I will share some of the most important experiences I have had.

My practice of *Hamsa*, as instructed by my Shri Gurudev, bore fruit in the form of darshan of Lord Shiva. Although he had appeared to me a few times early in my Sadhana, he had not revealed himself completely to me, nor spoken to me, until this time. He then started to appear to me in Meditation, sitting in front of me in full form, holding his trident. His hair was long and matted and he was a scintillating blue in color. In one vision, he gave me two contemplations that he told me to repeat to myself daily. *You are also welcome to use these contemplations, as well.* They are:

This world and the entire Universe is an unfolding of My Consciousness. The 5-Fold Act is an unfolding of My Consciousness.

And

I offer everything to Sri Maharudra (Lord Shiva) who is the great enjoyer.

After giving me these two contemplations, Shiva instructed me to go to a particular page in the Upanishads, and to also contemplate what I found there. The following is the prayer I found on that page:

I, who am an embodied being, endowed with intellect, life breath, and their functions, now offer up all my actions and their fruits to the fire of Brahman (God). No matter what I may have done, said or thought, in waking, in dreaming, or in dreamless sleep, with my mind, my tongue, my hands, or my other members; May all this be an offering to God.

I contemplated these daily, as Shiva instructed. Then, after a short time, I had a series of visions of him that occurred whether my eyes were open or closed. *These came spontaneously, starting with a vision in which Shiva gave me a mantra to chant and repeat.* He told me this mantra was for me to use whenever I wanted his darshan or needed to call on his power in this work.

For the purpose of this Chapter, I will call it the Mahapurusha mantra. When I performed this mantra, all impressions in me, all images, all thoughts, *everything* was immediately wiped completely clean, and there was nothing but the Bliss of the Absolute. And then I saw his magnificent form radiating everywhere, followed by streams of blue, gold and white light. I received Shiva's mantra in the following way:

Morning Meditation. I sit and repeat Hamsa mantra. As I do, I see the image of myself and Bhagawan Nityananda sitting together radiating light. I then see the Mahapurusha (Shiva) sitting in lotus posture above my head in Brahmarandra (sahasrara). He is the color of the blue pearl and is glimmering in the void. He speaks to me saying, "I am you and you are me." He then gives me a mantra and I then hear the mantra being chanted inside me. Shiva tells me to perform this mantra every day.

*   *   *

After being given my Mantra by Shiva, I had the following vision:

I was chanting. Bhagawan Nityananda was walking through aisles of people, dancing around people and offering his blessings to all. I saw myself in a chariot of pure gold. In fact, it was raining gold bindis. I was wearing a crown of gold. A consort was all around me and we were moving very slowly through masses of people in a place that looked like a huge garden.

All the deities were present in the form of those people. I became the Blue Being. It was him with my face. I am him. At the same time, I also saw my form turn to gold. It was like Vishnu and Shiva combined, with my face. I am them and they are me.

At several different times, I got out of the chariot to walk among all the people. At one point, I had one of my astras and I was giving people Shaktipat. At other times, I had my other astras and was using them to destroy demons and remove karmic obstacles. In this vision I was also working on people to heal their illnesses. This scene went on for a long time.

*   *   *

After this vision, I started to experience Shiva regularly. I also saw the *hundred Rudras*, the manifestations of *Shiva*. They have blue forms and often wear gold crowns. Often, when sitting for Meditation, I saw The Blue Being sitting above my head. At these times, he had snakes (serpents) moving in circles along his head and body.

At times, Shiva would appear in front of me and then dance around me in a circle. I then saw what I can only describe as a nuclear-type burst of light as he entered me. I came out of these meditations very stoned on Shakti and feeling completely rejuvenated at the same time. Some of the most profound experiences I have had of my Lord Shiva, were then corroborated in some way. This is something that is quite unexplainable in ordinary terms.

After having many of these visions and experiences, I began to have another experience. I can only describe it as being completely surrounded and absorbed in a scintillating Blue Consciousness, like a lake or ocean with no beginning and no end. I began to see myself as one with this Blue Consciousness at all times. I have more experiences to share of my magnificent Lord Shiva. But I can't share them just yet.

Chapter 22
The Dawn of Total Freedom

If I say that I am Self-realized, some will say that Kedarji is boasting for saying so. It is true that Sadgurus are self-effulgent and not self-proclaiming. If I don't speak of my own Self-realization, some will say that I don't speak of it because I have not attained *That*. Others may say that I am robbing them of the understanding of what the final state to attain is actually like.

The truth is, for Self-realized beings to share their experience of the final attainment, is like a gardener who has discovered an incredible garden paradise that he never imagined could be cultivated, because it was *discovered, by way the Grace of his Guru*. It's always been there in all its glory. It is like a chef trying to describe a taste that cannot be compared to any other dish, but must be shared anyway, out of spontaneous delight.

I am what my Master has made me. This Blessing of Grace is backed by a long lineage of Sadgurus. I do not have a resume. All I can rely on is a history of selfless service to the spiritual needs of my devotees and disciples. Those wanting verification of Kedarji's ability and authority to lead others to permanent spiritual transformation and realization of the Self can review the many video blogs at NityanandaShaktipatYoga.org, the posted experience shares there, and also speak with those who have served our mission and kept my company the longest. You can also come to programs that I lead and have an experience of your own to begin to decide what Kedarji's attainment is. These are really the best steps.

I share the following out of the spontaneous delight of doing so, and for the benefit of those seekers who want to have a better understanding of what Liberation means and is. This is my humble attempt at that.

"You are the one witness of everything, and are always completely free. The cause of your bondage is that you see the witness as something other than this."

~ Ashtavakra, from his Ashtavakra Gita

All I know is He, my beloved Master. I see only him everywhere. Whatever I experience, it is my Guru. I have lost myself in Him, and found myself in Him. By my Guru's Grace I know, without a doubt, that I am not this body, nor the objects of this world that I find manifesting in my life. By the Grace of my Shri Gurudev I know, without a doubt, that I am Shiva, that I am the Absolute, One God, the Supreme "I" Consciousness that manifests, sustains and withdraws this entire Universe. By His Grace, I know that I am THAT. There is never a time, during the course of my daily activities, when I forget this fact, not even for a mille-second. As a result, my life is completely rapturous, without interruption. **By my Master's Grace I know that the words "Liberation" and "Self-realization" are just words – words that die when language ceases to exist in the mind. By His Grace, I know that what I have is much greater than those words and their definitions.**

When God exists everywhere and in everything, what is Total Freedom? It is sometimes referred to as Self-realization or Final Liberation. But, if *That* is, always was and always will be, how can it now be called "final liberation?" When I did not have eyes to see, I sought after Liberation. Now that my eyes are opened wide, Liberation seems a strange notion. There is no place where *Shiva* is not, no corner of the Universe where *Shakti* does not reign supreme. This "Liberation" is a concept *that is useful up to a certain point only*. How can I explain it otherwise?

Still, how can I write just one paragraph on that which is at the heart of all religious and spiritual paths? **The Truth is there is a permanent state of Rapture, Supreme Joy, complete Knowledge and experience of God, *beyond which there is no other level to rise.*** So, I will try to speak a little about THAT which words cannot adequately describe.

What must be understood about this state is that it is a permanent, uninterrupted state of *Pure Perceiving Awareness*. One merges with this awareness that is the *Witness* to your mind. **This Pure Perceiving Awareness allows one to experience the fullness of Humanity in the constant delight of the inner Self.** So, the final state is rapturous by its very nature because in it, one is able to experience all of the aspects of Humanity as Divine expressions, movements in Consciousness that consistently expand this experience of rapture, of Bliss, in constant recognition of the inner Self, the Supreme Principle – *Purno' ham Vimarsha*.

This is a state in which all the expressions of Humanity, from thinking to the movement of emotions to sensory experience, are observed and enjoyed from the highest vantage point of the inner Self. In this permanent state, all that does not honor, glorify and invoke the Self has fallen away and dissolved in the ever-present recognition of Grace. *Then every mundane activity, every worldly interaction becomes a reminder of and experience of the Shiva-Shakti power within.*

This state of Liberation comes as a result of Sadhana (daily spiritual practice) under the direct leadership of a Sadguru. However, it is a state that *dawns*. Other than performing your Sadhana, you *cannot* plan for it to happen and you *can't* set your practice up in order to make it happen. Liberation comes to the Disciple *unsought*. It is a state that is bestowed (Para Shaktipata) on the Disciple by the Will of one's Guru (once The Guru is fully pleased with your Surrender), and by the inner Guru (the Self) directly; and sometimes after final initiation is given in the physical company of a Shaktipat Sadguru, or when such a being appears in the Disciple's Meditation.

After this dawning, Liberation is a mere after-thought and is perceived as a mere notion, just like all other notions or vikalpa; a falsehood that does not really exist. It is only a possible reality for those who have not yet attained it because, having merged with the Absolute, there is no such thing as bondage and, therefore, nothing to be Liberated from. What can I say. This is what I know of the subject.

I will share the following two experiences from my journal.

It is Maha Shivaratri. I sit for a second round of chanting Mahapurusha Mantra. I immediately see my great Lord sitting before me. He is blue and completely effulgent. His eyes are open and they are dark blue. His hair is radiating a light, silvery blue hue and it surrounds my being like an ocean. Shiva then starts to expand to fill the entire room. I see several flashes of brilliant light and I am carried to a place where the entire Universe is visible, but off in a distance from this blazing light.

Then I am in my Meditation room again, with my Lord sitting across from me. He is there even with my eyes open. He now has something in his lap that he is handing me. It looks to be a sword or column-like pillar with a tremendous gold handle on it.

Now I see that it is a huge blue column that looks to be light, stretching from this handle up into the heavens. Lord Shiva hands this to me. He tells me its name. He then gets up and enters me as he has before. The column then explodes into an ocean of brilliance, with rays flooding everywhere, vibrating like a magnet.

It then contracts to its original form and size, like a great sword, expanding and contracting in my hand. It then becomes the Blue Lake, stretching into an expanse that I can see emanating from me, but that I cannot describe. I sit with this vision for a while. I have seen the great Blue Lake of Consciousness!

*   *   *

3:45am. While taking a bath. I see a powerful white light blazing before me and all around me. It is the same blinding light I have seen before. I find myself at Bhagawan's feet in the Ganeshpuri Mahasamadhi shrine. I am lying in full pranam to Bhagawan. He sits up and places his fingers on my eyes. Then he puts his hands on my head and then on both of my temples, holding my head in his hands in this way. I see his form coming in and out of this white light. I then finish bathing and go to sleep listening to Brahmin Puja.

The next morning I sit for Meditation and chant Mahapurusha Mantra. I see a great golden light rising before me. As I continue to watch, thousands of brilliant blazing suns rise up before me. These suns encircle me as I have seen many times.

I then see and feel a Yajna in my being with a tall, blazing fire. I make offerings to the fire, specifically offering into the fire those things which I do not want to experience, and a prayer for the work I want to offer through our programs. I make a wish for my being, my body, my mind, my limbs to be used in service to Shiva.

The suns then turn into moons and Shiva, the Blue Being, appears before me. I am then submerged in the Blue Lake with Shiva sitting before me. I see the Blue Pearl and Visarga. These Visarga are represented by two white dots that are like magnetic poles on either end of a swirling dense blue field. I see the entire cosmos in this magnetic blue field, vibrating between these Visarga.

*   *   *

Amazing grace, how sweet the sound
That saved a wretch like me

I once was lost but now I'm found
Blind but now I see.

The final state of Liberation *is not* the vision of The Blue Bindu, although this vision is an important sign that Liberation is possible in the present life. It is not even the vision of Lord Shiva, as sublime as His Darshan is. The state of Liberation is known as *Purnaham Vimarsha* or Purest Vimarsha, also called Purno' ham Vimarsha, Purnahanta, Shiva Vimarsha or *Shiva Vyapti*. It is spoken about in many of the Agamas. **It is a state of constant rapture, permanent peace, unabated joy and ever-increasing stillness.**

It is everlasting Bliss. It is the *permanent* and *constant* awareness within the yogi of *The 5-Fold Act of Divine Consciousness*. It is the constant awareness "I am Perfect. I am God and God is me." It is the *constant* awareness of *Shivo'ham*, "I am Shiva, I am the Primordial Lord." It is this Shiva Vimarsha. *Above all else, it is the state in which the world and the Universe, as we know it, disappears*. And, most importantly, it is beyond the language I have just used in my feeble attempt to describe it.

> *Then (on attainment of krama-mudra), as a result of*
> *entering into the perfect I-consciousness or Self, which*
> *is, in essence, Chit and Ananda (Consciousness and Bliss)*
> *and of the nature of the power of the great mantra, there*
> *accrues the attainment of lordship over one's group of*
> *the deities of Consciousness that brings about all*
> *emanation and re-absorption of the universe. All this is*

the nature of Shiva.

~ Pratyabhijnahrdayam: 20

This final state of constant, uninterrupted Pure Perceiving Awareness (Purnaham Vimarsha) can only be experienced. It *cannot* be described. However, the *result* or the *effects* of that state of Liberation is what I can briefly share. Purnaham Vimarsha is the state in which one experiences *everything and everyone, everywhere* as God, as Divine, as the Shiva-Shakti power -- on a *permanent* basis.

Purnaham Vimarsha is a state so rapturous that what we call a Universe is really experienced as a *Play of Divine Consciousness,* no longer a world. If you have never seen Rama, Krishna, Vishnu, Parvati or Lakshmi, and yet, this is your experience, you have attained the highest state.

Purnaham Vimarsha is the state in which you experience your identity as being one with Shiva, one with the Self. Shivo'ham, "I am Shiva," becomes your identity.

Purnaham Vimarsha is the *constant* experience that it is God who owns this body. It is Shiva-Shakti who hears through these ears, sees through these eyes, tastes through these lips, smells through this nose, feels through these limbs. All experiences are only God's to enjoy. It is a state where you are no longer attached to the body and you no longer identify with the body and your limited "I" consciousness as just a person.

Purnaham Vimarsha is the state in which *all craving for and expectations of sense pleasures and worldly pleasures ceases.* This *does not* mean that a Self-realized being never experiences the people, place and things of this world. *It means he does not go chasing after them.* If, in the course of his/her daily activities and his/her offering to others, they come to him unsought, he accepts the experience of them. If they don't come to her *unsought* in due course of her activities, she does not actively engage in acquiring them.

Being completely established in this *Pure Perceiving Awareness* is the state in which the mantra *Hamsa* can be heard vibrating through one's being all the time. It is the state in which spontaneous Kumbhaka occurs regularly in Meditation and during the course of one's daily activities. It is the state in which the unstruck sound, *Anahata Nada*, like the crashing waves of the ocean or the vibration and buzz that can be heard standing inside a big bell that has just been struck, *can be heard inside all the time.* It is a state wherein the mantra Om or the six syllable mantra of this Kali Yuga age, *Om Namah Shivaya*, can be heard resonating from inside spontaneously on a regular basis.

In this state, the yogi is constantly and spontaneously aware of *The 5-Fold Act of Divine Consciousness* (taught in our Secret To Self-Realization Series of courses) and always aware of the *transcendental* and *immanent* aspects of every energy, over which one has full power.

In Purnaham Vimarsha, the yogi has merged in the *Nirvikalpa* state (the state where one is totally free of all thoughts and notions) and experiences an unbroken awareness of the Self, whether standing, sitting, working, playing, or moving about in any way. The yogi is able to dissolve her mind in the Shiva-Shakti power immediately, simply by directing her will to experience the Witness. In fact, this state becomes his permanent state, held in place by his constant remembrance of God, that is spontaneous remembrance of the inner Self.

This state of *Pure Perceiving Awareness* is the *permanent* realization that the yogi owns nothing, even though he may have things in his possession; that she possesses nothing and no one even though she may be surrounded by plenty; that he keeps nothing, even though people, places and things may flow to him; because all is God and all is experienced through God.

My Master's mantra is SEE GOD IN EACH OTHER. When this becomes your *constant* experience, that of seeing God in everyone, you have attained all that is worth attaining. In *Purnaham Vimarsha*, one goes *beyond* the tools of meditation, chanting, seva, yoga and the study of scripture. **And yet, the practices are now so rapturous, so joyful, that one continues to perform them.** But the *necessity* for doing them disappears. Even when this occurs, the experience of Total Freedom is relished over and over again through the ongoing experience of Devotion to one's Guru, God and Humanity.

Descriptions and actual accounts of *Purnahanta*, this *Shiva*

Vimarsha, can be read about in scriptures and sacred texts including *Chidakasha Gita, Yoga Vashistha, Shiva Sutras, Pratyabhijnahrydayam, Paratrishika Vivarana, Tantraloka, the Vedas, the Upanishads, Narada Bhakti Sutras, Shiva Dristhi, Sri Guru Charitra, Vijnana Bhairava, Shiva Purana* and *Amritanubhava.* Of course, better than reading about it is to reach the level where you experience it for yourself. Then there will be nothing to debate, discuss or research.

This state of Total Freedom *dawns* on the yogi *unsought* when the yogi *forgets* about becoming Liberated, when the yogi *discards* the thought of attaining anything *and simply becomes completely absorbed in Love and deep Devotion for daily spiritual practice, as instructed by a Sadguru.*

When daily spiritual practice (which includes the Shaktipat Kriya Process stated earlier) becomes a joy that you look forward to everyday, *with great anticipation and no worry of Self-realization,* Liberation or perfection in God will come looking for you. This is why it is said that perfecting the practice (Sadhana) is the goal.

> *Jivanmukti is firm abidance in Being,*
> *unaffected by scriptural or worldly ideas.*
>
> ~ Sri Ramana Maharshi

The concept of becoming Liberated is a difficult one for some people. "Total Freedom" is also difficult for people to grasp. *It's important to remember that "Liberation" is not about giving you what you already are. It is a process of burning away all that you are not.* I recently had a student leave our program after several of months of practice. She became suspicious of me and turned away from our offering after stating that Liberation was too lofty an ideal for her to even believe.

It is necessary for me to state clearly to my students and devotees, the goal of this approach, which is this Jivanmukti state of *Pure Perceiving Awareness* I have been describing. And if I don't state the effects or the result of this state of Total Freedom, from my own experience and that of the holy beings of our lineage, why should anyone take me seriously? So, if I didn't state these, others would insist that I am brainwashing people for my own personal use and gain.

If the concept of becoming free is too overwhelming for you, don't have it as your goal. **You can simply perform the practices for their own sake, without ever having to think of Liberation**. *This is actually the best way*. Then, as I stated earlier, "Liberation" will come looking for you.

In this state, the mind has merged and dissolved in the Supreme Principle. One sees from the perspective of the Divine. The Nirvikalpa state is instantly at hand. And Devotion turns into pure Bliss. This experience is no longer fleeting, but *constant*. This is the *Turyatita state*, the state beyond the Turya (turiya) or fourth state of Consciousness (this fourth state is known as the absence of the first three; waking, dreaming and deep sleep). It is beyond the Turya state because the states of waking, dreaming and deep sleep as separate states, *disappear* in the *Turyatita* state.

In the Turiya state, the mind becomes quiet. But in the *Turyatita* state, the mind is dissolved completely in the Shiva-Shakti power. *Then there is the realization that 'mind' is just a label for what happens when this Shiva-Shakti power recognizes/perceives itself as an object in Consciousness – that what we call 'mind' does not exist separate from this Shiva-Shakti power that is the only Experient and Enjoyer.*

The Universe as we know it disappears and everything, everyone, everywhere is perceived as that one Shiva, the inner Self. **As Sri Abhinavaguptacharya puts it, this is the state of Jagadananda. It is the Bliss of the Divine made visible as the Universe of all the worlds.**

In this book, I have placed a lot of emphasis on inner experiences and I have shared many visions that I have had. I have done this for the sake of my students, so that they can begin to understand *Chidakasha*, the vast expanse of the Inner Self. *As my Master did, I also want to warn my students that you can get hooked on the inner experiences of lights, sounds and visions and develop the wrong understanding about them by becoming egotistic.*

So, know that, although these inner visions are important, the state of *Purnaham Vimarsha*, its effects which I have just described, is the only true state of Total Freedom. It is the *Turyatita* state (state beyond the fourth state of meditation). **It is the only experience worth attaining and worth keeping. Nothing else is more important**. Conversely, one who does not experience the state that I have just described here, on a permanent, uninterrupted basis, cannot be said to be Liberated.

We live in a world full of scam artists and people who are not who they claim to be. "Insta-Gurus" can be found on every corner. *We also live in a world where people are unable to recognize true saints, a world in which many fear purity and refuse to allow a vision where Divinity is held in the highest esteem, a world in which evil is being embraced more and more by the hour.*

In this Kali Yuga age, in this most confused modern age, you will know a Self-realized being, whether he teaches or not, whether she gives Shaktipat or not, by the state I have just pointed to in this chapter. If you want an example to follow, to aspire to, that's the one, *Pure Perceiving Awareness*. When, through your practices, you begin to experience it for yourself, even if it is just a glimpse at first, you will know that it is possible to attain.

This state is acquired first by the Grace and instruction of a Sadguru, and then by Para Shaktipata, the final form of Grace bestowed from within by God, when your Guru is pleased with you. And the means to the second is the first. It cannot be attained by any other means.

I have been asked if my state ever leaves me, if my Meditation ceases when I am going about my day teaching, working, paying bills and handling administrative details. *It does not.* This state, this constant recognition of God everywhere and in everyone, this constant state of rapture does not cease for me.

The reason is, I have become the goal of the practice my Master instructed me in. I have become what *Shiva* has bestowed on me. *This is what happens when the Devotee dissolves his own ignorance through the Master's instruction.* **It can be the same for you, with practice.**

> *Those with physical eyes alone may See God in beautiful*
> *objects, Yogis see Him in the heart-lotus; Priests see*
> *Him in the sacred fire. The truly wise have a thousand*
> *eyes and see Him everywhere.*

Chapter 23
The Bond of Power

"A child cannot be born without a father and a mother. Clothes cannot be washed without water. There can be no horseman without a horse. So, without a Master, none can reach the court of the Lord." ~ The Poet Saint Kabir

Just as a teacher or mentor is required in the arts, sciences, athletics and so on in order to become really competent in those fields – So too, in the field of permanent spiritual transformation through Yoga Science, a competent Guru is required. In this regard, it is best for you to seek a Sadguru who has attained the goal that he espouses to others.

Also, as a reminder from previous chapters, spiritual growth is only spiritual growth when it is not skewed through the play of the Gunas and the Malas, and only when it is on a permanent trajectory to God-realization.

People generally think that a Master's body is guru. A man does not become a Guru by simply wearing sandals and counting beads on a rosary. One who talks "Brahma Jnana" (knowledge of the Self) and gives stones to his disciples is not a Guru. Whatever a Guru speaks in words, he must show it in action. First one must practice and, after Realization, he must begin to teach others. One who has thoroughly wiped off the idea "I am the body" is fit to be called a Guru. There is none higher than such a one. There is no god above such a Guru. Such a Guru is God, and God is such a Guru.

~ Bhagawan Nityananda
Chidakasha Gita

Gururupayaha --- The Guru is the means.

Shiva Sutras 2:6

"One can only know the formless Absolute (the inner Self) through the form of a Sadguru.

*"One who is without such a Guru is like a ship without a rudder.
...to a person who has no Guru, there is no safe place in the world."*

~ Bhagawan Nityananda
Chidakasha Gita

The word 'Guru' has been overused and abused on the internet and in other media. **The true Guru or Sadguru is a *strong spiritual leader* who has *earned* the right to lead others to permanent spiritual transformation.** Whether you believe in Saints or Self-realized beings or not, I think you will agree that, for anything worth attaining in life, for any skill or worth-while pursuit that is *life-changing*, one needs a *competent leader* to model after – one who will influence your thinking and habits to change for the better.

Sages of steady wisdom have a duty to influence our thinking and actions, *by any useful and powerful means,* to get us to change our understandings. This is done so that we can experience *the highest*, the greatest, the best that life has to offer. Such a being's only duty is to get you to experience and become awash in the highest Truth, *that you are the inner Self.* All the Master's effort toward leading you is for this purpose alone. **Once you experience permanent spiritual transformation in your direct experience of the Self, in a way that you have become *established* in that experience *after the tests of your attainment are complete*, the Master's job is done.**

The difference between a spiritual teacher and a Shaktipat Sadguru is that the living Shaktipat Sadguru *gives you the direct experience of what is being taught.*

Today, people are very apprehensive to follow a Guru and many advise against doing so. Due to all the entries on the internet, there is a wide perception that a Master is merely a personal truth seeker who can be found on any street corner, and that one does not need to be devoted or loyal to one Master or path. *This concept is flawed.* Also, due to the poor behavior on the part of some spiritual teachers, coupled with the weak intention of students who are mired in the 'god' trap (see later in this chapter), people are hesitant to fully embrace a true spiritual leader. I understand this. I was the same way, at first.

As I shared in the Introduction, a car is, for most people, a necessity for travel. Just as you would not stop buying a car simply because you purchased a couple of 'lemons' in the past, in spiritual life, if you desire permanent spiritual transformation, you should not stop seeking out a spiritual leader who can lead you, even if you have read about or have experienced one whose behavior was not pure and most useful.

In our approach there is a very profound and practical teaching embodied in the Shakta experience of Nityananda Shaktipat Yoga. This teaching is embodied in what is known as *Shiva-Shakti Trikona*. This is a reference to the *triadic heart* of Shiva (The Supreme Principle), having three points that all conjoin atop the Sahasrar – *Shiva, Shakti, Nara*. The meaning of this is that God (the Shiva-Shakti power), the living Sadguru and the individual bound soul are all one in the same.

If you remember that the true spiritual leader is a perfect reflection of your very own Self, if you remember that, when you hear the words 'Guru,' 'Master,' or 'Self-realized being' uttered, *you should also understand those to be a reference to your very own Self*; If you remember this, you will have no problem following the Master, once you have tested such a being (see Chapter 25 - Understandings Dictate Feelings).

The one who desires to realize God should seek a Guru because the Lord is known through scripture and scripture is known through the Guru. By destroying ignorance, through an enlightened understanding of the Guru's instruction, knowledge is attained and He (the Lord) is realized.

~ Bhagavadutapala

As I mentioned in an earlier chapter, the Shree Guru Gita is an ancient sacred text of our lineage *that describes both the transcendental and immanent aspects of the Guru-principle.* In this song sermon in which Lord Shiva imparts to Parvati the knowledge of how to attain permanent spiritual transformation and merge into the Absolute, Lord Shiva describes the importance of the spiritual leader in the living Master.

Some significant verses, relevant to this chapter are:

3. Parvati said "O Lord, by which path can an embodied soul become one with the Supreme Principle? Please have compassion on me, O Lord! I bow at your feet."

In the next four verses, Lord Shiva responds by saying:

5. The knowledge I impart to you now is difficult to obtain in the three worlds. Listen to it carefully. The Supreme Principle, that Shiva-Shakti power is none other than the Guru. O beautiful one, this is the truth. This is the truth.

6. The sacred texts and scriptures, such as the Vedas, the Shastras, the Puranas, historical accounts, and other written accounts; the knowledge of mantra, yantras, and so on; the traditional code of ethics, magic incantations…

7. The Shaiva and Shakta treatises, and other various sacred texts bring about in this world the downfall of those who are ignorant of the Truth and deluded by their false notions of worldliness.

(This is a reference to the fact that the time-honored and studied scriptures and sacred texts of our approach are purposely limited in their explanations of the Supreme Principle and how to know the inner Self. The understandings that these texts point to are left to be elucidated by a Sadguru. Otherwise, the interpretation of these texts is left to the worldly superimposition of the unenlightened, due to the 'god' trap I reference below. This is how one who doesn't have a living Master can actually contract in his/her understanding of these utterances.)

8. Those people are fools who engage in sacrificial rites, vows, penance, japa, charity and also pilgrimages without knowing the Guru principle.

**Excerpts from the Shri Guru Gita provided with permission by sanskrit.safire.com

The 'god' Trap

As I stated briefly in Chapter 4, many people today do not want to know the Supreme Principle or the sublime state of *Bliss* and *Love without distinctions* that can be experienced in the Self. *They want a God of convenience.* **They want a notion of God that conforms to their limiting desires and cravings for worldliness.** I call this is **the 'god' trap**. If you fall for this trap it means that you want God to become the product of your thinking and fantasizing, your imagination. You want God's 'stamp of approval' on your pursuit of pleasure in an attempt to avoid pain, *out of fear of loss*. You will *never* advance in any spiritual approach to permanent spiritual transformation with such notions.

Today, many seekers get caught in this trap. They are wooed into a 'department store' that promises that you can realize the Truth, that you can realize the Self, as if it's as easy as filling your shopping cart with teachings from aisle B and affirmations from aisle C. Aisle D is where you are told you can put any number of 'gurus' in your shopping cart (the more the better due to the volume discount that is being offered) before checking out at the cashier. And don't forget to use your credit card, instead of cash. That way, if you hear something that doesn't match *your fantasy* of spiritual attainment, you can charge the purchase back.

This reminds me of a story. There once lived a great alchemist who had the power to turn base metals into gold. One day the alchemist decided to teach and took on a small group of students. He began by teaching these apprentices how to stir the pot. A large fire was started. The pot was placed on the fire and filled with all kinds of base, worthless metals. The Alchemist put his long, wooden ladle into the pot and told the students to begin stirring the metals with the ladle while he intoned a series of secret mantras. The base metals began turning into gold before the students' very eyes.

At that point, the alchemist decided to step out for a moment. He told the students to keep stirring the metals with the ladle until *all* the metal had turned to gold, and that he would be right back. Little did they know that thi was the alchemist's way of testing their worth. The moment the alchemist left, the students began talking amongst themselves. "Look, there are gold pieces in there. We can get good money for them. Let's stop stirring and take this pot to the market to see what we can get for those gold pieces. Why should we wait any longer!?" With that, the students removed the pot from the fire and discarded the long, wooden ladle into the fire. Then they ran off.

The alchemist returned to find the ladle destroyed in the fire. He shook his head. "What fools," he said. "They ran off with a few pieces of gold and destroyed the only thing of true value, the one thing that transmutes all base metals into gold!"

This is the dilemma that seekers are faced with today and this is why a Sadguru with the power to transmit Grace is so necessary. My Master used to say that the false Guru market has grown so vast because the number of false devotees has grown so large. *To find the Truth, you first have to be looking for the Truth.* And then you have to look for it where it is, and *not* where it is not. In the story of the alchemist, the long wooden ladle represents your connection to God and the Sadguru, through following the instruction given for expiating your karmas and going beyond your mind and beyond your senses to where the true wealth is. Don't destroy the only connection that will turn your base leanings and tendencies into the gold of the inner Self!

The abode of the true Heart, that state of *Pure Perceiving Awareness* that is Liberation or Self-realization, **is an experience of the fullness of Humanity in the constant and uninterrupted delight of the inner Self.** This state is nothing like you've ever experienced in the fulfillment of your limiting desires and cravings. In fact, until you've attained this state, it is nothing like you have experienced in any area of your life.

It does not conform to your fantasies or popular notions of what God wants for your life. It cannot be experienced through the senses. It can only be experienced and realized by going beyond the mind and beyond the senses. **This state is experienced only when you let go of all notions and allow yourself to drown in the ocean of Bliss that exists there.**

How will you recognize it? Is it possible to recognize a house you've never been in or a street you've never been on without someone to lead you there? **So, a competent spiritual leader in a Self-realized Love being is a necessity.** *The Bond of Power that allows one to rise, by longing for and* *attaining the experience (and eventual state) of Pure Perceiving Awareness, this bond of power is your relationship with the Master, both inner and outer.*

There is a wonderful analogy uttered by the great beings of our lineage that supports the understanding of the 'god' trap and the necessity for the loving leadership and spiritual companionship of a Sadguru.

Very high up on a mountain plateau there was a tree with a huge beehive on it. The edge of this plateau overlooked a very steep and long drop into a rocky ravine, an abyss. This area of the mountain was frequented by wild bears.

One day, the beehive on that tree was dripping with honey. The beehive was situated on a branch that overhung the edge of the plateau, over the ravine. Now, bears have a very keen sense of smell and they love honey. So, on that day, a huge grizzly bear smelt the honey and rushed for that tree. It ran furiously toward the branch the beehive was on, not even looking to determine if the branch would hold its weight.

As the bear leapt onto that branch, the branch broke under the weight of the bear. The bear was completely oblivious to the fact that the branch it was standing on had just broke. It was too busy eating the beehive and licking the honey off of its fingers, as it fell to its death in that abyss.

Spiritual life and the effort at permanent transformation is just like this. Without the bond of power between the devotee and the living Master, *the fake sweetness of the 'honey' of worldly life (attachments, attraction, aversion) and worldly pursuits in an attempt to find happiness, is just like that bear and the honey tree.*

Attaining permanent spiritual transformation that allows you to find and experience happiness and peace where they actually exist inside, *is not hard. You are hard.* This attainment, however, does require vigilance and self-effort (by engaging in the Shaktipat Kriya Process – see Chapter 4) with patience – just like anything else in life that is worth attaining.

Retracing your steps back to God is very much like the oil company executive and the quest for oil. Oil companies are very wealthy. They are wealthy due to the resolve of the oil company executives. The seismic tests have been done. So, the oil companies know where to drill. They know the oil is there, due to the seismic tests. But drilling is not easy.

There is bedrock that has to be drilled through in order to get the oil out. So, they set up the oil rigs. Often they break the drill bits. So, a call goes out to the oil company executive. "We keep breaking drill bits. It's getting really expensive to replace them. What do you want us to do?" The oil company executive says, "I don't care what it costs. The oil is there. Keep drilling until you get all the oil out!" Sometimes, the oil rig blows up, taking lives in the process. Another call goes out to the oil company executive. "What do we do now?" The oil company executive replies, "Look. My job is to worry about the future of the oil Company. The oil is there. Rebuild the rig and keep drilling until you get all the oil out."

In Sadhana, we have to become like that oil company executive. **The wealth is there, beyond your mind and beyond your senses.** *As you begin to experience the inner Self, you are going to come up against your karmic obstacles –* all those leanings and tendencies that are preventing you from embracing and experiencing the fact that you are the Self. The Shaktipat Kriya Process, the mirror of the Sadguru, guarantees this. It is part of the Grace of the Sadguru that frees you (see Chapter 4). Those karmic obstacles are the bedrock that you have to "drill down through," by facing yourself in this Sadhana. The holy beings know that your treasure lies beyond your mind and beyond your senses. The 'seismic' tests have been done.

So, you have to keep digging. And *understand that, it's only when you start digging that the challenges arise.* Beyond all that bedrock is an ocean of Bliss, a sea of joy and happiness that is an unsurpassable delight. Your duty is to get to that ocean and to merge in it. The Sadguru's duty is to lead you, instruct you, remind you and act as your companion in overcoming the obstacles that will, inevitably, arise in your attempt to dig through the 'bedrock' – obstacles like fear, lack of trust, lack of faith, impatience, worry, doubt, poor inner and outer company and resistance (your obstinance).

The combination of your Grace in letting go and following the instruction for your self-effort *with great resolve and vigilance,* combined with the Master's Grace that allows that process to become spontaneous and free-flowing, while protecting you and supporting you through it – this is what is known, in our approach, as *the perfect relationship*. It is a relationship of pure Love and pure intimacy (a Love without distinctions where the devotee is never seen as an object, but as God) that becomes the focus of the devotee's longing. One develops this *personal bond of power* with a true spiritual leader by staying in that Guru's boat, so that he can take you across the ocean of worldliness to the distant shore of the inner Self.

Trust

In order to engage in such a process and relationship with a Shaktipat Guru who can lead you through Sadhana, *Trust* is required. As I shared in Chapter 4, when you begin the inner work that the Shaktipat Kriya Process demands, you are now past the honeymoon phase. Now the obstacles to your rising have to be addressed and faced. *This is why we say that, to make permanent spiritual progress, we have to face our karmas.* You can't successfully move through a process that you've never experienced before without leadership. There are too many unknowns. *Here's why the great beings of our lineage tell us this.*

As stated in Chapter 4, the Sadguru's Kriya Shakti is a mirror that reflects back to you all the useless karmic tendencies that you use to hide your true nature from yourself. **And it *is* a mirror.** For example, if you have a strong personality and are aggressive, manipulative, stubborn, egotistic or highly opinionated in your expression, *the mirror of the Guru will reflect that back to you in connection with the useless tendencies that are holding you back.* Without the right understanding about Kriyas, you will then see your own reflection in the Guru and insist that he/she has a strong, aggressive personality and is highly opinionated, stubborn and egotistic.

If you have a mild-mannered personality and are non-aggressive in your expression, this will also be reflected back to you and, due to your own superimposing, you may find the Guru to be mild-mannered, meek and non-aggressive. *But the Sadguru is none of these things. A Sadguru is the perfect reflection of the Supreme Principle in action, embodied in the fullness of Humanity.* To really understand this, it is necessary to hold the highest understandings of the holy beings of our lineage, that will allow you to experience, for yourself, who or what the living Master really is, and what is actually being brought out in the Kriya process that you are engaged in. **If you approach that Sadguru with a pure vision, the Master will always reflect that pure vision back to you and you will experience only the highest in the Sadguru's company.**

So, the understandings we hold as we keep the company of a Shaktipat Sadguru are vital to our participation and growth. The great poet saint Tukaram, in one of his most beautiful *abhangas*, states:

> *"Be careful when going near the saints. You might catch some of their shortcomings, some of their faults (that you superimpose on to them), if you don't have a pure understanding. Instead, turn within. Do not let your vision dwell on all the dualities of the world. Let it go into the inner Bliss."*

As Kriyas occur in the devotee due to the mirror of the Guru's Shakti, the devotee has to begin to discard his/her notion of being just a person or individual, *before* having fully resolved the identity crisis by becoming established in the Self. In other words, there is a period of time in one's spiritual growth where one has to discard the notion of individuality before having gathered enough evidence to fully embrace the fact that one is the Self.

So, for a while, there is a *gap* in direct experience. This leaves room for the limited and binding leanings and tendencies to foster fear and doubt in the devotee. Then the ego capitalizes on that fear and doubt with cynicism and other wrong understandings. Then the psychologists, the deprogrammers, family members, friends and lovers may say you have joined a cult and are being manipulated, and that all your experiences are simply due to the power of suggestion - **all due to this *gap* in experience where Faith and Trust are required, in the meantime, *until you close that gap with your direct experience of God.***

This is why I took a living Master and this is why one needs a leader and spiritual companion in such a being – *in order to take refuge in this bond of power*, in order to be reminded of these highest of understandings that allow one to go deeper in one's practice and inner experience. This is also why we study the utterances of the great beings in our sacred texts. Due to this gap in experience, you will need to embrace a *profound trust* in the approach and Grace of the living Shakta Adept, and give thanks to God for sending you to that Spiritual Mentor. *However, this is not blind trust.* You should never trust in a Master blindly. **Instead, the holy beings of our lineage all say that we should test the Guru.**

Testing The Master

A Self-realized being sees only Equality in God Consciousness everywhere and in everyone. In order to lead seekers in this world of forms *in which the notions of duality and diversity have become so entrenched*, **a Sadguru also has to use that perception of duality, within the fundamental experience of Unity, in order to lead seekers to permanent spiritual transformation.** *The true Spiritual Mentor is free of all duality, but must use your notion of duality in order to help you strike it down, permanently.*

A true Guru also gives devotees some of what they want, so that they will want more of what the Sadguru has to give. This giving devotees some of what they want and need, particularly in keeping those more in need in closer physical proximity than others, also occurs in the realm of duality that the Sadguru must use to reach people and wean them on to longing for the Truth.

It is due to this fact that the great beings of our lineage provide us with advice on how to properly recognize and test a Sadguru, as you take up the instruction of such a being. *People who are invested in the false notion of individuality, of being the body and just a person can only project or superimpose this false notion on to themselves and others, because this is all they know.* Because this is the case, over a period of millennia, the holy beings of our lineage have developed a series of tests for understanding whether or not you have chosen the right one.

Medical laboratories have tests for almost every disease, virus and physical malady known to humankind. These tests have been developed, refined and perfected over a period of many, many years. So, a new lab technician does not have to come with a test. He/she just has to be sure to use the test that has already been developed and proved, for the malady/deficiency, etc. that is being tested for. The tests of the Guru that are spoken of by the sages of steady wisdom of our lineage are like this.

In order to test the Guru, you will need to commit to spending some time in that beings' company, either in programs offered by the Guru or through some other form of personal contact. *The time required for this test varies dependent upon your longing for the Self.* But we're talking months, at a minimum. **Your test of the Guru should be based on your own inner experiences, the *quality* of those experiences and whether or not they deepen, over time, with your vigilance in following the instruction of that living Master.** Do you experience a desire to know God more fully while keeping the company of the Sadguru and his instruction?

The primary tests spoken of by the Sadgurus of our lineage are:

1. Ours is a Shakta approach (see Chapters 2 and 4). The full Kundalini Awakening is absolutely necessary to invoke the Shaktipat Kriya Process that allows you to make spiritual progress *in a way that is tested*, so that you know that your progress is permanent. **There are five primary tests of a Shaktipat Sadguru.** This is the first. After receiving Shaktipat from such a being, do you have inner experiences during and/or in the weeks and months after the receipt of Shaktipat that are verifiable by the utterances of the Shaktipat Gurus of a lineage of such beings? Did the receipt of Shaktipat catapult you into an experience of the inner Self that is worth your pursuing further?

2. The second primary test is this: Do you experience Kriyas (see Chapter 4) while in physical proximity to the Master, while attending programs in his school or center, or while engaging in the understandings and practices the Master has instructed you in? In other words, has your interaction with the Sadguru caused you to enter into the Shaktipat Kriya Process (Sadhana)? *If so, you know you are with a true Shaktipat Sadguru.*

3. Does the Guru have the knowledge and ability to lead you in rooting out *the Gunas and the Malas* (see Chapter 9)? Such a being should have the personal, direct experience of these being rooted out of his/her Consciousness, by the Grace and *tests* of his/her own Master. If not, your relationship with such a being will have no lasting impact on the permanent spiritual transformation you seek.

4. In order to properly test the Master, *you will need to follow that Master's instruction for a daily spiritual practice, and for addressing your karmas and spiritual life,* to determine if you are having worth-while inner experiences that are bringing you closer to the Self. *This is the fourth primary test.* You can't test the Guru without taking the Guru's medicine *for a while.* This *medicine* has been tested over a period of many centuries. It is *time-honored.*

   Just as you would not attempt to change the formula for a prescription you are given that has been proved to cure the disease you have, you should not attempt to change the instruction given by the living Sadguru for taking the medicine that will certainly cure you of your false identity.

   It's only through a *vigilant* effort at following the Master's instruction to the letter that you will be able to answer the questions "Is my mind getting quieter?" "Am I having experiences of going beyond the mind and the senses?" "Am I experiencing the thought-free state on a growing basis? "Are the practices causing me to deepen my understanding of the inner Self while experiencing Bliss?" "Am I becoming more content?" "Is my longing for the inner Self increasing?" "Am I experiencing a growing desire to retrace my steps back to God?" Of course, if you won't take the Master's medicine, by way of his instruction, *long enough to prove that the instruction works*, then you can't complain that the Sadguru is false.

5. *The fifth primary test is this*: Has the Guru been vested with authority and the Shakti power to initiate others, by

another Shaktipat Sadguru? Does the Master have a lineage of Self-realized beings that he/she participates in, or an acknowledged Sadguru who gave him/her the command to initiate others and guide others? And has the Master stored up the maximum amount of Divine Conscious energy necessary to transmit God's Grace-bestowing power to others through Shaktipat and the Shaktipat Kriya Process?

For example; Bhagawan Nityananda's power to give Shaktipat never diminished. It only grew as more and more people came to receive it. This was evident in the experiences that those people had, and that others observed.

In our experience, with respect to measuring the benefits of the instruction and practice taught, one should give this testing process a *minimum* of two years. For some, the growing inner experiences will provide the proof in less time. For others, it may take a little longer, if you're with the right one.

Back To Trust

You do not need to be Self-realized or God-realized to begin to have inner experiences that equal experiences that Self-realized beings have. Part of the Sadguru's Blessing and Grace is to bless you with some of these experiences as quickly as possible. So, even if you are not established in the final state, you can and should have experiences of that state. Having these experiences is a sign to you that the living Sadguru's state, the final state of Liberation, *is a state that you too can attain; And that, at the very least, you can experience permanent spiritual transformation that is evidenced in your changing for the better, in a relatively short period of time.* **But there are tendencies, leanings, understandings and poor company that can and will destroy your trust and patience, if you are not careful.**

As I shared earlier, in keeping the company of the Guru, *as you begin to acclimate yourself to heading in a new and powerful direction, there are unknowns that you will have to embrace.* The Shaktipat Kriya Process will spontaneously dredge up all of the base, limiting tendencies, false notions, beliefs, feelings and opinions that are keeping you from realizing your true nature, *that hold you back from resolving the identity crisis spoken of earlier*. In addition, any fear, doubt, worry and anxiety that has been festering in your subtle body for many lifetimes, will also be dredged up by the mirror of the Sadguru.

When this happens, there is a tendency on the part of the student/devotee to superimpose those weaknesses on to the Master and others – and to lay blame on them for the storm within the calm that has begun to erupt. This is a HUGE MISTAKE. What you need to remember while engaged in this kind of Sadhana, while standing in front of the mirror of the Guru, *is that ALL the karmic tendencies, false notions, emotions, etc. that are being dredged up* **were there already, embedded in your subtle body from many previous lifetimes and the present life** – *long before you met the Master*. The Master didn't cause you to 'manufacture' these or make these up, **and the Master is not responsible for their existence in your Consciousness – you are!**

For these reasons, it is essential that, after you have tested the living Sadguru to your satisfaction, that you address your doubt and cynicism so that you can inculcate the kind of Faith and Trust that will allow you to continue to rise, without ever looking back over your shoulder. **This is why we continually repeat that you are not a sinner. You are not small. You are not just a person. You are not just ordinary or delightfully weird. You are great. You are the Self. Your perfection is already with you.** *You just need to stop concealing this fact from yourself.*

All doubt on the spiritual path has its root in self-doubt – your denial or disbelief in the fact that you are the Supreme Principle, that you are that Shiva-Shakti power, the inner Self. This self-doubt arises from the fear inherent in the notion that you are separate from God. Even the slightest notion of your separation from the inner Self will allow fear, doubt and worry to fester in your being, *in a way that will slowly eat away at your spiritual awareness and cause you to slide back, over and over again*. This is why we teach that the understanding "Shivo' ham," I am God, I am the Shiva-Shakti power, should be held at all times in one's awareness, even while engaging in daily spiritual practice.

In today's world, there is *a lot* of peer pressure in the collective activity of the masses toward *doubt and cynicism when it comes to permanent spiritual transformation,* particularly connected to approaches where a living Sadguru is part of the approach. We recognize and embrace the necessity for a strong connection and intimate relationship with a mentor or leader for business, skill-centered education, wealth, life coaching, psychic predictions, healing, wellness, etc.

But when it comes to a living Sadguru, the 'god' trap that I share earlier in this chapter, is an obstacle, *along with another, very relevant stumbling block.* Especially here in the West, many people don't want to work for it. They don't want to put forth an extended effort for spiritual transformation. The amount of over-stimulation and brain-washing that causes people to pursue instant gratification, that causes people to define themselves by how they are stimulated by other people, places and things, *this also creates an attitude of cynicism toward what people can't immediately see and experience with their senses – because they are too busy chasing their limiting desires for pleasure, in an attempt to avoid pain.*

And then there is the identity crisis I have spoken of in earlier chapters. **People are slow to give up their false identity as the body, as a mere individual or person, especially if they are deriving pleasure and instant gratification (ego gratification) from pursuing and embracing this false identity.** As a great being has said, "We have the wealth to offer them, but they just want meat and potatoes."

The fact is, we have been *brainwashed* by the popular, collective notion (and subsequent assault on our senses, based on this notion) that happiness is to be found in the pursuit of worldliness, in the possession of people, places and things on some level. We believe we are *just* the body, *because the world tells us so.* We believe we are small, ordinary, just a person, *because our friends, family, lovers, husband, wife and popular culture tell us so. This* **is the power of suggestion that is truly suspect!**

Also, in our modern world, there are *so many distractions* that people become obsessed with. Modern technology, mobile devices and the internet have created an additional *universe of distractions* that keep us bound to objects of sense in a way that increases our attachment to the veil that covers our hearts!

It's important to realize that this is a *karmic trap*, part of your mental conditioning from many past lives of bondage and ignorance when you have pursued the honey from the 'beehive,' as in the story of the bear and the abyss that I shared earlier in this chapter. The first taint or impurity in your Consciousness (Anava Mala) is a karmic impurity that causes you to believe that you are separate from God, and that you are just a person, just an individual who has to make your life happen *because you believe you'll be happy when you can possess outcomes.* **But limiting desire can never quench desire. The restless mind, fueled by this limiting desire and craving, *does not* remain satisfied for long.**

From this impurity rises fear. Out of fear manifests doubt and it's partner – cynicism. Doubt in the fact that you are the Self is a useless tendency that expresses itself in your Consciousness as the belief that permanent spiritual transformation, that the experience of inner Peace and Bliss that leads one to become established in that which is beyond the mind and beyond the senses, is not possible for you – or that that it's just a myth.

When allowed to fester, this doubt then causes cynicism and sarcasm to rise within you, causing you to begin to put a contracting spin on everything and everyone you encounter. **This cynicism protects the energy of egoism** by forcing you further and further into the pursuit of worldly, limiting desires and cravings with the notion that you are the doer and that you have the right to possess people, places and things on some level. *The fact that this is an old karmic tendency means that you are probably not even aware of how cynical you really are.* This cynicism runs very deep. This is why the *mirror* in the Shaktipat Kriya Process is required.

Fortunately for us, God takes the form of the living Master to deliver us from this age-old karmic condition. So, as I finish the offering of this chapter to share with you the dynamic, profound and healing strength of this *bond of power* in the relationship with the living Sadguru, please set aside your cynicism and your ego for just a while. *Keep an open heart and mind as you read on.*

My Master used to say, "Can one who has lived in a ghetto all his/her life understand the life of the rich?" Similarly, can a person who has embraced the ignorance of worldliness for so long understand the wealth of the Guru's state, that is expressed in the fullness of Humanity from the constant delight of the inner Self? This is why we need a spiritual leader and companion who offers us Love, Grace *and the firm hand of spiritual discipline* in leading us to the experience of what is beyond the mind and beyond the senses.

The Bond of Power

The great poet saint Kabir has written, *guru janam janam ki tatak kholi,* "The Master has freed you from being stuck for many lifetimes." In the olds days of long-playing records, the phonograph needle sometimes got stuck and moved in the same one groove of the record, over and over again, without going forward or backward. In the same way, one can also become stuck in one's spiritual growth.

Lifetime after lifetime, the 'needle' moves in the groove of birth and death, pain and pleasure, contraction and limitation. But if someone were to lift the needle and move it over, the cycle comes to an end. Therefore, Kabir says "If you stick to the living Master, he removes you from the [groove] cycle of birth and death. One who sticks to the Master does not wander in the forest of worldliness." For this reason, the bond of power between the seeker and a true Master should be developed, nurtured and protected.

The challenge is loss of awareness that causes one to forget that he/she is the Self. **It is entirely possible for you to enjoy life to the fullest, while never forgetting your true nature as the inner Self.** To reach this glorious experience on a regular, and then constant basis, we have to be tested and reminded.

The tests given through the Grace of the living Master help us to understand where we're really at so that we can improve, so that we can become better at relishing in the Bliss of the inner Self, so that we get really good at recognizing everything as an expression of the Supreme Principle, as a Divine movement in Consciousness. This practice leads to an ever-increasing strength in our witnessing awareness. **The only mistake, the only sin or crime against our true nature is the loss of this witnessing awareness that causes us to turn away from the Light and Love once seen and experienced.**

The Sadguru, through the Shaktipat Kriya Process, shows us the karmic tendencies and leanings that we use to tear this awareness down, to become dull, to make ourselves small. The Guru then helps us to let go of these tendencies, and the subsequent mental conditioning, through the fire of his Love and the Grace of his tests. *Without this, we can never be reminded enough to break our habit of forgetting.* This is the great travesty that must be rooted out, that we forget that we are the Self. *To remember the Self is to wake up each morning with your heart singing and dancing in a state if indescribable Joy!*

Some of the karmic leanings and tendencies that we use to destroy our witnessing awareness of the Truth, to hide our true nature, this Joy, from ourselves are:

- Reaching for and holding on to the false notion that we each are just an individual, just the body, the mind and the senses, just a person, ordinary or delightfully weird.

- This false notion of individuality, the false notion that you are just the body, just a person, gives birth to the ego sense, the sense of doership that leads to attachment, attraction and aversion. This false notion of individuality that leads to the disease of self-appropriation is the chief culprit in keeping us bound to the imaginary ignorance of worldliness that we create for ourselves.

These two tendencies manifest all the others, *like a domino effect that becomes a landslide of understandings that keep us contracted in feelings of limitation, doubt and cynicism.* For this reason, I want to share with you what I and so many others were taught and experienced by taking and remaining devoted to a true, living spiritual leader.

Sadgurus can only give Grace. There is Grace in their talking, their walking, their eating, their laughter, their tough love and their every movement and gesture. *Around such beings it is always raining Grace.* If we don't experience this, it is due to our own inability or resistance to imbibing this Grace (see Chapter 27). We block it from entering us by our own obstinance and desire to remain small and bound. *For this reason, it is necessary to prepare ourselves for receiving and imbibing the Master's Grace that is the bond of power in this relationship.*

Some helpful guidelines are:

♡ There is a real art to keeping the company of the Sadguru. You will need the intelligence, courage and contentment that come with constantly cultivating Humility and Reverence for God, the Master and the approach being taught. Such Humility and Reverence will bode well for all the other areas of your life, as well.

♡ The spiritual leader in the living Sadguru has many faces and, at times, may appear to be very ordinary. This is due to the need for the Guru to reach you within your sense of duality (see earlier in this chapter), coupled with your habit of superimposing your own faults on to the Guru (fault-finding). In the company of a Sadguru, these leanings and tendencies are being reflected back to you by the Kriya Shakti of the Guru. If you mistake these for the Sadguru's tendencies, you will never be able to imbibe and follow Grace. Also, due to the karmic resistance *to being told* that most seekers have, it is often necessary for the Master to lead you with a firm hand and some tough Love. So, the Master may appear to you to be *forceful*, at times. For this reason, in verse 102 of the Shree Guru Gita, Lord Shiva tells us:

"Always remember the Guru for as long as you are embodied, even to the cosmic dissolution. One should never abandon the living Sadguru, even if he behaves in a self-willed manner."

♡ After having tested the Master to your satisfaction, using the tests recommended by those who have tested their own Gurus (see above), *you will need to embrace the Master fully, while letting go and giving over to Grace* (see Chapter 27).

♡ Do not worry or try to calculate when you will or when you should attain the Self. Instead, meditate, chant, pray, follow the living Master's instruction and command and wait, patiently, *while cultivating Love for yourself as the Self.* Learn to forget yourself, to lose yourself and your identity in Meditation. If you keep the

Master's company with great care and Humility, the right moment will come when you will realize the Self and discard your false identity as a mere person. Everything has its season for becoming ripe and yours will come too.

♡ Cultivate Faith by reviewing your experiences that have come to you while keeping the company of the Sadguru and following his instruction for retracing your steps back to God. **It is essential that you keep a journal of your experiences.** It is common that, especially in the early stages of the Shaktipat Kriya Process, one loses Faith and Trust. At these times, your ego will present you with all kinds of doubts, attempting to convince you that you've never had any worth-while experiences. When this happens, you will need to open your journal and review the experiences you have had, in order to renew your Faith and Trust. Faith and Trust are also cultivated by vigilance, a firm resolve in your practice of going beyond the mind and beyond the senses to collect the proof of your Bliss, the proof of your True nature.

♡ People who come to a Sadguru have varying levels of spiritual need, and their karmas are different. Some of these people require less outward attention from the Guru, others require more. For this reason, a Sadguru does keep some people in closer physical proximity than others. The degree of physical proximity to the Guru also manifests, based on one's Devotion and Longing for the Guru's state. **Everyone who comes to such a being receives the same transformative Grace.** *However, their direct experience of that Grace will depend on the degree of their Bhakti – whether or not they practice at imbibing that Grace or sabotaging it.*

In our approach, a spiritual leader in the living Master extends the Grace of the entire lineage to his devotees, in many different ways, dependent on the personality, karmas and changing spiritual needs and wants of the devotee. **For this reason we say *mind your own Sadhana.*** Retracing your steps back to God is a matter of you facing yourself with the leadership and instruction of the Sadguru, and the Blessings of God. *It's never about what is taking place between the Master and another devotee.* If you make it about that, you will fail.

♡ With vigilant effort, following the leadership of the living Master, *learn to rise above praise and blame, to rise above your habit of attempting to save face in order to protect your false identification with being just a person.* Of all the guidelines I could recommend for a newcomer to this approach, this is, perhaps, the most important, even if you forget the rest of the guidelines at first. You can review my own story related to this, in Chapter 4.

The *bond of power* between the living Sadguru and the student or devotee is the *easy* means for those who want permanent spiritual transformation that leads to the experience of the fullness of Humanity in the constant delight of the inner Self. The great news is that this state is entirely possible for anyone who wants it and is willing to become worthy of Grace. With the Grace that is bestowed through this *bond of power*, anything is possible.

There is an ocean of Joy, Love, Peace and Total Freedom within your own Consciousness, just waiting for you to discover it for yourself. Your true wealth exists there.

Chapter 24
Bhakti
The Transformative Power of Longing

*There is no other path as easy and pleasing as Devotion
in the three worlds, O goddess of devas, in all the four
Yugas generally and in the Kaliyuga particularly,
Knowledge (Jnana) and Detachment (Vairagya) have
grown old and have lost their lustre in the (present) Kali
Age. They have become decayed and worn out, as the
people who can grasp them are rare. In the Kali age
as in all the four Yugas there is immediate and visible
benefit in Devotion. I am subservient to a devotee in
view of the power of Devotion. ....*

*Why shall I say more, O Goddess? I am always subservient
to a devotee, always under the control of a person who
practices Devotion. There is no doubt in this.*

> ~ Lord Shiva addressing the Goddess Sati
> Shiva Purana

*Mukti (direct knowledge of the inner Self) is according
to the nature of our Bhakti. If you try hard, you get good
salary. If you try a little, you get a small salary.*

> ~ Bhagawan Nityananda,
> Chidakasha Gita

*na kasthe vidyate devo na pasane na kardame /
bhavesu vartate devas-tasmad-bhavam na samtyajet //*

The deity worshipped through an image does not
reside in the wood, stone, clay or body of which the
image is made, but in the feeling of the worshiper.
For this reason the feeling of Devotion must never
be abandoned.

To attain the Peace, Joy and Happiness of the inner Self,

you have to want it. The great beings tell us that God exists in our feeling and this is absolutely true. Without the Grace of a Sadguru, we cannot cross the ocean of worldliness. **However, no Guru, saint, Self-realized being nor God can help us if we don't cultivate and protect our Longing.** In the Vedas, it is called *Mumukshutva* – the longing to be free.

Without your Longing, your *Bhakti* (expressed as Devotion), the Master's Grace, in the form of his Kriya Shakti, cannot enter you. **Therefore, we say that your Grace, *embodied in this Longing,* is what actually burns away all that you are not.** For this reason, the sages of steady wisdom of our lineage consider this Longing, this Bhakti, to be the greatest component in attaining permanent spiritual transformation and attaining the inner Self. This Longing is what allows you to *steal* the Master's Shakti and to *fully* imbibe the Master's Grace. A bird needs two wings to fly. Your Longing is the first wing of the bird. The Guru's Grace is the second.

Furthermore, *permanent spiritual transformation takes time*. Karmas have to be dredged up and destroyed. The mental conditioning of so many past lives and the present life has to be reversed. Your bad habit of looking outside for what is inside you has to be addressed. For these reasons, permanent spiritual transformation takes time and *patience*. **Without your Bhakti, without your Longing, you will never be able to sustain the effort necessary long enough to achieve the goal**. This is why the cultivation and protection of your Longing is so necessary.

God exists in your feeling. It is the cultivation of this feeling of Love and Devotion, for the Guru and for God, that is at the heart of all spiritual transformation. Devotion is the nectar of Supreme Awareness. *It is that which causes God to come looking for you.*

Although indescribable, I will attempt to share with you now the experience of a state of intoxication so great, a state of rapture so profound, that it would seem to be complete madness! In my Guru's ashrams, we spoke a lot about the mad lovers of God, those devotees who, through their own mad love for God, drank the nectar of Self-Awareness constantly. *Devotion* is the fire that Sadhana is cooked in. For the devotee, this Devotion takes the form of *intense* Love. Directing all of one's feeling toward God, and especially the feeling of Love, is the bridge by which one crosses over the bondage of this worldly existence. *This is the Truth.*

Listen! Your spiritual attainment will always be equal to the level of intensity of your feeling. Progress on the spiritual path is completely dependent on the intensity of your Faith, the intensity of your Devotion and the intensity of your identification with the Shaktipat Guru, with God. You become what you think on the most. **The greater your intensity of *identification* with your spiritual leader in the Sadguru, the more of that Master's power (the Grace-bestowing power of God) you will absorb into yourself.** This is why I worshipped my Shri Gurudev. This Bhakti, this Devotion made me mad with Love for God. Here is an experience that I recorded in my journal.

> *I have become the fire! I have become the fire!*
> *I have become the fire! Who can describe such Maha Prasad!*
>
> *My Master's feet have appeared in my head. The feet of Baba, with the names So' and Ham have appeared in my Sahasrar!*
>
> *My Master's heart has become my heart.*
> *The gates to the palace have been thrust open.*
> *The gates to the palace have been thrust open.*
>
> *I have crossed the threshold to have Satsang with Shiva.*
> *I have crossed the threshold to have Satsang with Brahman.*
> *O, how sweet is his darshan!*
> *Who can describe this Maha Prasad!*
>
> *I have become the fire!*
> *I have become the fire!*
> *I have become the fire!*
>
> *Which bead am I on his golden necklace?*
> *I can no longer tell which one am I.*
> *I can no longer differentiate at all.*

Who is the knower?
Who or What is to be known?

Which bead am I on his golden necklace!?
Which jewel am I on his golden bracelet?
I can no longer tell which one am I.
I can no longer differentiate at all!

In this world of embodied beings, we have all developed the habit of attaching ourselves to forms. We've done this for millions of lifetimes and are experts at this. My Master used to ask us, "Do you want a formless husband or wife? Do you want a formless friend, lover or family member!?" Of course not. So, just as we often engage our emotions, our feeling through interaction with forms (falling in love, for example), in spiritual life, we direct this habit of being attached to forms to the form of the Sadguru in order to inculcate the Longing necessary to pursue the Self. Later, by the Master's Grace, the form of the living Master is transmuted into the genuine experience of the Supreme Principle, *as we lose ourselves in our Bhakti.*

"One can only know the formless Absolute
(the inner Self) through the form."

~ Bhagawan Nityananda

Now, I will share with you how I came to write the experience above from my journal. For years, I meditated on the form of my Guru. I did this with great intensity of feeling; So much so that I started to have visions and dreams where I received messages and premonitions, all of which came true. As my Devotion grew, my Longing for Liberation intensified. When my Longing for Liberation intensified, my Devotion for my Guru and God became even stronger.

Then I started to express this Devotion to my Shri Gurudev. As my Devotion deepened, I expressed my Love for my Guru directly to him. I expressed my Love for God and the transformation I was experiencing in this way also, directed to my Master with tremendous gratitude. During one particular period, whenever I went to visit the ashram to have the Darshan of him, I brought garlands of flowers. I also performed Guruseva. And I did one other thing. I let my Master know that I wanted nothing less than Liberation, complete realization of the Self.

My expression of Love in this way was not for the Guru's benefit. In fact, I did so with the complete understanding that the point of doing so was to cultivate more Devotion in my own heart. I wanted to attract even more of my Master's Grace. In this way, my Devotion intensified quickly and my longing for God grew. It is precisely this process that set the stage for the inner experiences I have been sharing in this book, along with the protection and Grace that I've experienced in my life.

It is my Devotion, my Longing, that caused my Master's Grace to dawn on me. Then my highest Lord, Shiva, appeared to me and took up permanent residence in me. All of this is due to the intensity of my feeling and identification with my spiritual leader in the Master and the inner Self, without making any separation between the two.

Now, I will share another secret with you. As my Devotion for the Master grew, I developed a very strong inner relationship with him. He would appear to me inside to give me messages and to instruct me. Then I would go to his physical form and ask him if he had appeared to me inside to instruct me or send me a message. Often, he would respond by repeating to me what I had heard from inside, thereby corroborating the message. As this occurred, *and as I used the prescribed method for installing my Guru in my heart*, I started to experience inner visits from many of the sages of our lineage who also counseled me. I then also began receiving Blessings for my material life, as well. *In this way, I learned to stop asking for any material boons of my Master.* I just inculcated *more Longing.*

Then I began to do something that I had read about in some of our sacred texts, but was hesitant to apply to my Sadhana, at first. *I began to attribute all the Blessings and Grace in my life to my Guru.* I did so with the complete understanding that Grace is in the giving, and also in the taking away. **This is the secret I wanted to share with you.** As I did this, my Longing for the Guru's state, my Longing for wanting to drown in the ocean of Bliss and *Love without distinctions* that is the Self, became much more intense! As I attributed *all* Blessings and Grace to the form of my Guru, my inner experiences intensified, my inner Darshan of Saints increased and my Love for God in all forms expanded! **This is the power of Longing, of mad Love for God, when directed to the form of the Master.** It is mysterious and profound,

And there is another mysterious and profound secret that I want to share. What I learned from what I share above *is to put everything before my Guru.* You'll notice that I just used the present tense here. Still, even now, I continue to put everything before my Shri Gurudev, as an offering to Shri Gurudev, as I was tuaght during the course of my Sadhana. If I had a question or concern, or I was experiencing some difficulty in my understanding, or I had contracted, or I was suffering in some way, I would take that directly to my Baba, either outwardly to his physical form, or by offering it inside. Often, I did not require an answer or comment from his physical form. At other times, I would hear from him, either outwardly or inwardly, often unexpectedly. Things were resolved just by my having placed it before my Guru in this way. This is the mysterious and profound power of Bhakti, Longing.

The experience of God inside me and everywhere only became real for me when I lost myself in complete and unwavering Devotion for my spiritual leader. This Devotion then became a supreme and sublime Love for the practices and teachings of my Master and our approach. In this way, the living Master took up residence in me and I disappeared. I became mad with joy, mad with intoxication of the Mantra, mad with inner Bliss. This "madness" crystallized into my unwavering commitment to become one with the inner Self. My contract was now binding. There was no turning back. *Longing, at this stage, is nonrefundable, non-returnable. It secures the goal.*

This Longing, this Bhakti cannot be cultivated without making the transition into the Kriya process (see Chapter 4). So, Longing cannot be had without moving from dabbling to discipline. Discipline is Bhakti. **Now, let me explain how this Bhakti is cultivated, strengthened and protected.**

If you have ever become infatuated with another by falling in love with that person, then you have had a glimpse of how longing can begin to open your heart. As another example, if you are a parent, you may have had a similar experience when observing the birth of your child, or in the process of raising a child. At some point during this relating, you may have even had a glimpse of unconditional Love, what we refer to as *Love without distinctions* that caused your heart to open even further, perhaps temporarily.

So, dependent upon what form (person, place or thing) you have directed your longing or desire to, you have experienced a degree of Love and a shift in your heart. *This happened because you had a form to direct your desire, your longing to.*

In spiritual life, a *form* to direct our Longing to is also necessary, *for a time*, until one becomes *established* in the *Pure Perceiving Awareness* of the Self. And, since leadership is required for permanent spiritual transformation, we cannot make permanent progress by directing our Longing to a picture or a statue, etc. A picture or statue will never be able to lead you through the Shaktipat Kriya process of Sadhana. A picture or statue will never be able to administer *the necessary tests* for your spiritual growth either. *For this, a live catalyst is required.* That catalyst is the Sadguru.

The experience I shared earlier of my meditating on my Master's form inside and expressing my Love and Devotion to my Baba, and by serving him, is what is known in our approach as *Guru Bhavana.* This practice, this type of worship leads to mad Love for God. With reckless abandon (not compulsion), that was borne of my gathering the evidence of the inner Self, by going beyond my mind and beyond my senses, **my Longing, my mad Love caused God to come looking for me!** The Self-realized Love beings of our lineage also describe it in this way.

Now, having read to this point, you may be thinking what many people think who have never tasted the nectar of this Bhakti. "This sounds like worship of a man or woman, like a cult." Well, that might be true if the Sadguru were a man or woman. But, before we go down that road, be honest with yourself for a moment. Haven't you ever worshipped a man or woman before!?

Only the Supreme Principle, only God is innate. Everything else is a superimposition, a projection into Consciousness and on to other people places and things. Some superimpositions are not useful in spiritual life, as they keep us contracted in ways that destroy our Longing for the Self. Others are very useful in that they turn our attention to God and increase our Longing for the experience of what is beyond the mind and beyond the senses. After delivering us to this Abode of the Heart, they dissolve.

Given this fact, before reacting to the possibility of great value in following a living Master and time-honored approach to the Self, *consider the Truth about where your notions and understandings about living life come from.* You have parents whom you were born to. You accept the fact that your parents are your parents without ever questioning if, in fact, they are your parents. You accept that they are your parents because they tell you so.

You accept most of the notions and understandings that the society in which you live has popularized *by mass acceptance.* Most times, you don't question these. You do as society tells you to do. You even accept the notions promoted by popular culture without questioning theme. You may also accept and incorporate beliefs and opinions into your life that you have become attached to through your favorite TV shows, movies, Youtube, FaceBook, Instagram, online communities, etc., simply because you have been told that they are popular. *You are also attracted to many of these things due to the mental conditioning established in your being over many, many past lives.* **In this way, your past karmas also dictate which understandings, beliefs and opinions you gravitate to.**

My point is, before inquiring into the nature of the Self and the Supreme Principle whose sacred law rules here, we all have assumed a life, based on what we've been told by family, friends, lovers, husband, wife, teachers in and out of school, popular media and the widely-accepted notions and pursuits of the culture in which we live. And we have done so without questioning many of these, due to 'peer pressure.' Isn't some of this brainwashing?

In this *Play of Divine Consciousness*, everyone has an object of worship. Some worship money. Others worship sex. Still others worship food. Some people worship political power while others worship fame. And those who criticize ritualistic worship are usually involved in some form of ritual themselves. Even coffee and donuts taken at the same time each morning is a ritual, *a form of worship*. Depending on what you worship, how you worship and your attitude during worship, you either advance in life or fall further into the abyss. Then there is the type of worship that causes *real spiritual transformation* to occur.

There are a number of circumstances and situations in which worship of an individual is accepted and embraced in our modern society. Depending on what the sexual preference is (men and women, men and men, women and women) people in our society worship each other. Relationships between lovers and spouses are not only accepted but promoted in every aspect of worldly life. Romance is hyped as the ultimate life experience, just ahead or just behind sex (with family running a close second or third), and people who find themselves intimately involved, worship each other openly.

In fact, the very essence of infatuation, that of being *in love*, is worship by one individual of another. People flaunt worship of each other all over the internet. So many feel that they are only sharing their lives in a meaningful way if they are showing off their worship of each other with 'in your face' posts on Facebook, Instagram and elsewhere, or long phone calls about the intimate details of the relationship. Such people are mad with worship!

Again, this type of worship is not only embraced by modern society but promoted as healthy and normal. Knowing full well that we are born alone and die alone, modern society still embraces the notion that we need someone else to complete who we are. *This is also worship*. It is common to find pictures of husband, wife, family and lovers decorating the desk and walls of a person's office or home and Facebook page. Go into certain bars and auto repair shops and you will find pictures of naked women and men on the walls. Worship, in this context, is never labeled a cult.

Then there is also worship of one's parents, something promoted by scriptural injunction in most religions. Then there is the worship of rock idols, pop idols and rap artists. I knew a woman whose son worshipped a popular rock band. His room was decorated with pictures of each member of the band. These pictures were everywhere, including above the bed and at the foot of the bed. In addition, her son had tattoos of their faces all over his body. He blasted their music constantly on his stereo. He lit candles at night, invited his girlfriend over and, together, they smoked pot and sniffed cocaine, while worshipping the band.

The mother thought nothing of this. After all, rock is a widely accepted part of our culture, as is pot smoking and other recreational drug use. Then one day, her son cut his hair, took all the pictures down, cleaned his room, stopped smoking pot and doing cocaine, broke up with his girlfriend, and took up Transcendental Meditation with Maharishi Mahesh Yogi. **The mother was beside herself!** She hired a deprogrammer and attempted to sue TM, even though the boy's entire outlook on life had improved!!

In fact, rock and pop idol worship is widely accepted in this country – so much so that the "groupie" phenomenon surrounding rock, pop and even jazz idols is promoted regularly on television and in other media. And if you don't believe that, you need to watch MTV, VH1 and E or any of many reality TV shows! Or just log on to Yahoo News to view the hundreds of stories about exposed celebrity body parts and who claims to have 'hit that.' No one has ever pointed to these as cults. And the media would never do anything to cast itself or its *human products* in a negative light.

Celebrity worship is another example. Our society embraces the idolizing of movie stars, television personalities, sports heroes, etc. Celebrity fan clubs define a celebrity's career. Fans are known not only to hoard pictures and other mementos of the celebrity, but they also send money to the celebrity's charity and other projects that the celebrity deems worthy. And they pay money to attend expos in which they dress up as the celebrities they worship. The portrayal of these fantasies continues on YouTube.

In business and education, we are in the habit of worshipping those overachievers who represent the ultimate that we feel our quality of life has to offer. In our professional pursuits, we are taught, and eventually have to acknowledge, that specializing in a given thing for a long period of time, perhaps a lifetime, is what is necessary to have a successful career. We worship those who have gone before us in this manner.

The wealthiest CEOs, the greatest attorneys, the most

prominent political leaders, the greatest activists, the most popular artists, all have walls decorated with pictures of their most adored and revered champions whom they constantly remember for their excellence. *This is also a form of worship.* No one has ever complained of this practice being cultist. Reality TV shows about the lives of the rich and famous have become very popular. Is this not worship?

The act of taking a true Spiritual Guru or Master, as a means to permanent spiritual transformation, is similar to these forms of accepted worship in our society, *with one profound difference*: Worship of the Grace-bestowing power of God, inherent in a Shaktipat Guru *is not* worship of the body. *It is worship of the inner Self in form and it leads one to the highest realization of the inner Self.* It leads one to the greatest identity one can have; that of being completely Divine, that of being God. In this way, the worshipper is set on the path to the formless Absolute.

In the beginning, your senses need a form with which to accomplish this aim. This is the principle that is the basis for the relationship between the Master and the Devotee. This is how the living Sadguru, and the relationship between that Master in a human form and the Devotee, has become such an important part of retracing one's steps back to God.

There are obstacles to Bhakti that have to be overcome with the Love and guidance of the Guru. In the Yoga Vasishtha, a great sacred text that embodies the recorded instruction that Lord Rama's spiritual Master, *Vasishtha*, imparted to him, Vasishtha tells Rama that there are all kinds of people who come to a living Master. Some have very worldly agendas, while others want what the Master really has to give. He tells Rama that some who come to a Sadguru are very dull and not interested in discipline. Others who come hold the Master in contempt and go on their way. He counsels Rama that this is quite common where a Sadguru is concerned.

The difference that makes the difference is Longing, Bhakti. That is the one aspect of Grace that seals the deal, that carries one to permanent spiritual transformation. A foundation needs to be built in order that this Bhakti be *protected and allowed to flourish.* And you have to remember that God exists in your feeling.

In spiritual life, and especially if you receive genuine Shaktipat initiation and enter into the Shaktipat Kriya process (see Chapters 2 and 4), you will need a *security detail* that you should never go anywhere without. This security detail is comprised of two, armed security guards, standing on either side of you. Their names are **Humility and Reverence**. Cultivate Humility and Reverence first, and Longing will naturally follow.

Most spiritual seekers are not born with a lot of Humility and Reverence. Some don't even know what these are. I have found that the best way to cultivate these is to keep the company of holy beings. In doing so, I began to understand and experience these for myself, through the example set by Liberated sages of our lineage.

Humility is a state of Grace, born of Equality Consciousness and steeped in Awe. To be humble, the complete *recognition* of Grace is required. *The recognition of Grace is the right understanding that nothing here belongs to us.* Everything in this world of forms is ephemeral, transient. We come into this world by ourselves and we leave the same way. The body is on loan to us. And whatever we acquire here, while embodied, we have to leave here. We didn't bring any of it with us and we can't take any of it with us.

Therefore, Humility is the realization of how impermanent, how temporary and fleeting life in this world of objects is. This realization brings the understanding and experience that God alone exists – that the nature of the Shiva-Shakti power stomps out all belief in a *separate* world. When remembered, this awareness of how fleeting life is leaves us in the experience of *Humility and Reverence* for that One who gives us our time here while embodied.

In this way, Humility is also a reminder that we don't own anything that is on this stage on which we have climbed, temporarily. *This is the recognition of Grace and this recognition must be present for the experience of Humility to be imbibed.* Humility is borne of Equality Consciousness. *Equality Consciousness is the constant remembrance that the Self, the Supreme Principle exists equally in all* – that you are neither greater or lesser than anything or anyone else. You are equal. *You respect yourself because you respect the Self and all others as that same One God.*

Even though my attainment was not yet equal to that of my Master's, knowing that we are all equal in God, and that he and I were also equal in God, increased my Faith in and Longing for attaining his state. **Equality Consciousness is your willingness to live in this awareness, and living in this awareness is Humility.**

Having learned this by keeping the company of some of the great beings of our lineage, *Reverence* began to manifest in my Consciousness. As I practiced approaching my Guru and the teachings, instruction and practices he taught me, *with Humility*, my inner experience of the Self grew and grew. Then I began approaching my Sadhana with great Reverence for God, the living Master and the reflection of the Supreme Principle as this world of forms. **This Reverence grew out of my practice and experience of Humility.** *These two inculcated great Faith in me.*

As my eyes were opened wide by the experience of going beyond the mind and beyond the senses, I developed a *burning desire* for the experience of the Bliss I found there, and for the company of my Master's Love and Grace that caused this experience to grow in me. **This burning desire became my steady and deepening Longing for my Master's state**.

This Longing, this Bhakti blazed a trail through my heart, and into the *Abode of the Heart*. This is how I was shown that Bhakti is the Longing to merge in the Self and to dwell there. It is the Longing to know the Truth of one's identity. **Bhakti is the Longing to open and purify one's heart in order to see God in everything and everyone, in order to revere the manifestation of this world from the highest vantage point of the inner Self.** A Bhakta is one who is filled with Bhakti, and this is what Bhakti is, *and nothing else*. The holy beings of our lineage give this definition, and it is the Truth, it is the Truth, it is the Truth.

Keeping the company of this Longing, while also keeping the company of the understandings, the wisdom of the Sadguru and the holy beings of our lineage, while also keeping the company of the daily spiritual practices instructed by the Guru – this will cause you to become mad with *Love without distinctions*, mad with Love for God, mad with Love for the Master and the spiritual practices. **When this Bhakti intensifies at this level, *all that you are not* is burned away by Grace**. Then you will see your own Self everywhere and in everyone, at all times. *Your heart will never close. It will remain wide open.*

This Love without distinctions is the greatest power in the Universe. It is the most powerful weapon and the most useful tool. Bhakti, this Longing I speak of, *in its fullest expression, becomes this Love without distinctions.* After burning away all that you are not in the madness of your Longing, this Bhakti allows you to experience the *fullness of Humanity*, from the highest vantage point of the inner Self. This is the dawning of true freedom.

When you arrive there, you will be able to extend unconditional Love to all, even when the roles you play dictate varying levels of interaction. *You will live better, you will love better, you will work better, your kindness will grow and you will learn to rise above attachment, attraction and aversion.* What a glorious state this is! How full of Grace it is! *I am able to share this with you because this state dawned on me by the Grace of my Shri Gurudev, and by the Grace of my Longing, my Bhakti.* This Longing keeps one fully engaged in the instruction for the practices that deliver the goal!

However, this Longing has to be protected. You have old friends that are just waiting in the wings to destroy your Bhakti. *These old friends are your karmas – tendencies and leanings such as fear, doubt, worry, anxiety, self-loathing, the false notion of individuality, etc.* **Until these are rooted out of your Consciousness, you must guard your Longing**. Here are some important steps to take in doing so:

Keep the most useful company. By company we rise and by company we fall. Therefore, if you want permanent spiritual transformation that comes with Bhakti, you will have to keep good inner and outer company. This instruction is so important that I have devoted a separate chapter to it (see Chapter 26).

Facing yourself and your karmas with Grace and delight. In any true spiritual approach, everything is between you, God and your spiritual companion in the Sadguru. **If you ever hold the understanding that someone or something else is the cause of your suffering, you will fail. If you ever hold the**

understanding that someone or something else is the cause of your happiness, you will also fail. The only way to true happiness, peace and joy is to discard these notions, to discard duality, in the experience of the Shaktipat Kriya process (see Chapter 4) that allows you to perform the inner work to untangle yourself.

Taking the Guru's medicine. Once you have tested the Guru, obey the Guru's instruction and command for your Sadhana. If you don't take the medicine for the prescribed period of time, or if you attempt to alter the proven formula, there will be no cure. If you won't take the medicine, don't blame the doctor.

Taking the understandings of the Master and the sages of our lineage over your own, in order to protect your Longing. The understandings you reach for and hold dictate your feelings and the way in which you vibrate. And the way in which you vibrate dictates your karmas, the people, places and things you continue to attract to you. For this reason, understandings impact Longing, Bhakti. If your Longing for the Self, your Longing for the means to attain the Self, your Longing for the Master's state, if this Bhakti begins to wane, you know you've gone off course. I have devoted the next chapter to this vital part of our approach.

Firm vigilance and resolve in performing the daily spiritual practices instructed by the Sadguru for going beyond your mind and beyond your senses. Longing is inculcated by your inner experiences of the Self, that Shiva-Shakti power that is the Ultimate Reality and cause of everything that you experience through your senses. You can only prove this to yourself by establishing a firm discipline in the practices that are the means for going beyond your mind and beyond your senses. As you do so on a daily basis, you will prove to yourself how beneficial your Longing to be free is.

The journaling of your experiences. During the stages of retracing one's steps back to God, it is common for people to begin to experience fear, doubt, worry, lack of trust, etc. that become obstacles to the profound trust needed to overcome one's false sense of individuality, of being just the body (see Chapter

23). During your Sadhana under the guidance of a Shaktipat Guru, you will experience cycles of contraction when the energy of egoism tells you that you haven't attained anything from your practice and the instruction of your Guru, and that you are wasting your time. (This contraction usually occurs when one moves out of the honeymoon phase and begins to undergo the *tests* inherent in the Shaktipat Kriya process – tests that bring out all of one's karmic resistance to letting go of the false identity that one has been fed by the restless mind and the senses). *This wrong understanding will tear down your Longing.* For this reason, it is essential for you to keep a journal of the experiences you have while engaging the practices for going beyond your mind and beyond your senses.

Major breakthroughs in your experience of Peace, Bliss and the Love of the true Heart should also be recorded in your journal because, *it is during those cycles of doubt, anxiety, fear, frustration and resistance, that you will need to turn to your journal for the evidence that you have actually made progress.* Otherwise, your Bhakti will gradually disappear. As you engage the Shaktipat Kriya process, keeping a journal will also help you remember that your fears, doubts, etc. were already there in your Consciousness *before* you ever met the Guru and decided to take up a spiritual approach – and that they have not been planted by the Kriya Shakti of the Master, *but that they are, in fact, being rooted out by the Shaktipat Kriya process* (see Chapters 4 and 9 regarding the three malas).

Learning to let go and give over to Grace. Permanent spiritual transformation cannot take place without the transmission of God's Grace bestowing power. Part of this transmission of Grace to the devotee includes being taught how to recognize and imbibe God's Grace, in all its forms. This is an art that comes with leadership, training and practice because the doership that you have been engaged in for so many lifetimes that has caused you to sabotage Grace has to be rooted out. This is why I took a Sadguru as my leader. Without the Blessings of my Guru, I would never have been able to protect my Longing. For this reason, I have devoted a separate chapter in this book to Grace.

Obedience of the Master's instruction. You may think yourself to be quite independent. But the fact is you are ruled by the understandings you embrace (see the next chapter) that have caused you to operate under a false identity, the false notions that you are just a person, just an individual, just ordinary or just like your friends, lover, family, etc. You obey your senses now. You obey what your restless mind tells you. You obey your limiting, binding habits. In order to keep those friends whose company you have become attached to, you obey what they tell you. You also obey the brainwashing of the popular culture that you have come to love.

So, you already obey something or someone. Obeying the instruction of the living Sadguru, as a command for addressing and expiating your karmas to realize the ecstasy of the inner Self, is similar to this, with one difference. When you obey the spiritual Master's instruction (not blindly – see Chapter 23), your Longing to be Free, that Bhakti that will purify your heart and open your eyes to the magnificence of your true identity, will be protected and will expand and expand! This is my experience and the experience and utterance of the Sages of steady wisdom of our lineage.

These are some of the ways in which you can cultivate and protect the Devotion that you may not have in the beginning. **Bhakti is everything. This mad love delivers the goal.** *God exists in your feeling*. Therefore, the great beings tell us to protect our Longing.

The pure-hearted person fulfills the supreme purpose of life through the instructions of his spiritual Master, even though they be casually imparted. The worldly-minded person studies and enquires throughout his life, yet remains unenlightened.

Ashtavakra Gita 15:1

Chapter 25
Understandings Dictate Feelings

The only thing required for spiritual growth is detachment from worldly pleasures. If you don't listen to this, you will fail in the end. The thoughtless state, the state of detachment, is the highest state. How can there be desire in the state of detachment? It is not the world the yogi gives up, it is desire for worldly sense pleasure. The true yogi is full and content whether he is a pauper or a rich man. If pleasurable things come your way, experience them, but never go looking. Always be content in yourself wherever you are and whatever your circumstances.

~ Bhagawan Nityananda of Ganeshpuri

It's important for each of us to examine where we get our understandings from. It's important because understandings always dictate our feelings. How we are vibrating, from moment-to-moment, is dictated by the feeling we experience in that moment. Our vibration immediately begins to attract to us the people, places and things that will reinforce that vibration. This causes us to hold other understandings (that will dictate other feelings) that will keep us wedded to whatever state we find ourselves in, by way of the understandings we have been holding, and the subsequent feelings and vibration that manifest out of those understandings.

For this reason, if we want to change how we feel, we need to change our understanding. You can take from this that understandings are vital to whether or not you will experience your true nature from the vantage point of the paradise of the Heart, that indescribable Joy. The understandings you hold either keep you bound to lack, limitation and contraction, or they free you to experience the Joy and Peace of the true Heart – from which you are able to invoke changes in your life that enhance your living, *without* compromising your Shanti (peace) and your true worth – *without compromising your Human Dignity that is the essence of the experience of the Absolute.*

I have covered some crucial understandings in Chapter 4 that relate to what I am continuing to offer in this chapter. In

Chapter 24, there was a discussion of where we tend to get the understandings from that we fashion our lives after. These understandings often come from embracing the popular and widely-accepted notions about who you are, *based on what society, the collective consciousness of the masses, your husband, wife, friends, family members, lovers – based on what they all tell you.* If you believe yourself to be a 'liberal,' you identify with what the liberals tell you. If you are a 'conservative,' you fashion part of your identity after what the conservatives tell you. If you have a favorite celebrity, you accept the ideas and notions that the celebrity has made popular. You may even believe that the roles celebrities play on the internet, in movies, TV and other popular media have an important message for you.

You may believe that you are the body, just a person, just ordinary, an individual who has to make his/her life happen – you accept these things *without even questioning them* because these are the understandings you have been taught by the company you keep and the society and collective consciousness that you choose to embrace.

These understandings cause you to feel very passionate about those things that you have accepted without questioning. As a result, you vibrate in a way that continues to attract the people, places and things to you that reinforce these understandings. **In this way, you have created karmas for yourself that continue to dictate the mental conditioning that controls your life.**

Even when this is the case, many complain that spiritual paths that embrace a living Master are vehicles for brainwashing, yet they are already so thoroughly brainwashed by the understandings given them by society, collective consciousness and the company they keep. They question the instruction of spiritually-perfected beings, yet they never question the understandings they have come to embrace, just because those understandings are popular and have been affirmed by the collective consciousness. For this reason, the great beings say "O man, O woman, please wake up! When will you awake from this dream!?"

The same psychologists who regurgitate the notions of popular culture and society for how to lead one's life, also sell themselves to the very companies who brainwash you into buying their products. For example, if you've ever been inside a major advertising firm (I have) then you know what goes on there. Ad firms are brainwashing machines that, with the help of modern psychology, have become very skilled at manipulating all areas of popular culture and the widely-accepted understandings that societies embrace, in order to walk around in your head to cause you to become attached to products and services that they want you to continue to buy. *And you accept this form of brainwashing.* (This reminds me of a good example of what I've just stated, portrayed in a movie comedy entitled *How To Get Ahead In Advertising* – 1989, starring Richard E. Grant.)

The entertainment industry makes products of those who, in their early careers, just wanted to be artists. In music, for example, in order to make a steady living at it as a career, you need a record deal. If you are not business savvy enough to sell your own records (and enough of them to make a living), and if you're good enough and sexy enough, *and willing to compromise your human dignity* and intention as an artist, you'll get a recording contract. Then you become the product of the record company and you have to do what they say with respect to tunes that you write and record – all based on what they have determined will sell millions of records by appealing to the largest (and often most base) common denominators of the record-buying public (I spent many years with a career in the Performing Arts – now known as the entertainment industry). This is also a form of brainwashing. And many accept this also.

Once, while in a local laundromat, I overheard a confrontation coming from the TV. A well-known and very popular prime time show was on, and I caught the last half of an episode on sexual 'dysfunction' in marriages. A team of sex therapists (all pimping their new books from the NY Times bestseller list) was grilling a couple on their problems. It seems that the husband had an ongoing complaint about the lack of sexual gratification in their 15-year marriage and the celebrity star was there to help (?). The focus of the 'therapy' turned to the wife. From what she was sharing, it was clear that she had just grown tired of simply 'putting out' for her man. She was just tired of sex and appeared to want a break (nothing wrong with that).

Well, the sex therapists didn't ask her why she wasn't

interested in ongoing sex. Instead, they suggested that she had a lot of sexual inhibitions. Then she made the mistake of admitting that her father was a pastor in a local church that she grew up in. Boy, did they jump all over that!, insisting that her father must have raised her in a way that prevented her 'sexual' success.

Then, before the woman could get a word in, she was told that, now that she was married, she should no longer concern herself with purity. The sex therapists (both of them female embodied beings) chimed in with all kinds of suggestions about how she should please her man in the bedroom by embracing understandings that will make her an object, a tool for sexual gratification! And so it goes with the understandings popular culture has embraced. They managed to brainwash the poor lady into believing that something is wrong with her, without even hearing her understanding of the situation. Well, I understand that's television but that also has an impact on the viewing public's understandings. Now, Kedarji is not for or against sex (see Chapter 7). *He's against the compromise of Human Dignity.*

Now, there are societies on the planet where the popular understandings that are embraced, as part of the popular culture or widely-accepted notions of society, *are quite different than in the West or Europe.* For example, in Eastern India, the popular culture and societal norms embrace the understanding of a higher power that allows people to perceive this world as an expression of the Divine. The culture there is imbued with the understanding that life exists to pursue, experience and glorify the Self.

This understanding is reflected in the popular culture of many regions in their society. Instead of growing up on Batman and Lady Gaga, they grow up reading and embracing the understandings offered in the *Bhagavad Gita* and other sacred texts. It is this way in certain parts of Asia, as well. Unfortunately, the collective consciousness in some of these regions is moving toward contraction and a lower vibration, due to the fact that people there are following the example of greed and excess set here in the West. This is also due to brainwashing.

The Truth is, *this entire world is a play of the Shiva-Shakti power.* The great beings tell us that gold fashioned into bracelets, earrings and necklaces is still only gold. The sweet known as Halva is still sesame seeds. In the same way, this one Shiva-Shakti power has become all the forms, from a blade of grass, to an insect to a human being. Furthermore, this same power becomes our ability to perceive and name objects. This is also what leads to the *imaginary* sense of duality and diversity.

This is why the sages of steady wisdom also tell us that, just as gold fashioned into various objects with different names remains gold, in the same way the Shiva-Shakti power, that Supreme Principle, while fashioning itself into the multitudinous forms of this world-appearance is still just that One Shiva-Shakti power. That inner Self pervades all people, places and things. That same power is the witness to your mind. This power contracts and expands of its own free will, bringing countless universes into being, sustaining those universes and then withdrawing them back into the cosmic, formless Absolute – all without any materials with which to do so, and without any dependence on anything or anyone. This power is supremely independent, and *That* is your true nature.

It is this Consciousness that speaks, walks, talks, sleeps, etc. The great sages tell us that the notion of individuality is false, imaginary, contrived and that the body is just a nest, a vehicle in which the Self comes and goes here. This Truth can be experienced for one's self by going beyond the mind and beyond the senses. But to accomplish doing so, you will have to set aside the false notion that you are an object, the false notion that you are just the body, the senses and the mind.

The pursuit of objects (people, places and things) is the expansion of the false notion that you are just a person, just an individual, just ordinary or delightfully weird. Objectification is the spiritual disease of our modern age. I have known some very unfortunate beings who, upon waking, will not meditate or perform any spiritual practice. Instead, they rush for their morning coffee, and then they sit at their mobile devices or their computers, trolling their Facebook pages for new comments or posts that they then leave a comment about, in order to extract a comment in return. They perform the same ritual throughout their day, and before going to bed. Then they sleep worrying if they will still have any friends who have 'liked' their posts when they check their account the following morning. Their children are raised in the same way, with stout rituals of Instagram, Youtube, Facebook and all the rest!

As I have stated previously, this cultivated and limiting desire for constant, outside stimulation and instant gratification has become a trademark of many societies. This kind of spiritual crisis is what adds to the identity crisis that prevents one from experiencing the Bliss of the inner Self. *In this way, even your notion of being independent, or the notion of what it is to be independent, is derived from the collective consciousness and popular media of the society that you embrace.*

The objectification inherent in the pursuit of worldliness is due to understandings. As stated in the previous chapter, there are Superimpositions and then there are superimpositions. What you project into Consciousness, beginning with the understandings you hold, determine how you feel about a particular person, place or thing.

For example, you experience a song or musical tune as being 'happy' or 'sad,' usually based on the *understanding* you hold about the tune and/or the lyrics, *and not the music or lyrics itself.* Furthermore, you may have accepted that understanding by way of other understandings that you are in the karmic habit of reaching for, or by way of the understandings given you by others or through popular culture or peer pressure, or based on who or what you attract, *by way of how you are vibrating.* Regardless of the understanding, your feeling about a person, place or thing is always due to the understandings you hold.

Going back to the music example, music becomes popular and accepted with respect to its 'emotional' content, due to the repetitiveness with which the music is heard. Stephen Sondheim (a partner of the great Leonard Bernstein), one of the greatest composers of musicals on the planet, once told me that a composer's music becomes popular due to air time, and not necessarily because the music is even noteworthy. Here he was referring to the necessity of getting one's record played on the radio and in other popular media where people will become attached to a composition by the mere fact that they hear it a lot, or all the time. The mind loves the places it frequents the most!

Everything is a superimposition, a projection in Consciousness. The principle of *Superimposition* is something we study at length in our approach. The popular culture and the ideals of any society are based on the widely-accepted understandings of that society, based on the ideas imparted by the collective consciousness of the masses, that also breed many other understandings. These popular understandings are popular, only because people embrace them. Coupled with the understandings you come to through your life experience, acquired through the lens of the false sense of individuality (your 'personal truth'), you have created a world of inner impressions that you carry with you from birth to death and birth again.

When your understanding of a person, place or thing changes, your feeling about that person immediately changes, and you vibrate in a different way, as a result. For example, you fall in love with a person and believe that the person is your soulmate, and that everything you believe you lack that person is going to complete for you or fulfill. Then, one day, that person does or says something that crosses you in a way that you feel is irreconcilable. So, you break up. The breakup was caused by the fact that your *understanding* of that person and your *understanding* of the relationship with that person changed. Therefore, your feeling changed. Someone you once loved and proclaimed as your soulmate is now dead to you – all due to the change in the understanding you chose to embrace.

Let me give some other examples that I believe you will be able to easily relate to:

Location. Maybe you've been living in a particular place for a long time or you live in a city or town that you grew up in. And maybe life wasn't so good for you as you were growing up in this location. Perhaps mistakes you made began to haunt you, or you had a series of bad relationships that caused your reputation to become tainted. Or maybe you've been unable to launch the career you want or find the husband or wife you're seeking in this location. One day, you decide you're going to move to a place you think will be better, or you just long for a change in surroundings, believing that this is the best way to leave your past behind you. So, you move to a different city or town and soon forget about your previous location. Your feeling about both the old and the new location is due to the understandings you hold about both.

Identity. Maybe you have been addicted to drugs or alcohol. One day you decide to get professional help for your addiction. Part of that professional help includes some kind of therapy, or maybe a 12-step program. As you are weaned off of your addiction and regain awareness of what it's like to make choices that are not driven by your addiction, you start to realize that you are not the person you thought you were (most addicts have this experience in rehab). This realization came about due to the change in your understanding about you and your relationship to other people, places and things.

Labels for Sexual Preference. Perhaps you are 'gay' or 'straight.' One day, you decide that you are no longer 'heterosexual' and you decide to become 'gay' or vice versa. This decision was due to a change in your understanding. Understanding yourself to be an object of sexual desire, an object of attraction for others or just the body (that's what this kind of objectification is about), you label yourself after the understanding of gender. Changing your sexual preference then, is a matter of a change in your understanding – from one label as an object of attraction as the body to another (attachment to attraction is always karmic, as is any underlying 'biology.')

In each of the above examples, you can easily understand how a change in feeling, and the subsequent change in behavior is due to a change in the understandings that are embraced. *For this reason, the great beings tell us that understandings always dictate feelings.* **If you want to change your feeling, you have to change the understandings you reach for and embrace. For this reason, if permanent spiritual transformation is the goal, the understandings one holds are vital.**

In our approach, there are understandings that allow you to go beyond the mind and beyond the senses to what is real, that paradise of the Heart where you embrace and acquire purer understandings of what actually is and what takes place, based on the power of what actually is there, when all thoughts subside.

We are yoga scientists here. We treat understandings like a good scientist uses an hypothesis. The dictionary definition of 'hypothesis' is (surprisingly) in perfect alignment with our Shakta approach and the understandings of the Saints of our lineage. Here it is:

Hypothesis...

1. a proposition, or set of propositions, set forth as an explanation for the occurrence of some specified group of phenomena, either asserted merely as a provisional conjecture to guide investigation (working hypothesis) or accepted as highly probable in the light of established facts.
2. a proposition assumed as a premise in an argument.
3. the antecedent of a conditional proposition.

The arc of our approach to understandings is based on a group of hypotheses which we refer to as better, more useful understandings – imparted to us by those Sages of steady wisdom who have attained the inner Self that we are seeking to attain, in the fullness of our Humanity. In this way, their understandings are the *Wisdom* that leads us. The Arc of this movement of the Divine Consciousness energy is:

- Understandings always dictate your feelings.
- How you are vibrating from moment-to-moment is dictated by the feeling you experience in that moment.
- What you are putting out (projecting or superimposing into Consciousness) immediately begins to attract to you the people, places and things that will reinforce that vibration and cause you to hold other understandings (that will dictate other feelings) that will keep you wedded to whatever state you find yourself in -- by way of the understandings you have been holding, and the subsequent feelings and vibration that manifest out of those understandings.

So, in understanding what it means to face ourselves to expiate and destroy the karmas preventing us from rising to the experience of our own Bliss, we begin with the following, primary understanding or hypotheses that we hold in order to have a frame for proving or disproving it in the laboratory of our own existence. That laboratory is beyond the mind and beyond the senses where the witness to the mind dwells. This is where our witnessing awareness is magnified and becomes the microscope under which we observe what is actually taking place in our Consciousness, along with the root cause. The Truth about everything, about everyone and every situation and circumstance exists in that 'laboratory,' in that state of the Observer.

The first of our three Primary Pillars of Understanding (hypotheses) is:

You are the Self. All other beings in your life are that One Self also. Others are your reflections in Consciousness. Therefore, God alone exits here, everywhere.

As with any other understandings, this first primary point of Wisdom gives rise to other, very useful understandings that allow us to deepen our experience of *That* which is beyond the mind and beyond the senses – in a way that we are able to prove the hypotheses to ourselves. In this way, we become the voice of experience, rather than the idol chatter of mere opinion and belief. And you can't argue with direct experience of the inner Self. Some other useful understandings are:

♡ The truth is objects do not have any agency without the power that has caused them to manifest in your Consciousness. That power alone is real and all people, places and things appear to be real to you, due to that power. When you attribute everything to that Shiva-Shakti power, you are able to reach for and hold the highest, the purest of understandings that will allow you to experience who you really are, by way of a purer feeling and vibration.

♡ The ego does not exist. It is only the *perception* of ego that exists. It is important for devotees, for spiritual seekers to understand this. *Otherwise, your seeking will never come to an end.*

It is the Shiva-Shakti power, the inner Self that contracts to conform to your false notion of individuality, the notion that you are just the body, just a person with a separate personality, just ordinary or delightfully weird. As long as you embrace this notion, you will experience differences and distinctions in duality that will keep you bound to lack and limitation, and entangle you in the false notion that you are the doer and that outcomes belong to you. This contraction of the Shiva-Shakti power is what is referred to as the 'ego,' or 'ego sense,' or 'energy of egoism.' In fact, it is the Shiva-Shakti power of the Absolute that becomes these false notions. So, how can there be a separate thing called 'ego.'

Therefore, it is really important to understand that egoism is not necessarily connected to any particular type of behavior or manner of speech that you may find 'pleasant' or 'unpleasant,' for these notions exist in the imaginary realm of duality only. In truth, the ego does not exist.

When you direct the Shiva-Shakti power in such a way that you hide your true nature from yourself by coming to believe that you are just a person, just a body, just the mind and the senses – and when you self-appropriate all the activity in your life to this false notion, what manifests due to this act of self-appropriating the activity in your life to this false sense of individuality, again, is what we call the 'ego.'

This is how karmas are created and become binding. From this you can understand that activity, interaction, the enjoyment of life – these *are not* the culprits. *The culprit is your wrong understanding of who or what is actually experiencing.*

♡   Understanding this, if you attribute your false notion of individuality (the false notion that you are just the body, the senses and the mind) to the movement in your Consciousness of the One God, the Self, *from your witnessing awareness*, you will have another experience that will take you higher. See for yourself what is there when you consciously discard the false notion of being just a person, when you let go of that false notion and give over to the inner Self in meditation, chanting, japa and selfless service.

♡   Therefore, reach for the highest understandings, the Wisdom imparted by the holy beings, the spiritually-perfected Love beings. These understandings, when reached for and embraced, will deliver you to the experience of the witness to your mind – that sacred place beyond your mind and senses. As you spend more and more time in meditation on the inner Self, these understandings, after helping to deliver you there, will begin to dissolve, leaving you in the experience of your true nature, your true identity, the Self.

In our approach, we practice *Witness Consciousness* so that we can observe the understandings we reach for, how they impact our feeling and vibration, and what changed in our understanding and why. As you work back and forth in this Shaktipat Kriya process with the leadership of the living Master, you will begin to experience for yourself how imperative your understandings are to your permanent spiritual progress.

Retracing our steps back to God in this way, in the way that we are able to embrace the fullness of Humanity from the highest vantage point of the inner Self, leads us to a life that is so much better, so full of the nectar, the ecstasy and purest delight that life has to offer us.

This state cannot be had without the loving leadership and firm hand of the Sadguru. You can't learn this by teaching others what you have not yet imbibed. That would be leading others astray with your own ignorance. Can you learn to be a heart surgeon by simply operating on people and teaching others, when you have not been trained and mentored by an expert heart surgeon? The passage to the inner Self is even more delicate than that. For this reason, *the Sages of steady wisdom tell us that only the one who obeys can command.* One who has never followed and served another living Master cannot become a true spiritual leader.

In Sadhana, until you have fully realized the Self, there is where you think you are at, and then there is where you are really at. You can't know the difference without being tested (see Chapter 4). How do you know that you have learned math well? You only know because the math teacher tests you and grades you. How do you know that you have become a good enough athlete to compete in events like the Olympics? You only know because you have surrendered to a coach who tests you severely so that you know what you have to do to improve, in preparation for the Olympics, in preparation for excellence. In the same way, you only know of your spiritual attainment (and what you need to change to improve), and whether or not it is permanent, by way of the tests given by the Master. So, just as in other areas of life where you want to attain something really worth-while, understand how great it is to be tested by the one who has attained what you seek!

>   1. *Mano-buddhya hankara-chittani naham*
>   *Na cha srotra-jihve na ca ghrana-netre*
>   *Na cha vyoma bhumirna tejo na vayu-*
>   *Chidananda-rupah shivo ham shivo ham*

I am neither the conscious nor unconscious mind,
Neither intelligence nor ego; Neither the ears
nor the tongue nor the senses of smell and sight;
Neither ether nor air nor fire nor water nor earth;
I am Consciousness and Bliss. I am Shiva! I am Shiva!

>   2. *Na cha prana-sajjno na vai pancha-vayur-*
>   *Na va sapta-dhaturna va pancha-kosha*
>   *Na vak-pani-padam na chopasthapayu*
>   *Chidananda-rupah shivo ham shivo ham*

I am neither the prana nor the five vital airs,
Neither the seven body components nor the five
sheaths; Neither speech nor hands nor feet nor
anus nor sex organ;
I am Consciousness and Bliss. I am Shiva! I am Shiva!

>   3. *Na me dvesharagau na me lobha-mohau*
>   *Mado naiva me naiva matsarya-bhavah*
>   *Na dharmo na chartho na kamo na mokshas-*
>   *Chidananda-rupah shivo ham shivo ham*

Neither aversion nor attachment, neither
avarice nor delusion, Neither arrogance
nor the feeling of jealousy, at all, Neither
righteousness nor wealth nor pleasure are mine;
I am Consciousness and Bliss. I am Shiva! I am Shiva!

4. *Na punyam na papam na saukhyam na dukham*
   Na mantro na tirtham na veda nayagnah
   Aham bhojanam naiva bhojyam na bhokta
   Chidananda-rupah shivo ham shivo ham

I am neither virtue nor vice, neither pleasure
nor pain, Neither mantra nor sacred place,
neither Vedas nor sacrifices; I am neither the
food nor the eater nor the act of eating;
I am Consciousness and Bliss. I am Shiva! I am Shiva!

5. *Na mrtyur-na shanka na me jati-bhedah*
   Pita naiva me naiva mata cha janma
   Na bandhur-na mitram guru-naiva shisyas-
   Chidananda-rupah shivo ham shivo ham

Neither death nor doubt nor caste distinction,
Neither father nor mother nor even birth are
mine, at all; I am neither brother nor friend,
neither guru nor disciple, indeed;
I am Consciousness and Bliss. I am Shiva! I am Shiva!

6. *Aham nirvikalpo nirakara-rupi*
   Vibhutvaccha sarvatra sarvendriyanam,
   Na chasangatam naiva muktir-na meyas-
   Chidananda-rupah shivo ham shivo ham

   Shivo ham Shivo ham

I am without thought, without form;
I am all-pervasive, I am everywhere, yet
I am beyond all senses; I am neither
detachment nor salvation nor anything
that could be measured;
I am Consciousness and Bliss. I am Shiva! I am Shiva!

Nirvanashatkam of Shri Adi Shankara

Chapter 26
The Importance of Keeping Good Company

"What is served for others, should not be eaten by us. We must place a separate plate for us and eat our food."

~ Bhagawan Nityananda of Ganeshpuri
Chidakasha Gita

In our approach, we *do not* criticize or condemn any other spiritual approach, path or religion. Our approach is backed by a time-honored offering of a lineage of Saints that is many centuries old. It is an approach that is *proved* by the spiritual attainment of many Self-realized beings. For these reasons, without negating any other, we offer this approach, along with its wisdom and practices, with great intention and authority.

The sages of steady wisdom tell us that it takes *only one drop* of sour curd to spoil an entire vat of milk. Every true spiritual approach speaks of the importance of keeping good company, if one wants to attain permanent spiritual transformation. My Master spoke about this regularly. Your outlook on life, your life experience and your destiny are all determined by the company you keep. Therefore, the importance of good company can never be underestimated. When I speak of the company you keep, I am talking about two kinds of company; the company you keep on the outside and the company you keep inside. **The great beings tell us that by company we rise and by company we fall. And this is so true.**

KEEP THE MOST USEFUL INNER COMPANY

Throughout this book I have talked about thoughts and their relationship to action. I have also spoken about the nature of the mind, vikalpas (thought constructs and notions), the ego, the intellect and the workings of Karma. So, by now you have an idea of how important it is to discipline your mind and control your thoughts, as well as, how important it is to keep your mind thought-free whenever possible.

The company you keep inside are the thoughts, notions and

fancies, including the limiting desires and cravings you choose to entertain or find yourself entertaining without complete awareness. Those thoughts and notions that you entertain most frequently constitute your inner company. As stated in previous chapters, your inner company will determine the understandings you reach for. Those understandings will dictate how you feel and the subsequent vibration you put out. How you vibrate creates the circumstances and situations you find yourself in, as well as, the people you attract into your life. This sets the stage for more of your Karmas to be created. And then you keep cycling around.

This is why every Saint, every Sadguru implores us to think only the highest of ourselves and others. This is why the great ones repeat over and over again, "You are Divine. You are great. God dwells within you as you. You are Shiva-Shakti. Your essence is pure and untainted."

This is why the living Master constantly challenges the devotee to merge his/her limited identity into the Self *by the practice of going beyond the mind and beyond the senses.* This is the act of keeping the most useful inner company. *The mind loves the places it frequents the most. You get what you meditate on. You become what you obey.* For this reason, if you want lasting spiritual transformation, it is essential that you embrace the practice that will allow you to calm your restless mind and experience that ocean of Peace and Joy that is the paradise of the Heart.

The ego is like a black bug on a black rock
on a moonless night. How will you ever
recognize it to eradicate it, without the Grace
of a Sadguru?

~ The Poet-Saint Kabir

You can keep the inner company of the *Mantra* instructed by the living Master. You can keep the company of *pure* thoughts. You can keep the company of the form of your Master inside. You can meditate and chant every day.

Keeping the most useful inner company is cultivated through this kind of daily spiritual practice, and through Selfless Service and Devotion to God and the living Master. This is how you are able to embody your true identity, to experience your true nature *in such a way that you can protect yourself from the limitation of the ego that is always ready to pounce on your Bliss.*

As I just mentioned above and previously, there is an incredibly useful and powerful practice that, during my Sadhana, I found to be invaluable. It is known, in our approach, as *Guru Meditation* or *Guru Bhavana*. For years, I began each meditation by meditating on the form of my Master. I started by gazing at a picture of him to begin each meditation, while repeating the mantra he gave me.

Then I was able to remember and recall his form into my Consciousness at will. This caused my witnessing awareness to become so strong that, over time, I was able to observe how the energy of egoism, the contraction into the false notion of individuality began to form, *and I was able to arrest this in the moment, to stop that limitation from manifesting in my Consciousness.* This is the power of Meditation on the form of the Sadguru. One is able to 'steal,' as it were, the Guru's Kriya Shakti.

KEEP THE MOST USEFUL OUTER COMPANY

The company you keep outside is equally important. **For some, this is, perhaps, the greatest challenge to engaging in retracing one's steps back to God.** What I say now is directed to those who sincerely want to know God and who intend on performing the instruction/practices that result in liberating themselves from the bondage of ignorance of the inner Self.

When I first took a Guru and started performing spiritual practice as instructed, I was very vulnerable to what others thought about what I was doing. Having just embarked on the spiritual path in earnest, I was a "young lion" at best and, therefore, very susceptible to people's comments and opinions about my spiritual practice and my chosen approach.

I was also living with my girlfriend at the time and I was particularly concerned with what she had to say about it. What started to happen is that, **based on the comments and criticism of those who had *no* personal experience (nor desire) of the path I was on, I started to question the true transformation I knew was occurring in me.** *I started to doubt my decision to follow a living Master, and I started to question experiences that I knew were true* (fortunate for me, I kept a journal of those experiences).

I later recognized this vulnerability, this concern for what others thought, as a weakness on my part that I had to face and address in my own best interest. After all, I chose a spiritual approach because I wanted to know the Truth, because I wanted to experience God and, through that experience, become a happier, stronger and better person. I thought to myself, "Certainly those who really love me for who I am will have no objection with this reasoning."

Well, this is when I found out who my real friends were and who really loved me and accepted me without selfish motive. **This was an eye-opening experience**. I found out that my girlfriend really didn't love me for who I was. I found out that her motives were entirely selfish and that she really had no interest in who I was becoming. **The minute she realized that her complaints about my spiritual seeking were not going to sway me away from my Guru, she left me.**

Although my false identity as just a person suffered at first, I eventually realized that this was the best thing that could have happened, as it opened the door for those people who were right for me and the direction I was headed in to step into my life.

Several of my friends showed their 'real colors' when they found out I had taken a Sadguru. Instead of embracing me and welcoming the person I was becoming, they openly (and some secretly) criticized me. I lost them as friends. *This was also the best thing that could have happened to me.* Some of my friends continued to embrace me and we remained friends.

Of course, my family members, especially my parents, became concerned *in the beginning*. **But once they saw useful transformation occurring in me, and once I made them understand that my pursuit of the Self was not a sign that I was going to stop loving them or seeing them, they relaxed and embraced my decision.** Only one family member continued to have concerns. But he was a self-proclaimed agnostic, so nothing I could have done or said would have made a difference. Our relationship changed and found its own level in that context.

Now, some of the people who I have had intimate relationships with in the past, although being quick to recognize my transformation, have refused to accept my transition to the role I am now engaged in with this offering. Some of these people are those who can't stand the fact that the nature of our relationship changed when I lost the craving for partying and proliferating, and turned my full attention to God. Others are those who will no longer embrace me, now that I no longer have the desire to succeed in business as a multi-millionaire. This is unfortunate, for them. As I said earlier, one thing is certain; I had quickly learned who my real friends are!

The truth is, even before taking a Master and embracing a spiritual path, there were points in my life when, as I changed as a person, people fell away and others entered my life. I believe this is true for most people, regardless of whether there is a spiritual transformation or not. We do change, some of us for the better. As we change as people, there are and will always be those who resist that change in us and, therefore, don't want to continue a relationship with us. This is a part of every life.

Unfortunately, spiritual matters are seen by many as being entirely different than the rest of life and, therefore, less tolerable in the context of how they affect relationships. **This is why, as a practicing yogi, you have to keep the most useful company.** This is what I had to do. *I had to seek out better company for me.*

You can also understand it in the following way: A parent regulates who his/her child spends time with, counseling the child about the child's friends and who and what else the child has contact with. In this way, a parent ensures that the child doesn't fall into the company that will cause the child to develop bad habits, etc. This is done until the parent feels that the child has sufficiently learned the parent's teachings and wishes, as the child grows up and has to face life. Keeping good company to support spiritual life and growth is like this. While spiritually young, before becoming established in the inner Self, it is extremely important to accept and embrace the living Master's instruction in this regard.

Now, there is a word that I have been using a lot in this discussion, CHANGE. If you want to know the Truth, if you want to embrace your Natural, Free State of Being and become who you have forgotten you are, if you want to be *eternally happy*, experiencing your own Joy, Bliss and Freedom on a *consistent and even constant* basis, *you will have to learn to embrace change.* As your ignorance falls away, over a period of time, you will become a different person. **Change is inevitable for the true seeker.** And you *should not* keep the inner company that says you are a proverbial seeker. *Seeking should come to an end in finding what you seek.* This is the purpose of a relationship with a Sadguru.

Some of those people you are in relationships with now, *especially those close to you who are not themselves on a similar course of change and growth*, will resist the changes they see in you. This, in many cases, may necessitate a shift in how you relate to each other, or a severing of ties all together. *You should not fear this.*

If you keep the company of those who are also growing spiritually and involved in spiritual practice, if you keep the company of those who are also devoted to God and want to know the Truth, you will have no problem with these changes.

In India, it is common for people who are traveling long distances by train, bus or on foot, to carry machetes with them for cutting down the wonderful variety of tropical fruits that are often growing along the roadside. One day, a man stopped by a very tall mango tree. His trip was long and he was very hungry. So, he began climbing the mango tree to get to the mangos at the top of the tree. He was unaware that there was someone sitting across the road from the mango tree, watching him as he climbed.

The man climbed all the way up to the top of the tree, cut away a couple of mangos, and then began his descent down the tree. Just as he reached the bottom of the tree, the man watching him from across the road began to yell, "Be careful! Be careful! Watch where you put your feet!" When the man landed back on the ground, he asked that person, "Why did you wait until I climbed all the way down the tree to caution me!? It's a huge tree. Why did you not yell up to me when I was near the top of the tree?" The man responded *that it is when people think that they are almost to the possession of their goal that they often take their skill and understanding for granted.* And this is when they need to be most aware. When this is the case, you can understand why the holy beings caution us on the company we keep.

The principle of keeping good outer company *is not* **taught to us in order to put others down. It** *is not* **given by the saints for us to engage in thoughts of "I am higher, he is lower."** Here we recognize all beings as the Self and know to separate the person from the deed. We also understand that all the energies of interaction in life belong to that one Shiva-Shakti power. *We also know that people have free will in how they direct that power, and some people direct it in a way that is self-destructive, counter-productive, contracting, and in way that negates the inner Self.* For this reason, Shri Ramkrishna, a great sage in our Shiva lineage, has said, "God exists in everyone equally, but you don't hug a wild, untamed tiger." I think you get his point.

For those earnestly seeking to experience the Truth, for those who want to know the inner Self, *good company is everything.* Here are some guidelines that I suggest you follow:

- Keep the company of holy beings whenever possible. Keeping the company of a Sadguru is the same as keeping the company of God. All the holy beings of our Shiva lineage say this.

- Keep the company of those who serve your chosen Master and participate in the same approach and spiritual community of your Master. This is very important. If you can't do this, at the very least, keep the company of those on a similar path where people are moving in the same direction that you are going spiritually, with the same desire for permanent spiritual transformation.

- After testing and choosing your spiritual leader in the living Master, avoid the company of those who criticize or condemn the Master you have chosen. Exposure to such people will sway even the strongest off their chosen path.

- Make absolutely sure that loved-ones, family and close friends understand that your choosing a Master and a spiritual approach *does not* mean you no longer love them and no longer want to spend time with them. Have them understand that, although time commitments may change when you see each other, that your commitment to your own spiritual growth will not affect the fact that you will spend time with each other and share your love. This is *very important* to convey. Loved-ones and family members usually react in opposition because they don't understand or have an experience of your chosen spiritual approach or Guru, or they disagree with the approach, or they fear losing your love.

- Avoid those whose behavior is not in alignment with the new behavior you are attempting to foster within yourself through spiritual practice, *especially* in the early stages of your Sadhana. As an example: Can someone who wants to stop drinking ever break the habit by keeping the company of those who drink? You get my point. Exercise this caution out of your growing spiritual awareness, *not out of fear and judgment.*

- If you are going to seek feedback about your chosen path and spiritual companion from those who have no prior direct experience of your chosen path and Guru, I strongly suggest you put those opinions in their proper perspective *by considering the source.* Someone who has never experienced your chosen path and Guru, and who does not have more than a cursory exposure to them, probably *does not* have good, solid feedback to offer you.

- Take the feedback (regarding your spiritual practice and approach) of others who are important to you into consideration, *but also trust your own experience and discernment.* Use your own discernment to decide what feedback may be useful or not, based on your growing inner experience of the Self.

- The Self-realized beings tell us that we have been going in the wrong direction for a very long time. Because this is the case, they say that we have to go (away) for a while, so that we can return. "**Go so that you can return**." They mean that we have to *remove the distractions* to our practice of the instruction received from the Master (including our daily spiritual practice and the unfolding of our spiritual lives) *for a period of time, in order to create boundaries of solitude around us,* **long enough to be able to change our direction permanently** – long enough to turn the runaway train around, so that we get on the right track, so that we transform our ordinary perception into that of the Divine. Then we can *return* with a new vision, a Divine vision of a Heart full of Love and Light. *In such an elevated state, our spiritual awareness becomes so strong that we are no longer swayed by the vibrations of others.*

These are the important guidelines to keeping the most useful outer company. **One other strong suggestion**: In the early stages of your Sadhana, it is usually best to keep your inner spiritual experiences (lights, visions, sounds, etc.) to yourself to allow those experiences and your contemplation of them to grow.

You will find that, with respect to spiritual practice under the instruction of a Shaktipat Guru, everyone has something to say about it. Naysayers are very good at instilling doubt in the weak. These naysayers may even be students of the same Guru. As you perform your practice, and as Devotion for God and your chosen Guru increases in you, you will feel more confident and more comfortable sharing your inner experiences with others.

Also, as you practice "in secret" so to speak, your inner experiences will take on new and profound meaning for you. For many years, I shared my inner experiences with no one, except my Guru or when I was in the company of other devotees and asked to do so. Later I started sharing some of my experiences with certain family members and my wife of that time. Still, many experiences I kept to myself.

It is not possible to progress on the spiritual path without keeping good company inside and out. For those serious about removing the ignorance that causes bondage, the ignorance that veils the Self, good company is essential.

Chapter 27
Grace Is All There Is

Grace begins with a grateful heart. The cultivated practice of giving thanks to God for the living Sadguru, for the relationships that support you in facing all your circumstances, and for the privilege of praise and worship – this practice is the beginning of becoming fit for imbibing Grace. Therefore, in our approach, we have a saying that has become a daily offering for many: *Thank you Lord for another day to glorify you.*

God, Shiva-Shakti, your own inner essence, is pleased when you merge your individual identification with your body, mind and senses, into God. When you allow your consciousness to rest in God permanently, in every thought and action, by giving God the glory, by attributing everything to the Self, by seeing God in everything and everyone everywhere, by remaining absorbed in the constant state of Blissful rapture that is the inner Self, *Grace comes looking for you and fills your life.* **In this way, you please God. And pleasing God attracts even more Grace into your life.**

Attaining this state frees you from all bondage, all worry, all fear, all entanglements. It frees you from ignorance forever, so that you can experience Perfect Peace, Perfect Happiness, Perfect Joy, Perfect Abundance, Perfect Gratitude, Perfect Love, Perfect Giving and Perfect Receiving. What's there not to love about this state?! So, why do it? You tell me! This is the part where everyone says, "Great! Wonderful! I'm there. I can do it!"

But there is another part that some people get very hardheaded about. How does one acquire this state? *This state is not attained without the Grace and leadership of a Sadguru.* Every Saint, every spiritually-perfected Love being in our lineage says so. This is the truth.

Make no mistake about it. If you are seeking the inner Self, the goal is *permanent spiritual transformation* that is had by the Grace of a spiritual leader who lives in an uninterrupted state of Grace. ***Even without being Self-realized*, you can have and continue to deepen your experiences of the Self, that can equal the state of the Self-realized beings.** When you follow the instruction for becoming established in these experiences, the Master is pleased and God is pleased. So, the first step is to please your Guru in this way, by following the instruction and obeying the Shaktipat Kriya Process for facing yourself. This is the way you attract the Grace necessary to experience and realize your true nature.

Grace is all there is. My Master used to say that it is always raining Grace. It's just that people put their umbrellas up and keep Grace out. People do sabotage Grace. When it is the Supreme Being who sees through your eyes, hears through your hears, smells through your nose, feels through your limbs, when this is the case, it is Grace that rules your life. *There is nothing but Grace.* **If you don't experience it in this way, the reason you don't experience it as such is that you have not yet aligned your will with God's Will. That is the only obstacle.**

This Grace also takes the form of pure, Supreme Love; God's Love, the *Love without distinctions* that is experienced in the company of Saints. This Love also takes the form of the Grace-bestowing power of God that is transmitted by the Shaktipat Guru through full Kundalini Awakening, and the Master's Kriya Shakti that engages you in Sadhana. For this reason, Bhagawan Nityananda refers to our approach as Gurukripa Yoga, the Yoga of Guru's Grace. Lord Shiva refers to it as the *easy* means. Lord Krishna refers to it as the *only* means. **And, above all else, this Grace is God's Love, the Love of the true Heart.**

Although one can begin to cultivate Bhakti by embracing God's Grace when one directs one's Longing to the formless Absolute, the sages of steady wisdom of our lineage refer to this as an *inferior* means that will only lead to glimpses of the opening of the highest spiritual center. This is why the great beings tell us to direct our *Bhakti*, our Love and Longing *to the form* of our chosen Sadguru. This is the easiest and quickest means of attracting and imbibing the Grace-bestowing power of God. This is due to the ultimate power of *Will* that requires a form to properly direct – *and your Longing* that causes the Master to direct his *Will* to your receipt of more and more Grace.

Muralee bajat akhand sadaaye

The flute of the infinite is played without ceasing,
And its sound is love:
When love renounces all limits, it reaches Truth.

How widely the fragrance spreads! It has no end,
nothing stands in its way.
The form of this melody is bright like a million suns:
Incomparably sounds the vina, the vina of the notes
of Truth.

~ The poet saint Kabir
from Songs of Kabir

As we imbibe more and more of this Grace, we come to understand and experience *living in a state of Grace*. This state of Grace is all-encompassing Love. This Love is without any distinctions, completely unconditional. It is a state of indescribable Joy! **Those who are in the habit of making distinctions in love have tainted themselves in such a way that they find the true Love of the Heart suspicious**. *Ignore these suspicions*. Rise above praise and blame by the hand of this Love. Once you begin to experience the Love that living in a state of Grace delivers, don't engage in politics. Don't ever close your heart again lest you sabotage this Grace.

A great being has said that God is bought with Love alone. If you want sublime intoxication that is so much greater than the intoxication of drugs, alcohol and sex, **if you want inner rapture, *first become your own beloved.*** Through Love this entire Universe of all the worlds comes into being. Through Love the sun shines, the moon glows, nature sparkles, the seasons change and the clouds shed rain. This is the power of Grace. Therefore, the great beings tell us; *Make this Love without distinctions your life*. **Make Love your worshipful deity and become a Love addict. Love all as your very own Self. Conquer yourself with this Love that is Grace.**

In the Yoga Vasishtha, there is a wonderful story that Vasishtha imparts to his disciple, Rama. There was a great forest that was huge. In it were millions of square miles, like the space within an atom. In this forest, there was just one person who had a thousand arms and limbs. He was forever restless. With a mace in one hand, he beat himself and then ran away from this beating in a panic. Then he fell into a blind well. When he climbed out of the well, again he beat himself with the mace and ran away in a panic, this time into a forest. Then he came out of the forest, beat himself again and went into a banana grove.

Although there was no other being present to fear, he wept and cried aloud in fear. He kept running as before, beating himself all the way. Vasishtha, with the power of his Grace, restrained the man for a moment. He asked him, "Who are you?" But the man was completely distressed and called Vasishtha his enemy. The man wept aloud and laughed aloud. Then he began tearing his body apart, limb by limb.

Immediately after this, another person appeared there, running like the first, beating herself, weeping and wailing. When Vasishtha restrained her, she began to abuse him and ran away, intent on her own way of life. In similar fashion, Vasishtha says that he came across several persons like this. Some listened to his words and, abandoning their previous way of life, realized the Self. Others ignored the great sage and even held him in contempt. Still others refused to come out of the blind well and the dense forest.

The world itself is that forest. Vasishtha tells Rama that this world-appearance is like a great void that can only be properly understood by *frequenting the inner Self*. He says that this is inquiry into the Supreme "I" Consciousness. This wisdom is accepted by some and rejected by others, who then continue to suffer. Those who accept this wisdom and embrace it, realize the Truth.

Vasishtha then tells Rama that, the person with thousands of arms is the mind with countless ideas, thoughts and manifestations. The mind punishes itself by its own latent, karmic tendencies and, restlessly, wanders the world. The blind well in the story is hell, and the banana grove, heaven. The dense forest of thorny bush is the life of a worldly person, with numerous thorns of *attachment* to wife, husband, lover, children, wealth, etc. that entangle a person all the time. The mind wanders into hell, now heaven, now into the world-appearance of human beings.

Often, even when the light of wisdom shines on the life of the deluded mind, it foolishly rejects it, considering that wisdom to be its enemy. Then it weeps and wails in distress, while increasing its attachment and attraction to the false notion of individuality. In this way, Vasishtha explains to Rama how all bondage, all contraction and limitation is *self-imposed*. He then goes on, in this story, to explain to Rama why the Master's Grace is so necessary.

I have already spoken, at length in this book, about the methods and approach for attracting more and more Grace into one's life. **The Truth is, we can never have enough Grace in our lives.** And that Grace is dependent on the spiritual merit gained through spiritual practice and the application of the understandings taught us by the spiritually-perfected Love beings.

There are obstacles to imbibing Grace that cause one to sabotage Grace. Here are some important ones to be aware of:

♡ **Identity and the poor little ego**. I feel that this one is worth repeating from Chapter 25. In Nityananda Shaktipat Yoga, our understanding is that we have already attained the highest, the formless Absolute. You are already one with that formless Absolute. Great Masters of our Shiva lineage such as Swami Lakshmanjoo (whose videos and writings you can find online), state that our approach is concerned with how to make the experience of that fact (that each is the inner Self) manifest *constantly* in our lives – *how to make the experience of the fact that you are one with God, manifest constantly in your life.*

The inner Self cannot be known without the direct experience of *the fullness of Humanity.* The issue *is not* the expression of this Humanity. *The challenge is in understanding who or what is doing the expressing.* So, you have to begin with the false notion that you are just a person, just an individual. This is what the words 'ego' or 'egoism' are references to – this contraction in your Consciousness, due to how *you* direct that Shiva-Shakti power that you are *to contract.*

Ego has nothing to do with a particular expression, mood, tone of voice or behavior that you may find 'comfortable' or 'uncomfortable,' or that you might find fault with. If you believe you're just a person, *ego,* in the form of *doership* is *automatically* engaged. If you know, from direct experience and from your heightened witnessing awareness, that you are the Self, there is no ego *because there is no contraction in your Consciousness that leads you away from the fact that all the expressions of Humanity belong to that inner Self and actually emanate from the Self, the Supreme Principle.*

The understanding I have just shared with you will free you from any false notion of what egoism is, *by way of helping you to imbibe Grace.* If God alone exists (which is true) how can there be such a thing as an ego sense? So, this false notion is *self-imposed* through the *imaginary* sense of individuality – the false notion that you are the body and the senses (known in our Shaivism as Anava Mala – see Chapter 9). You can prove as much to yourself by a strong practice of Witness Consciousness.

♡ **There is almost nothing that will sabotage Grace faster than fault-finding.**

"The purity of a Mantra also depends
On the understanding one has of it.
The purity of actions depends on their
Being offered to the inner Self.

According to the Vedas, that which appears
to be pure can in, in reality, be impure
while that which appears impure can,
in reality, be pure. Thus the words of
the Vedas cut off, at the root, categorical
judgment of what is pure and what is
impure.

Someone already on the ground has no
further to fall. Actions that would debase
one person may not have the same effect
on another. These things will depend on
the status of the one performing the action."

~ *Lord Krishna*
From the Uddhava Gita,
Lord Krishna's final teaching
Before his passing,
Uttered to His disciple, Uddhava

"What is called Bliss or Samadhi is seeing and experiencing the

One in all. By practice, one must conquer the six enemies of limiting desire, fear/anger, greed, emotional attachment, pride, jealousy. A devotee, especially a beginner in retracing one's steps back to God, should not talk ill of others. If he/she does so, his progress will be retarded – like that of a sprout on which a heavy stone is placed. A seeker must not relax his spiritual practice even for a ghatica (24 minutes). The mind should be ceaselessly engaged in the practice."

~ Bhagawan Nityananda of Ganeshpuri
Chidakasha Gita

Where or how does this fault-finding begin? Sometimes, it is *self-directed*. At times, you may be too hard on yourself, judging yourself for your weaknesses and mistakes in such a way that you beat yourself up – maybe you guilt yourself on a regular basis. At other times, fault-finding is learned *by example*, by the company we keep. But it is always based on superimposition or the way you project your limited life experience into Consciousness, *from the false notion that you are just a person.*

The sages of steady wisdom say that everything is between you, God and your chosen spiritual Master alone. They also tell us that *fault-finders and those who criticize, condemn and complain can never make permanent spiritual progress.* In our approach, we are very focused on removing this habit, because it is such a great obstacle to spiritual attainment.

Also, right understanding in this regard is vital. If you are enrolled in a science or history class, for example, the teacher has the responsibility to correct your weak knowledge of the subject matter, and to have you submit to tests in order to determine how well you have learned and applied the subject matter. In the same way, the Guru has the duty to point out to you the weaknesses that are 'stunting' your spiritual growth, and also has the duty of testing you so that you know where you are really at, and how much further you have to go to become truly free. This *is not* fault-finding or criticizing.

At various chapters in this book, the statement has been made that we are all that One Supreme Principle, that we should see each other as God and that God alone exists. When this is the case, as one of the great poet saints of our lineage has said, *God is below you, above you, to the right of you, to the left of you, in front of you and behind you.* There is no place where the Self is not. Therefore, everything and everyone is a reflection of that Divinity. If we hold this understanding, then we come to experience the reflection of our very own selves in others. In this way, we can learn something useful, even from a blade of grass!

A great being has said that your shortcomings and weaknesses are obstacles. *Let them be criticized,* but don't criticize others. An ignorant person can indulge his/her own limiting cravings by maligning others. *It's so easy to blame others in order to justify a position that you have attached yourself to, but it is a mistake to do so.* This is what happens in fault-finding. Indulge in virtue by not finding fault in others. A pure heart sees everyone as pure.

So, in our approach, we are taught to turn fault-finding into *fact-finding* within ourselves. For example; Let's say that you are engaged in a conversation with someone and that person says something that causes an immediate reaction in you. You then feel the urge to 'hit back,' to criticize or find fault with something the person just said. And, maybe the energy of your reaction does not match the energy of the conversation.

In this moment, you should ask yourself, "Am I finding a fault or useless tendency that is actually a reflection of my own weakness or fault?" Fact-find within yourself in this way. Is the other person mirroring back to you a tendency that you are *hiding from yourself,* that you need to take responsibility for? Because, *often this is the case.* Then you stop there and, instead of fault-finding or criticizing the other person (as in this example), you address that same weakness within yourself.

If you ask this question of yourself and honestly determine that a fault of your own *is not* being reflected back to you, then (using this example) you may decide to offer feedback to the other person. Here are some important guidelines for offering feedback in a *heart-centered* way that will help you *avoid* merely criticizing out of your own superimposition, *thereby keeping you in alignment with Grace.*

♡ Never offer feedback if you are not prepared to offer concrete examples of that which you are calling the person's attention to. For example; You decide that another person doesn't communicate properly or speaks in an 'egotistic' or harmful manner. Where are the examples of this? Be prepared to offer them.

It's much more useful to offer examples so that you are sure not to confuse your own emotionality about a thing, or your superimposing a fault of your own on to another, so that the feedback you are offering is actually useful. Otherwise, you're just complaining, condemning or criticizing.

♡ It's best that, when you do offer examples, you combine those examples with a personal experience of how what you are suggesting actually could be an improvement. Pictures are worth a thousand words. Sharing a personal experience, connected to the examples you are giving will be much more helpful.

♡ Before you even decide to give feedback, put yourself in the other person's shoes *first*, and contemplate the feedback you want to offer *from that perspective*, to determine whether or not the feedback is still valid, *before* offering it. I'll offer the following story as an example:

One day, in one of my Master's ashrams, a person decided to bring her own tea bag for tea in the dining hall. An argument ensued over hot water. The person who brought the tea bag went to the local press the next day to file a complaint about the ashram. The news got back to Baba. Later, in a large public program, Baba addressed the complaint. At the time, the ashram policy was that if people brought their own tea bags, they were given hot water in a ceramic cup. The person had refused the ceramic cup and demanded a styrofoam cup which she was then asked to pay for. Baba explained that the ashram had to charge for the styrofoam cups because the ashram had to pay for them over and over again (due to their not being reusable), that the person was not charged for hot water, but for the styrofoam cup.

Well, upon hearing Baba state this in a program with three thousand people present, I thought to myself, "That's ridiculous!

Why does a Sadguru like Baba feel he has to defend himself and the ashram over a stupid complaint over hot water!?" So, I went to one of the trustees to complain. I told the trustee that I thought Baba had made a mistake in making such a public announcement, that he came across as having to defend himself, and that it made him look small and petty. Why couldn't he have just talked to the person directly, or had one of the trustees send a note to the local press?

The trustee sat me down and spoke to me very lovingly. He asked me if I had any experience running a global foundation like Baba's. I replied that I did not. He asked me if I had any experience in public relations for large foundations or high profile spiritual leaders. I said "No." The trustee then explained to me some of the situations they had run into during my Master's world tours, where gossip and misrepresentation had spread so quickly that it was impacting the ability of people coming to programs to focus on the experience of Bliss and inner Peace being offered in the programs – and that Baba was simply taking action, based on past experience of these kinds of distractions that were also false claims.

In this conversation with the trustee, I realized that I had not put myself in my Guru's shoes before complaining. I hadn't even considered the possibility that there was another side to the circumstance that could have been weighed. Later, I also realized that I had just resorted to fault-finding and was superimposing my own opinion on to the situation. I had not engaged in offering loving feedback and I did not have examples, from my own experience, to offer for how my Master could have approached the situation differently.

♡ If you are offering feedback or advice to another for spiritual life, be sure that, in addition to the points made above, you are not giving feedback based on mere opinion or belief. Everybody thinks they are the next great intuitive, but how do you know that it's not your ego talking? How do you know that you are not superimposing from your false sense of individuality?

Sheik Sahib used to give discourses in coffee shops. He was a flamboyant personality and loved to talk. (Some Sadgurus also come across as 'flamboyant' and love to talk. How do you know the difference? - by the inner experiences you begin to have in the company of such a being.) One day, Sheik Sahib was giving some very pointed advice to those present in the coffee shop. "If you want God, don't smoke or drink," he said. "Stay away from women and fornication and avoid bars and wild parties."

At that moment, a man stood up and said, "Sheik Sahib, isn't that a pack of cigarettes you have there in your pocket?" "Yes, yes. I smoke." Another person yelled, "Khan Sahib, I see a bottle of liquor in your inside jacket pocket right now!" Sheik Sahib replied, "Oh yes, I drink." Another person stood up and asked, "I'm in the park everyday. Don't I see you with a different woman in the park everyday?" "Oh yes, I have many girlfriends. I love women." Then Sheik Sahib continued, "I just give you teachings. I don't actually follow them myself."

Don't be like Sheik Sahib! Be sure that your spiritual advice is based on experiences you can also share *of going beyond your mind and beyond your senses,* so that you are not merely engaged in complaining, condemning or *universalizing* your own opinion. *Especially in spiritual life, opinions are not useful.* Inner experience of the Self is all that matters.

♡ When giving feedback or advice, do so without any expectation of the outcome, otherwise it's not feedback. Many people don't want to change and are not willing to accept Love in the form of loving feedback or advice. Be prepared for this fact when you offer feedback by having no expectation of the impact of your advice.

♡ When accepting feedback or advice from others, always consider the source, *first.* Does the person offering advice to you have any personal experience in what he/she is calling your attention to? Or are you just being offered an opinion or belief that the person giving you feedback has universalized?

Grace is everything – the beginning, the middle and the end. Again, here I am speaking of the *transformative* Grace that causes one to let go of the false notion of individuality (the false notion of being the body, the mind and the senses), while engaging the instruction that allows one to experience the inner Self on a consistent basis. *This Grace comes from a Master*, and your understanding of whether or not you are imbibing or sabotaging that Grace comes by way of your realizing the level of your spiritual attainment. By attainment, I mean the level to which you have fully let go of your false identity as an individual, as just a person, as just ordinary – *the level to which you have let go of all that you are not,* including the false leanings and tendencies that form the veil that covers your heart.

As stated in previous chapters, to really know where you're at with this, *you need to be tested.* The tests that occur in the Kriya process are the only way you will be able to discern the difference between *where you think you are at* and *where you are really at. These tests are actually the Grace of God at work in your spiritual life* that the Shaktipat Guru is the catalyst for. These tests are Grace, so learn to welcome them and imbibe them. **During my own Sadhana, I was taught how great it is to be tested.** This should be your attitude, because this understanding will allow you to weather the tests of the Guru in such a way that you will continually attract more and more Grace into your life.

We can never have enough Grace for our lives and spiritual transformation. Your Grace, inherent in your increasing Bhakti, your Longing, coupled with the Master's Grace – this is the proven formula that allows you, *armed with that Longing,* to burn away all that you are not in the fire of your Love and the living Master's Love.

A picture of a saint does not have the ability to administer these tests. A set of teachings that may *appear* to be the same as what the great beings utter – although the practice of these teachings may help you to gain more spiritual awareness, *the teachings themselves will never be able to test your attainment.* For such tests of Grace, you will need an outside, living catalyst in a Sadguru. I accepted this Truth, and all I have to give is due to my Guru's tests, both inside and out. *In order to be properly administered, these tests require that the Will of a Shakta Adept be directed to your attainment in the Shaktipat Kriya Process.* **This Will is Grace.** It is the Shiva-Shakti power in it's fullest capacity to deliver you from the ignorance you have used to hide your true nature from yourself.

The act of imbibing Grace is a practice of letting go and giving over to Grace. What are you engaged in the practice of letting go of? The only obstacle to your permanent spiritual transformation – your false identification with the body, the senses and the mind, your false identification with being just a person, just ordinary or delightfully weird. When you practice letting go in this way by giving over to the Master's instruction and embracing the Master's Love in all its forms, with complete Devotion/Longing, God is pleased. Why? Because That Supreme Principle knows that, over time, you will realize the inner Self! In this way, Liberation can be accomplished quickly. I say this for one reason only. This is how I have attained *That*. This is how many beings in our lineage have gone across. It is evident in this way.

At times, devotees of a Sadguru fall prey to the 'god' trap (see Chapter 23) in their understanding of whether or not they are receiving the Grace that is transmitted by such a being. Others become spoiled after having very tangible experiences of that Grace in their lives, *wrongly believing that the only time they are blessed with this Grace is when it is revealed in very tangible ways that can be perceived through the senses.* Understand that Grace is cumulative, *and sometimes it cannot be perceived through an event or outcome that the mind and senses can grasp.* **It is always at work on behalf of the Devotee, nonetheless.**

Ultimately, Grace is always between you, the catalyst in the living Sadguru and God. In the end, as in the beginning, everything is between you and that Supreme Principle, the inner Self that you are.

People are often unreasonable, illogical and self-centered. Forgive Them Anyway.

If you are kind, people may accuse you of selfish, ulterior motives. Be Kind Anyway.

If you are successful, you will win some false friends and some true enemies. Succeed Anyway.

If you are honest and frank, people may cheat you. Be Honest and Frank Anyway.

What you spend years building, someone may destroy over night. Build Anyway.

If you find serenity and happiness, they may be jealous. Be Happy Anyway.

The good you do today, people will often forget tomorrow. Do Good Anyway.

Give the world the best you have and it may just never be enough. Give the world the best you have anyway.

You see, in the final analysis, it's all between you and God. It was never between you and them anyway.

~ Mother Teresa

NITYANANDA SHAKTIPAT YOGA

With Great Respect and Love
We Welcome You With Our One Heart

I extend to you a warm invitation to find out more about how you can begin to experience the Peace, Joy and Love of the inner Self.

Nityananda Shaktipat Yoga programs and events include Shaktipat Meditation, *full Kundalini Awakening* in weekend Shaktipat meditation retreats, Chanting, *Witness Consciousness Centering* methods, Mantra Yoga, wellness events and more. We also offer week-long Shaktipat meditation retreats and global, live webcasts over the Internet. Products as aids to the instruction given are also offered in our bookstore and online store.

In Nityananda Shaktipat Yoga, we place the greatest emphasis on the weekend Shaktipat Blessing retreats in which full Kundalini Awakening (Shaktipat) is given.

Our experience is that Love is the highest goal of Human life. Here we examine and experience how to immerse ourselves in that *Love without distinctions.*

Information about Nityananda Shaktipat Yoga and how you can benefit from our offering can be found at our web site at NityanandaShaktipatYoga.org.

I dwell in the paradise of my Shri Gurudev's Love and Blessing. And what a Blessing it is!

Yoga, the transformation of limited and binding awareness of the mundane world, into the highest spiritual witnessing awareness of the Self or God, is not psycho-babble, witch craft, spiritualism or voudou. With the right leadership and methods, it is an exact *Siddha Science* that can be verified in the laboratory of one's own existence. https://nityanandashaktipatyoga.org/spiritual-path/

This Siddha Science is the Yoga of the Siddhas, the spiritually-perfected Love Beings. It is the Science of the sacred law that rules here. **As such, it is also the Science, the Yoga of Guru's Grace**. This Yoga Science has been taught and handed down in an oral, time-honored tradition and approach, from Sadguru to Devotee/Disciple, in an unbroken lineage that dates back to the Pre-bronze age. It exists to this day, in the Sadgurus of our lineage, expressed through the living Shaktipat Guru.

We live on a rock that hangs in a void of space, spinning on an axis in an orbit around a fireball! And there is an order to it all that no nation, no standing army, no President, no dictator, no corporate conglomerate and no sovereign wealth trust can influence or change. It is a higher order, a greater law. Wherever there is law, there is a lawgiver. Now, let that fact sink in for a moment.

As human beings, as spiritual entities and as a species we are evolving in every way. We are evolving back into That Supreme Being that is embodied in the energy substratum of everything and everyone.

It is a fact that, in any evolutionary process, only the species that adapts will survive. Therefore, the key to our survival, growth and freedom is in our ability to adapt.

We cannot move toward the fulfillment of any potentiality that is not already inherent in our existence, no more than a caterpillar can decide to, one day, become a frog, rather than a butterfly.

So, our ability to adapt must be based on this inherent potentiality. This chapter is for those who have an interest in the place that well-being takes in our Siddha Science.

In Nityananda Shaktipat Yoga, we also speak of and teach methods for Well-Being, since all of well-being has a spiritual foundation in the energy substratum – that Shiva-Shakti power that is one with the Supreme. Kedarji's Ecology of Wellness expressed in the offering of Nityananda Shaktipat Yoga, embodies 4 pillars of Joy In Daily Living that are the essential nature of that ecology of wellness. This is founded on the journey to well-being that naturally evolves to the realization of its fullest potential, by way of this inherent potentiality.

The ancient wisdom of many Sages of Siddha Science has already proved this. Modern science is now beginning to make this same proof also.

Ecology

I call this offering *The Ecology of Well-Being*. The dictionary defines 'ecology' in the following way:

- the set of relationships existing between organisms and their environment
- the set of relationships existing between any complex system and its surroundings or environment

Environment can also be understood as any force that acts on or shapes the existence of a person, place or thing. This would include the inner and outer company we keep and the inner environment dictated by our mental and emotional states.

Environment can also be understood as the extra cellular matrices that cells form in the process of building connective tissue around organs and muscle, as it is a scientific fact that our cells form 'communities' in which constant communication via energetic exchanges is taking place every second. These energetic exchanges are also known as *cell signaling.*

Often, when we think of the word 'ecology,' we think of places like the Amazon rainforest. In fact, until recently, over 90% of all our pharmaceutical drugs and the base for most of our vitamins came from nutrients and chemicals mined in the world's tropical rainforests. These rainforests contain a vast, magical and complex ecology known as *the biosphere.*

The biosphere, when left alone to operate naturally, relies on a subtle and perfect balance of all its component *energies*, in order to continue to produce the wonders of the world that also include much of our natural and synthetic medicines.

So, when we think of 'ecology,' *delicate, harmonious balance* is what comes to mind. Kedarji's Ecology of Well-Being that I speak of infers that a delicate, harmonious balance must be struck in our beings, *and maintained*, for us to get well and stay well. So, connected to our well-being, each of us also has an ecology or ecological makeup. And this delicate, harmonious balance to be struck is vital, right down to the cellular level.

In order to provide a simple structure for attaining this balance, I have created Kedarji's 4 Pillars of Joy In Daily Living. I will, briefly, elucidate here how each of these 4 Pillars are active, relevant and impactful for improved well-being and vibrant health, all the way down to our cells.

These 4 Pillars are:

1. The Spiritual Power
2. Improved Mental State
3. Emotional Resilience
4. Vibrant Health

In Siddha Science, there is the consistent examination of what we refer to as the *two aspects* of the one Divine Conscious Energy or energy substratum. These are known as the *Transcendental* aspect and the *Immanent* (worldly) aspect, the immanent being an expression of the transcendental. In other words, everything here in form has these two aspects at play in the myriad expressions that comprise life – *all the way down to our cells.*

Prior to breakthroughs in the science of Quantum Physics, the now outdated Newtonian model of matter and the Universe had us believing that the atom is the smallest particle of material existence. Thanks to Quantum Physics and Quantum Mechanics, we now know that atoms contain subatomic particles that are actually the smallest material particles in the Universe. And even that statement becomes a dubious one, when closely examining what such particles are actually made of (invisible energy)! Upon close, scientific examination, we know that atoms comprising molecules are actually like wobbly, spinning tops radiating their own identifying energy patterns. This means that *every material structure* has an *energy signature* that is *the substratum* of its compound makeup! These energy signatures are also known as energy vortices, and these vortices are quarks and photons that makeup the structure of all atoms. (For more information and references to many studies, see the book *How To Live Strong & Be Happy With Kedarji's 4 Pillars of Joy In Daily Living* which can be purchased at https://www.nityanandashaktipatyoga.org/books-by-sadguru-kedarji/)

Ultimate Power Source

So, modern science has confirmed that there is, in fact, an energy substratum of all things, right down to the molecular structure of our cells. However, this fact has been known and applied in the East and Asia for centuries. In both the societies and spiritual paths originating in these places, *Energy* is honored as the principal/primary factor in wellness, including vibrant health!

We say this energy substratum is Spiritual. Why not? It would have to be. In my experience it is, because these energy exchanges are happening in an orderly fashion with their own power source. Just like this rock that we live on, that hangs in a void of space, spinning on an axis, in an orbit around a fireball – and in an orderly fashion, 365 days a year, twenty four hours a day. Who decided that? Who or what? Who decided that females will bare children rather than males? Who decided that we would have two eyes, two ears, two hands, two legs, rather one hand or four heads!?

So there is an order here. We can't argue about that. So why label it in any other way except to recognize it as an order – as in a *higher order or sacred law* that has an energy base?

I like to think of this as the *Ultimate Power Source*, and the *science* of how that power source is *expressed.* So, there is this Ultimate Reality and the Science of how it expresses itself *as our existence here.* Physicists and other scientists will find this to be in alignment with their own findings, with respect to examination and application of Einstein's theory of relativity (now qualified as his theory of special relativity) and E=MC squared. Scientist Buckminster Fuller's work also supports this principle. Quantum

Physics is also considered to be the philosophy of the science that is specifically examined and expressed in Quantum Mechanics (considered to be a branch of or contained in Quantum Physics).

So, to further understand the impact of these 4 Pillars on joy in daily living, I group these pillars in the following manner.

1. The Transcendental or Ultimate Power Source = Spiritual Power, Pillar 1.
2. The Immanent or Science of how that power source is *expressed* (in human beings) = Improved Mental State, Increased Emotional Resilience, Vibrant Health (Pillars 2, 3, and 4).

Further, as you may be getting by now, *"how expressed"* is the understanding that is vital here – because it is the key to observing and understanding how each of these 4 pillars is expressed, even at the cellular level. And, how you *choose* to express the energy substratum, meaning how you choose to direct that Ultimate Power Source, will determine whether or not you attain an improved mental state, emotional resilience and vibrant health.

Joy and Matter

This raises another understanding: You are responsible for how the first aspect is expressed as the second in your existence here, all the way down to how your cells are communicating (epigenetic expression).

Then there is another matter to address. If not stored under optimal conditions, milk spoils very fast. A gold bracelet that is mixed with silver or bronze is no longer pure gold and its value is greatly reduced. A silk garment mixed with cotton or, worse yet, polyester, is considered to be a useless knock off. In each of these examples, the worth or power of a thing has been skewed or tainted by the way in which choices were made in how they are *expressed.* By this I mean that a gold bracelet is, essentially, just gold. A carton of milk is just baby calf growth formula that has been processed and packed. Silk is still, essentially, the eggs of the mulberry silkworm, albeit altered.

Similarly, if your expression of the energy substratum, that Ultimate Power Source, is tainted, your mental state, emotional resilience and vibrant health are degraded. In other words, *you have the power to decide how that Ultimate Reality is expressed in your existence here*, thereby impacting the expression of the last three pillars.

Raw energy, in the hands of someone who doesn't know how to properly use it, can result in fatality. So, in Nityananda Shaktipat Yoga, we focus on helping people to use the ultimate energy, The Spiritual Power, to enhance the immanent (the other 3 pillars), in way that that enables them to *harness* this energy *optimally*.

It can further be understood in the following way: **Joy and Matter are connected** – *meaning that any thing material can be impacted and improved by the experience of Joy (Bliss of the Inner Self) that breeds peace and content.* This Joy is an inner state that calms the restless mind, opening the floodgates to spontaneous inspiration. Writers do their best work when it's quiet and they experience an environment of peace and calm that is conducive to an inner experience of Joy and Inspiration. Inventors and cutting-edge scientists and innovators report that, often, they get their best ideas when they are not focused on manifesting an idea itself, but rather are focused on nothing apparent (allowing Joy to arise spontaneously due to a quiet mind). When I attended master classes in music conservatory, great, world renown artists like Itzak Perlman, Isaac Stern, Max Roach and Dizzy Gillespie each told me that their best performance occurred when they got out of their own way and allowed an unseen power to take control of their hands and minds, giving way to a state of Joy!

So, another way to understand the grouping of the 4 Pillars that I mention above, is to recognize the relationship between Joy and Matter – a relationship that you can begin to experience more fully within your own being, with the right methods for doing so. If you were to examine modern physics, you will also see that modern physics supports the interconnectedness of Joy and Matter. Of course, we also see this in Nature – that there is a higher power in the orderliness of Nature that is joyous to behold, and that surely must have at its foundation Love and Joy.

Grouping the 4 Pillars of Joy In Daily Living in the context of these two aspects will help you to embrace and seek to nurture The Spiritual Power, without succumbing to fears of the unknown or ridiculous notions heaped upon you by popular culture or people who are frightened by what they don't understand.

The Spiritual Power

This entire book is about The Spiritual Power, and how my Shri Gurudev led me in harnessing that power. This is how Nityananda Shaktipat Yoga has come to be. Still, in examining this energy substratum of all sentient and insentient things, we don't need to argue about the labels of God, Yahweh, Spirit, Islam, Shakti, Shiva, Christianity and so on. Labels are there to get and keep our attention long enough to engage the methods for understanding and experiencing *That* which is beyond all labels – *That* which gives power to all labels. Part of increasing spiritual power is getting past being stuck on these labels, getting past seeing differences and distinctions caused by attachment to labels. The labels are simply indicators of something greater that, when experienced, allows us to discard the fear created by the perceived differences in them.

At the core of it, regardless of what the label is, the one thing that we can all agree on, the one thing that medical doctors can agree on, that scientists, spiritualists, meditation masters and spiritual leaders can agree on – we can all agree on one thing: That there is, indeed, an energy substratum to our existence here. This is irrefutable. Why is this irrefutable?

Because we live on a rock that hangs in a void of space with nothing material with which to support its hanging there, a rock that is spinning on an axis in an orbit around a fireball! And no nation, no government, no sovereign wealth trust, no army, no wealthy individual or corporate conglomerate, no drug cartel or organized crime entity any where can change this fact or exert any influence over it whatsoever!

This brings us to another, irrefutable fact connected to The Spiritual Power. There is an order here in this realm, on this planet in which we live that is dictated *by force of law*. The Sun rises and sets. The moon waxes and wanes. Weather patterns and seasons come and go. Trees, grass, flowers grow like clockwork in seasons, rivers run and oceans rise and fall, often in predictable ways. This signals the fact that there is an order to these cycles, along with the birth and death and rebirth of all things here that is dictated by this law. I call it Sacred Law. And, in the words of the great Mahatma Gandhi, where there is *law*, there is always a *lawgiver*.

At the very least, considering the energy substratum as a

spiritual power allows for the examination of this hypothesis, connected to the other 3 pillars – and in such a way that we can test and embrace the understanding and experience of an Ultimate Power Source *that can be harnessed for well-being.* In the Ecology of Well-Being that I offer, there are proved methods that are taught for either proving or disproving this hypothesis for yourself, in the laboratory of your own existence. **This is an important point because facts can be argued, interpreted and reinterpreted,** *but you can't argue with direct experience.*

What You Risk If You Don't Increase The Spiritual Power

I have just discussed the energy substratum and how we need a power source for the function of everything. And I've also stated why you should access the purest, highest power – *because it is inexhaustible!* It is this kind of power that is required to convert old, bad habits into new and more useful habits that will support your journey to well-being in your entire existence here.

We are all creatures of habit. *And the truth is that most people love good news about their bad habits!* Are you like this? I was. I only raise this point because we all know how hard it is to break bad habits, even when well-intentioned thinking is expressed. With an increase in The Spiritual Power, discarding useless habits for more useful, liberating ones is easy and, over time, effortless. Why?

To begin with, a restless mind can only produce habits that have their foundation in fear, doubt, worry, frustration, anxiety, sarcasm, cynicism, depression, anger and….well, you get my point. Therefore, particularly where wellness is concerned, nothing useful comes from a restless mind.

To make the restless mind quiet on a lasting basis, *without reaching for recreational drugs and other devices that are limited and are not without side effects that are harmful*, you need The Spiritual Power! The great thing about The Spiritual Power is that you already possess this treasure. You only need to be taught the methods that will secure your complete access to it, permanently.

In fact, we are all energetic beings who operate on this spiritual power. We search for it outside, like an ignorant person who lives by a river or stream, and yet searches for water in a desert! Merging in The Spiritual Power *is your birthright*. It does not have to be sought after in caves, castles, money or relationships. It is there and has always been right there inside you. You just need to stop concealing it from yourself.

Once recognized and fully realized, this power source transforms the restless mind into a sharp, golden wonder, upon which wellness *beyond your expectations* can be enjoyed. *With the harnessing of The Spiritual Power and the most effective methods in doing so, you are carried beyond the mind and beyond the senses to a sacred space of Joy, Peace and Inspiration!* That's the easy part to discarding old, useless habits, along with your attachment to wanting good news about your bad habits.

The risk you run in not acquiring the means to this spiritual power permanently is that you will never be fully able to improve your mental state.

Improved Mental State

Witness Consciousness or the State of the Observer. This is an experience in which you are able to watch your thoughts, emotions, notions, etc. come and go *passively, without judgment* and without any reaction or response that allows the energy of egoism to arise. It is a state in which, from that Witness to your mind, you are able to observe that Source from which all thoughts rise, are sustained and withdrawn. In Nityananda Shaktipat Yoga, as part of helping people to improve their mental state, we lead people in a practice I call *Witness Consciousness Centering*. In the many years I have offered this Meditation method, our case studies show that the majority of people who practice the method as instructed, even on the very first attempt, experience a silent mind in less than 3 minutes.

The purpose of practicing Witness Consciousness Centering is to begin the important process of *Remembrance*, as you go about your daily activities. The great beings tell us that Remembrance means resolving one's identity crisis by identifying with the Self, with our True nature, in every movement of thought, emotions, notions, etc. in our Consciousness. Again, I refer to this true nature as *the energy substratum of all things*. At our core, we are energetic beings, inhabiting a human form, just for a short while. Without that energy, that Highest Power, the body dies.

Therefore, the body is actually inert, with no agency of its own. It is that energy that gives the body its life and luster.

Why do you need to be reminded of this? Because you have forgotten who you really are. Through so many karmas (mental conditioning) of so many past lives and the present life, you have developed the false notion that you are just a person, a mere individual, that you are the body with an exclusive personality, that you are small, ordinary or delightfully weird. Without remembering who you really are, without being reminded that you are the Self, that Highest Power, there is no hope for permanent spiritual transformation or long-term wellness. Finding true peace and happiness then becomes a fading dream, mostly due to the raging river of worldly distractions.

What to do? The first step in addressing a poor mental state is to understand the Witness to your mind. For example, you know when you are thinking but *how do you know you are thinking?* How do you know you have slept? How do you know you have dreamt? You know because there is a higher power, a power that I refer to as the Knower, the Witness, the Shiva-Shakti power or Supreme Principle. There is no point in arguing about the labels. There are as many labels for grapes as there are languages on the planet. We're still talking about the same grapes! Likewise, this Highest Power, the Self is that which even gives us the power to perceive differences and distinctions in this way. This Witness is beyond the mind and beyond the senses. *That* is what observes these changing states of experience. That Witness is who we really are.

Reaching for this Witness Consciousness state, with practice and the Grace and leadership of a really good spiritual Master, leads to your awareness merging in the experience of the Witness. It is through the experience of this Observer, this state of *Witnessing Awareness*, that you are able to watch where your mind goes. You are able to observe all of the manifestations of the restless mind. And this is the first step in reigning in the wandering, restless mind, *in order to improve your mental state.*

To begin to understand and to experience this state of Witnessing Awareness, it is necessary to hold and to contemplate the fundamental instruction of this approach. This instruction is framed in the utterances of the Sages of steady wisdom who tell us, See God In Each Other. The Self (that energy substratum) exists equally in all. In order to practice and perfect Witness Consciousness Centering, we begin by holding this highest understanding.

In fact, your perfection is already with you. The great travesty is that you forget who you really are. You lose awareness of this Highest Power or energy substratum, the awareness of your own Divinity. You lose this awareness by concealing from yourself the fact that you are The Spiritual Power inherent in the energy substratum of your being. This is how the mental state becomes degraded. So, using methods to regain the experience of The Spiritual Power, to remember the experience of it by accessing it again and again, is how you will improve your mental state.

STOP HERE FOR A MOMENT AND TAKE A DEEP BREATH. Witness Consciousness Centering has been examined in detail in Chapters 2, 4, 12 and 25. It's good for you to review these chapters.

What You Risk If You Don't Improve Your Mental State

Every wellness mechanism in your being that God has provided for both your Joy and your enjoyment of life is compromised by a poor mental state. And a poor mental state is your creation. Therefore, you are responsible for improving it. This can be easily accomplished with the right, proved methods for doing so on a lasting basis.

As I stated previously, a mind that is the embodiment of fear, anxiety, worry, doubt, anger, cynicism, sarcasm, lack of gratitude and content *cannot produce anything useful where wellness is concerned.* On the other hand, a quiet, calm and content mind, with the right spiritual practice, can become a superconductor for the power of the Ultimate Reality, inspiration, spontaneity and Love and, ultimately, Freedom.

- The mind loves the places it frequents the most.
- Whatever the mind meditates on regularly, it becomes.
- You become what you obey.

These three utterances of the Sages of my lineage embody the risk you run in allowing your mind to wander into and relish in (by way of attachment) fear, anxiety, worry, doubt, anger, cynicism, sarcasm, lack of gratitude and content. **Once you become these, well-being is destroyed and health severely diminished.**

In fact, the connection between a poor mental state and chronic health conditions and pathways to disease is well documented. For example, within the membrane of each of our cells, there is the nucleus of the cell itself. There is also the nucleus of the Mitochondria, the 'cell burners' within each and every cell that convert nutrients into the energy and signaling processes that keep our bodies healthy. *These are separate nuclei that interact with each other.*

Due to the excellent work of Dr. Bruce Lipton and his medical team, a discovery was made that has changed our knowledge and understanding of what impacts cellular health. The science of this is known as *Epigenetics*, a science that has proved that cells change, grow and mutate based on communication (epigenetic expression) that is taking place both inside the cell membrane and between cells in extra cellular matrices (in connective tissue and organs). *This epigenetic expression can be altered in many ways, without changing the underlying DNA coding.* **This means that, in fact, disease-causing genes and be switched off and health promoting genes switched on, regardless of inherited genetic predisposition** (genetic inheritance only represents about 3-5% of all disease causes).

Within the non-encoding RNA, contained in the 'dark matter' of each cell nucleus, there are integral membrane proteins (IMPs). These are divided into *effector proteins* and *receptor proteins* (Lipton 2015, (6)). These two proteins talk to (signal) each other on a constant basis. *And here's the connection to poor mental state.* The receptor proteins' ability to properly signal to keep the cell functioning properly *is directly impacted by signals they receive from outside the cell and outside the body* (environmental factors). This is how medical science now knows and acknowledges, for example, that stress kills. In fact, *stress* is now considered to be *one of the leading causes of chronic health conditions and diseases such as heart disease, diabetes, stroke and cancer.* There are many other examples of factors that change receptor protein signaling, including food toxins and environmental toxins.

There is only one way to reduce stress and that is to engage time-honored, proved methods for calming the restless mind and turning it within and upward to the power source – *The Spiritual Power*. These are methods that include true meditation, kirtan chanting and contemplation of the Highest.

So, the risk you run in allowing your mind to remain restless is a poor mental state that traffics in lack of well-being, poor health and disease!

Emotional Resilience

Then there's the third pillar of *Emotional Resilience*. Emotional Resilience simply means this; we want to be able to express our humanity. Here, we believe that we should enjoy life, but there's a lot that gets in the way of enjoying life. And one of the things that gets in the way of enjoying life is *riding the emotional roller coaster*. Being dragged back and forth, from one emotion to another, to another. This makes you a slave to your emotions and this is not useful for your well-being. This does not produce happiness and content.

In fact, as we know from medical science and all other forms of science, riding the emotional roller coaster is detrimental to your health and well-being. For example, stress has now been moved up on the list of chronic health conditions that cause cancer. Stress causes cancer and a host of other diseases. Just stress alone can do this, due to the way stress has been shown to increase insulin resistance and disrupt cell signaling pathways. *Therefore, stress is a toxin.* When we become slaves to our emotions, we place ourselves under a great deal of stress.

Emotional Resilience on the other hand, allows us the freedom to express our humanity - to express our emotions, *but from a place of sheer delight* connected to the first pillar of The Spiritual Power. That's why we need The Spiritual Power. This power frees us from the prison of emotional enslavement so that we are able to express our emotions, *without becoming entangled in them.* To be able to express our humanity without becoming slaves to our emotions, what's wrong with that? We all want that.

This is Emotional Resilience and it is a state. Now, having said that, it's not possible to attain Emotional Resilience without first improving your mental state. Because if you have a lousy mental state, you cannot attain a state of emotional resilience. These two work synergistically, in conjunction with Spiritual Power.

Again, an improved mental state is reliant on The Spiritual Power, as is Emotional Resilience. Without an improved mental state you cannot attain lasting emotional resilience. Instead, you remain a slave to your emotions. And that really has the effect of degrading your well-being. So, how do you increase your emotional resilience?

It's important for each of us to examine where we get our *understandings* from. It's important because understandings always dictate our feelings. How we are vibrating, from moment-to-moment, is dictated by the feeling we experience in that moment. Our vibration immediately begins to attract to us the people, places and things that will reinforce that vibration. This causes us to hold other understandings (that will dictate other feelings) that will keep us wedded to whatever state we find ourselves in, *by way of the understandings we have been holding*, and the subsequent feelings and vibration that manifest out of those understandings.

For this reason, if we want to change how we feel, we need to change our understanding. You can take from this that understandings are vital to whether or not you will experience your true nature *from the vantage point of the energy substratum of your being – the power source of your well-being*. The understandings you hold either keep you bound to lack, limitation and contraction, or they free you to experience the Joy and Peace of the true Heart – from which you are able to invoke changes in your life that enhance your living, without compromising your Peace and your true worth – without compromising your Human Dignity that is the essence of the experience of The Spiritual Power.

Often, we tend to get the understandings that we fashion our lives after from embracing the popular and widely-accepted notions about who we are, based on what society, the collective consciousness of the masses, husband, wife, friends, family members, lovers – based on what they all tell us. If you believe yourself to be a 'liberal,' you identify with what the liberals tell you. If you are a 'conservative,' you fashion part of your identity after what the conservatives tell you. If you have a favorite celebrity, you accept the ideas and notions that the celebrity has made popular. You may even believe that the roles celebrities play on the Internet, in movies, TV and other popular media have an important message for you.

You may believe that you are the body, just a person, just

ordinary, an individual who has to make his/her life happen – you accept these things without even questioning them because these are the understandings you have been taught by the company you keep and the society and collective consciousness that you choose to embrace.

These understandings cause you to feel very passionate about those things that you have accepted, *often without questioning them*. As a result, you vibrate in a way that continues to attract the people, places and things to you that reinforce these understandings. In this way, you have created karmas for yourself that continue to dictate the mental conditioning that controls your life. And this is what has *downgraded* your emotional state.

Even when this is the case, many complain that spiritual paths and strong spiritual leaders are vehicles for brainwashing, yet they are already so thoroughly brainwashed by the understandings given them by society, collective consciousness and the company they keep. They question God, Spirit, that Highest Power, yet they never question the understandings they have come to embrace, just because those understandings are popular and have been affirmed by the collective consciousness of the society in which they grew up. *For this reason, practicing the most useful methods for increasing Emotional Resilience is vital to well-being.*

More Examples – How A Downgraded Emotional State Works Against You

Some of the same psychologists who regurgitate the notions of popular culture and society for how to lead one's life, also sell themselves to the very companies who brainwash you into buying their products.

For example, if you've ever been inside a major advertising firm (I have) then you know what goes on there. Ad firms are brainwashing machines that, with the help of modern psychology (Sigmund Freud's nephew, Edward Bernays, used his Uncle's approach to psychology to start the first and most popular PR and advertising firm here in America), have become very skilled at manipulating all areas of popular culture. They use the widely accepted understandings that societies embrace, in order to walk around in your head to cause you to become attached to products and services that they want you to continue to buy.

This is accomplished by encouraging you toward senseless emotionality. And so many people accept this form of brainwashing. (This reminds me of a good example of what I've just stated, portrayed in a movie comedy entitled *How To Get Ahead In Advertising* – 1989, starring Richard E. Grant.) Ad firms have very strong PR (public relations) teams that have now become the 'go to' for politicians and CEOs of major corporations, due to their skill at what I've mentioned above. **Perceptions are easily manipulated when Emotional Resilience is lacking.**

The entertainment industry is another great example. Due to the power of music, combined with popular perceptions, records, TV, movies and other media, these are, absolutely, designed to invoke emotions – with the intention of making those emotions *memorable*. **The challenge is that many of these induced emotions do not serve our wellness**. For example, if you research the body of movies on Netflix or Amazon, you will notice that, as part of our popular culture and worldview, we are obsessed with crime, guns, drugs, sex, lies/deceit and revenge.

So much of what sells falls into these categories, reflecting the mental/emotional state of the masses. This is an indication of where so many are at with respect to the triggers they reach for which degrade their Emotional Resilience.

These are just some of many examples regarding how so many people formulate the understandings they reach for that dictate how they feel, often without even questioning those understandings. In this way, many do not even bother to examine the subtle yet profound impact the above has on their awareness.

However, there are societies on the planet where the popular understandings that are embraced, as part of the popular culture (or widely-accepted notions of society) are quite different than in the West or Europe. For example, in Eastern India, the popular culture and societal norms embrace the understandings that embody the wisdom of Siddha Science that allows people to perceive this world as an expression of the Divine. The culture there is imbued with the understandings that the ancient science of Yoga provides.

This understanding is reflected in the popular culture of many regions in their society. Instead of growing up on portrayals of humankind, indicative of TV shows like *The Sopranos*, *Sex In the City* or *Breaking Bad*, they grow up on Yoga for wellness of the whole being. It is this way in certain parts of Asia, as well. Unfortunately, the collective consciousness in some of these regions is moving toward contraction and a lower vibration, due to the fact that people there are following the example of greed and excess set here in the West. *This is also due to a downgrade in their emotional state, as a result.*

Excess stimulation and instant gratification has become the hallmark of many societies. This impacts Emotional Resilience as well, by way of the understandings people reach for. In this way, even your notion of being independent, *or the notion of what it is to be independent,* is derived from the collective consciousness and popular media of the society that you embrace.

For example, you experience a song or musical tune as being 'happy' or 'sad,' *based on the understanding you hold about* the tune and/or the lyrics, and not necessarily the music or lyrics themselves. Furthermore, you may have accepted that understanding by way of other understandings that you are conditioned to reach for, or based on who or what you attract, by way of how you are vibrating. Regardless of the understanding, *your feeling about a person, place or thing is always due to the understandings your hold.*

Going back to the music example, music becomes popular and accepted with respect to its 'emotional' content, due to the repetitiveness with which the music is heard. Stephen Sondheim (a partner of the great Leonard Bernstein, one of the greatest composers of musicals on the planet), once told me that a composer's music becomes popular due to air time, *and not necessarily because the music is even noteworthy.* Here he was referring to the necessity of getting one's record played on the radio and in other popular media where people will become attached to a composition by the mere fact that they hear it a lot. The mind loves the places it frequents the most! This is important to understand with respect to increasing your Emotional Resilience.

Understandings Are The Parent of All Emotions

When your understanding of a person, place or thing changes, your feeling about that person immediately changes, and you vibrate in a different way, as a result. For example, you fall in love with a person and believe that the person is your soul mate, and that everything you believe you lack that person is going to complete for you or fulfill. Then, one day, that person does or says something that crosses you in a way that you feel is irreconcilable. So, you break up. The breakup was caused by the fact that your understanding of that person and your understanding of the relationship with that person changed. Therefore, your feeling changed. Someone you once loved and proclaimed as your soul mate is now dead to you – all due to the change in the understanding you chose to embrace.

Let me give some other examples that I believe you will easily be able to relate to:

Location. Maybe you've been living in a particular place for a long time or you live in a city or town that you grew up in. And maybe life wasn't so good for you as you were growing up in this location. Perhaps mistakes you made began to haunt you, or you had a series of bad relationships that caused your reputation to become tainted. Or maybe you've been unable to launch the career you want or find the husband or wife you're seeking in this location. One day, you decide you're going to move to a place you think will be better, or you just long for a change in surroundings, believing that this is the best way to leave your past behind you. So, you move to a different city or town and soon forget about your previous location. Your feeling about both the old and the new location is due to the understandings you hold about both.

Identity. Maybe you have been addicted to drugs or alcohol. One day you decide to get professional help for your addiction. Part of that professional help includes some kind of therapy, perhaps a 12-step program. As you are weaned off of your addiction and regain awareness of what it's like to make choices that are not driven by your addiction, you start to realize that you are not the person you thought you were (most addicts have this experience in rehab). This realization came about due to the change in your understanding about you and your relationship to other people, places and things.

Labels for Sexual Preference. Perhaps you are 'gay' or 'straight.' One day, you decide that you are no longer 'heterosexual' and you decide to become 'gay' or vice versa. This decision was due to a change in your understanding. Understanding yourself to be an object of sexual desire, an object of attraction for others or just the body (that's what this kind of objectification is about), you label yourself after the understanding of gender. Changing your sexual preference then, is a matter of a change in your understanding – from one label as an object of attraction to another.

In each of the above examples, you can easily understand how a change in feeling, and the subsequent change in behavior is due to a change in the understandings that are embraced. For this reason, the great beings tell us that understandings always dictate feelings. If you want to change your feeling, you have to change the understandings you reach for and embrace. For this reason, if permanent spiritual growth and wellness are the goals, the understandings you hold are vital.

In Kedarji's Ecology of Well-Being, there are understandings that allow you to go beyond the mind and beyond the senses to what is true, that paradise of the Heart where you embrace and acquire purer understandings of what actually is and what is actually taking place in the moment (from moment to moment), *based on the power that is easily experienced, when all thoughts subside.* This we call Wisdom!

In our Siddha Science, we treat understandings like a good scientist uses a hypothesis. The dictionary definition of 'hypothesis' is (surprisingly) in perfect alignment with our Shakta approach and the understandings of the great mentors of my spiritual and well-being lineages. Here it is:

Hypothesis...

1. a proposition, or set of propositions, set forth as an explanation for the occurrence of some specified group of phenomena, either asserted merely as a provisional conjecture to guide investigation (working hypothesis) or accepted as highly probable in the light of established facts.
2. a proposition assumed as a premise in an argument.
3. the antecedent of a conditional proposition.

The arc of my approach to understandings is based on a group of hypotheses that, in Siddha Science, we refer to as better, more useful understandings – imparted to us by those Sages of steady wisdom who have attained the full awareness of *That* Highest

Power (the energy substratum) that we are seeking to attain, in the fullness of our Humanity. The Arc of this movement of the Divine Consciousness energy is:

1. Understandings always dictate your feelings.
2. How you are vibrating from moment-to-moment is dictated by the feeling you experience in that moment.
3. What you are putting out (projecting or superimposing into Consciousness) immediately begins to attract to you the people, places and things that will reinforce that vibration and cause you to hold other understandings (that will dictate other feelings) that will keep you wedded to whatever state you find yourself in -- by way of the understandings you have been holding, and the subsequent feelings and vibration that manifest out of those understandings.

So, in addressing and increasing Emotional Resilience (Pillar 3), there are methods that I teach for embracing and fully realizing both the principle of *The Arc* and the practice of it. To begin with, in this approach to our Siddha Science, we treat every understanding as an hypothesis, the efficacy for wellness of which must be first proved or disproved in the laboratory of our own day-to-day existence. Knowing, from direct experience, the power of the practice of The Arc, understandings that don't support continued and permanent spiritual growth and wellness (as in total well-being) are discarded and replaced with those that do. *In this way, Emotional Resilience is attained and maintained.*

What You Risk If You Don't Increase Your Emotional Resilience

There is a lot of talk these days about wellness being, in part, dependent upon community and connectedness. Doctors, medical professionals and health and healing practitioners have all jumped on this bandwagon. However, the best way to connect with others is through inner strength – *the inner strength necessary to stand on your Human Dignity and command respect* **by way of knowing your true nature and adjusting your life accordingly.**

Therefore, connectedness *is not* had through dependency. It is reaped and enjoyed by way of inner strength and respect for Human Dignity.

This *inner strength* rises from increased Emotional Resilience *and is what makes community and connectedness truly great*. It allows you the ability to fully express your Humanity but, as a great being in my lineage of spiritual Gurus used to say, from the 'upper story' of the serenity and happiness of the inner Self.

On the other hand, if you lack emotional resilience, you become a slave to your emotions. That is to say that you ride the roller coaster of emotions, moving your emotional 'baggage' from one shoulder to the other and back again – while you allow your ego to convince you that you don't have any emotional baggage!

People who lack emotional resilience and suffer in this way have very restless minds. This is the hallmark of degraded emotional resilience – that it always leads to a poor mental state due to lack of the inner strength necessary to take on life's challenges - and to thrive on such challenges in a way that they make you stronger, while increasing human dignity. Therefore, Emotional Resilience is necessary for an improved mental state that, in turn, relies on increasing The Spiritual Power. I think you see how Kedarji's 4 Pillars of Joy In Daily Living are connected and integrated by necessity, based on harnessing The Spiritual Power.

Again, lack of emotional resilience also equals a poor mental state. When these two conditions begin to collaborate, the result is degraded well-being and poor health.

Vibrant Health

The 4 Pillars of Joy In Daily Living form the foundation of The Ecology of Well-Being and *are also active at the cellular level*. In this section I will present hypotheses and active, dynamic principles of holistic lifestyle medicine and medical science that is based on the new physics (Quantum Physics), to support what has just been stated. That is that

1. The Spiritual Power
2. Improved Mental State
3. Emotional Resilience
4. As well as, Vibrant Health

are active at the cellular level in a way that supports our application of all 4 pillars to attaining vibrant health, as part of long-term, lasting well-being.

Years ago, I had the privilege of serving the community in which I lived during a severe outbreak of sickle cell anemia. 1 in every 3 people in the community had been diagnosed and was suffering from this disease. Local labs were inundated with testing requests and did not have enough pathologists to review the thousands of tests for which a diagnosis had to be formulated.

At the time, my mother was dating a pathologist from one of the local labs where these tests had to be reviewed. He actually lived up the block from us. Due to his workload, he recruited me to help him in the lab. He taught me how to find sickle cell under a microscope, so that he had help in identifying in-vitro samples that required his attention for a diagnosis. So, for several months, I was afforded the experience of studying blood cells under a microscope to identify characteristics and patterns that might indicate the presence of sickle cell anemia. This turned out to be a magnificent experience for me in the universe of cellular biology – an experience that taught me a great deal about the magical world of our cells.

It is based on this experience, among many other similar experiences, that I share this with you now. Connected to vibrant health, it is most useful to think of our cells as *energy transformers*, **as powerful entities that transmit, transduce and transform energy**. In fact, energy transduction, the conveyance of energy from one donor electron, for example, to another (a receptor), changes that class of energy and the very structure of the molecule. This energy is part of a *power source* that must be made to *adapt* to support the function of our physical bodies. In this way, it's useful to think of our cells as our partners in supporting the body's energy needs, so that we can function optimally in the 'nest' that we find ourselves in. **Most importantly, our cells are the most important component of the function of our bodies.** So, for vibrant health, it's urgent that we have a basic understanding of the function and makeup of our cells, *from both the energetic standpoint and the physical/physiological standpoint.*

The Body Is The Temple

With regard to the energetic component, my spiritual Guru taught me that *the body is the temple in which God resides.* Everything I offer connected to vibrant health is offered with this understanding. And who wants to dwell in a broke, filthy (as in diseased) temple? For me and so many others whom I have helped, this understanding has helped me to honor my body in the greatest of ways, as a gift or Blessing of Grace – and to remember that the gift of this body, this nest, is not given us forever – *that we have a finite period of time in which to honor this vehicle that we reside in, to make the best use of our time here.*

Therefore, it certainly pays for us to remember an irrefutable fact that I posited in the opening of this work: **We live on a rock that hangs in a void of space, spinning on an axis in an orbit around a fire ball!** This dwelling place that we call Earth is actually defined by a sacred law that no one here established and that no one here can change. And everything connected to that law, including the configuration of our 'nest' or 'temple,' has an order to it that is subject to a higher principle or energy.

I'm choosing my words carefully here because there is a tendency today, particularly amongst the masses in the West, to refute Siddha Science or any other science that does not have, as its basis, American Science, a.k.a. Yankee ingenuity.

Particularly where vibrant health is concerned, when examining how our cells function, the Science is very clear. There are some 47 trillion cells in our bodies. And there are millions, if not billions of energetic exchanges taking place every moment, in and outside of our cells in tissue and organs. These energy exchanges are part of *signaling* that is constantly taking place by cells, as part of their epigenetic expression (Sheldrake, 2009 (7) – Lipton, 2015, (8), Sayerji, (9), Dotta et al., 2012, (10), Bókkon, et al., 2010, (11)). *Electrons* and *protons* are coupling and uncoupling, for example, at a phenomenal pace. **In others words, energy transmission, transducing and transformation is occurring constantly.**

The Air We Breathe

Here is where I would usually interject an utterance of one

of the Sages of my spiritual heritage (lineage), in order to support my foundational premise that The Spiritual Power (the first of the 4 Pillars) is at the core of even our cellular function. But, before I do, let me offer another example in the accepted Science of it that will make the spiritual point.

The physical body, in order to function at all, let alone optimally, *requires a power source at the cellular level*. Our cells need power *first*, that they use to then act on the nutrients we feed them, to convert those nutrients to the energy our bodies need – without which our bodies could not function.

At the heart of this need on the part of our cells is the necessity to engage the following conversion cycle:

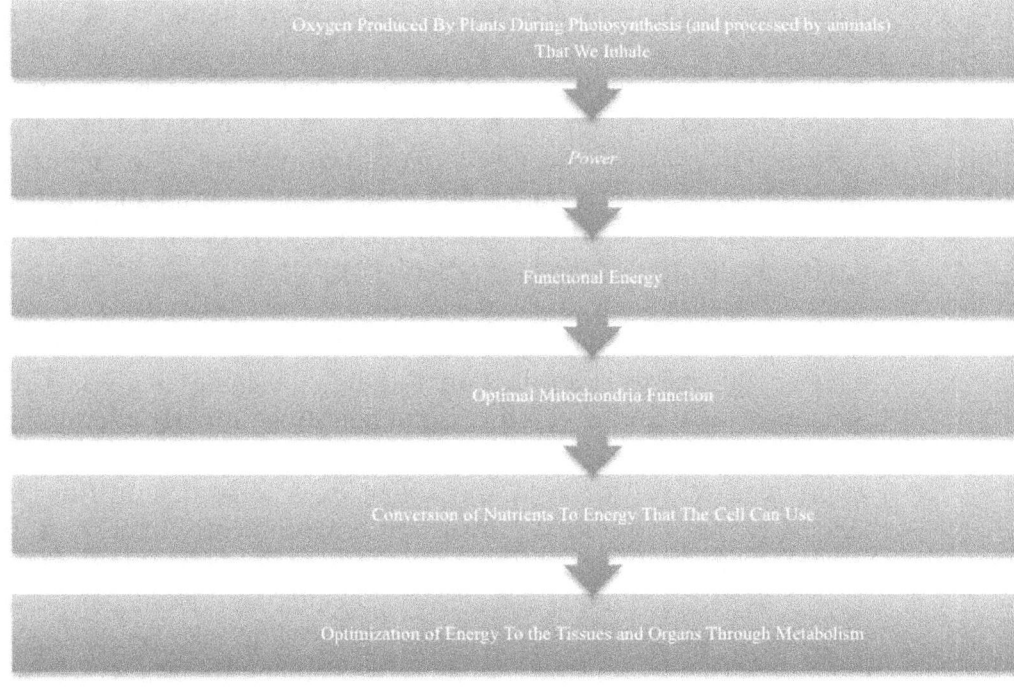

The key is optimal *cellular respiration* within the mitochondria, cytoplasm and cytosol of the cell. Cellular respiration is a set of metabolic reactions and processes that take place inside the cell to convert biochemical energy from nutrients into ATP, after which waste is released and dispensed with.

So, we have the cell burners, the *Mitochondria* that, in the third step above, when functioning optimally, produce 36-38 ATP (Adenosine triphosphate – a cellular chemical needed for cells to function properly to support vibrant health) molecules per cycle, from each glucose molecule. This ensures that the cell is respiring optimally. It occurs as part of *glycolysis* (breakdown of glucose) through OxPhos (Oxidative Phosphorylation).

In other words, cellular respiration is a process whereby, in OxPhos (as opposed to substrate-level phosphorylation using aerobic or anaerobic fermentation – *The Warburg Effect*) (Seyfried, 2012, (12)), energetic transmissions are taking place within the Mitochondria that produce chemical reactions involving electrons, protons and proteins.

In this process, cofactors/coenzymes such as NAD (Nicotinamide adenine dinucleotide is a cofactor found in all living cells) is converted to NADP and NADPH. These are best understood as 'shuttles' for transporting electrons, oxygen, hydrogen and carbon dioxide from the cytoplasm into the Mitochondria. This dynamic, energetic process also initiates homeostasis, of which things like the Krebs cycle (also known as the TCA or citric acid cycle) are a part (Doerr et al, 2014, (13), Krulwich, 2011, plus rap tune video!(14)).

When a cell (and specifically the mitochondria) is not respiring properly through OxPhos, it executes a process of reliance on energy transduction through unhealthy means. This happens by way of the cell that is not respiring properly attempting to stay alive by a process of fermentation (with or without oxygen) to produce ATP. However, this reliance on fermentation (due to lack of proper respiration) creates an environment within the cell that produces ROS.

ROS are reactive oxygen species that are carcinogens and mutations that damage the mitochondria, while also producing a mutation of the cell leading to dysregulated cell growth. Once the cell is mutated, it is now capable of bypassing the immune system's signal for apoptosis (cell death of unhealthy cells) and begins to develop communities of these rogue cells. This is the basis for all chronic health conditions, as well as, metastatic cancer by way of the stimulation of malignant cells. I share this so that you understand what can and does happen when optimal cellular respiration is degraded. So, where does the power come from on which the mitochondria act?

The lung function of pulling in oxygen is required for the Mitochondria to burn sugar (glucose) and remove CO_2 (carbon dioxide), after breaking down the glucose. The Mitochondria in our cells can't burn glucose well without the oxygen that the lungs provide.

The point here is there is an exact Science to the function of our cells. If you reread the above chart, you'll notice that everything starts with *inhalation*, the air we breathe that has been produced by the Calvin Cycle (Koning, 1994, (15)) in plants, due to photosynthesis.

The Calvin cycle has four main components: carbon fixation, reduction phase, carbohydrate formation, and regeneration phase. Energy to fuel chemical reactions in this sugar-generating process is provided by ATP and NADPH, chemical compounds that contain the energy plants have captured from Sunlight. Plants release this energy into the air we breathe. That air is captured by our lungs to provide the ingredient necessary (oxygen) to support OxPhos in the Mitochondria, for proper cell respiration.

Let There Be Light

Indeed, the function of our cells is light-dependent, relying on the plant photosynthesis of light for oxygen. Without our inhalation (and subsequent exhalation even on the part of plants and animals), our cells could not function at all.

Not only is the physical body light-dependent, but science has now proved that our bodies, in particular, our cells are also comprised of Light. This scientific breakthrough comes about through the study of biophotons. The science of Quantum Physics, for example, states we are more than the atoms and molecules that make up our bodies and our cells are actually comprised of Light. The human body emits, communicates with, and is made from Light! Biophotons are emitted by our cells in a pulse or beat pattern. According to the research, they exhibit patterns that are fundamental to the epigenetic expression of our cells. Considering that the human body is light-dependent, relying on the air produced from the photosynthesis in plants that forms our food (food as condensed sunlight), it should be no surprise that our cells transmit light.

Why can't we see this light shooting out of our cells and

body? These biophotons, known as UPEs (ultraweak photon emissions), are emitted in particles of light/waves that are 1,000 times less visible than what our naked eyes can see. They are 380-780 nanometers in size and are only detectable by very sensitive instruments. (Herbert Schwabl, Herbert Klima., 2005, (16)) (Hugo J Niggli, Salvatore Tudisco, Giuseppe Privitera, Lee Ann Applegate, Agata Scordino, Franco Musumeci., 2005, (17) – also see GreenMedInfo.com). Nevertheless, biophoton emissions are connected to energy metabolism and oxidative stress in human tissue and cells. This means that our cells, DNA and Mitochondria use biophotons in the process of cell signaling, *including storing the memory of epigenetic expression between cells.*

This signaling transfer is much faster than chemical diffusion. According to a 2010 study, "Cell to cell communication by biophotons has been demonstrated in plants, bacteria, animal neutrophil granulocytes and kidney cells." (Masaki Kobayashi, Daisuke Kikuchi, Hitoshi Okamura., 2009, (18)). Some researchers have demonstrated that "...different spectral light stimulation (infrared, red, yellow, blue, green and white) at one end of the spinal sensory or motor nerve roots resulted in a significant increase in the biophotonic activity at the other end." This finding suggests that "...light stimulation can generate biophotons that conduct along the neural fibers, probably as neural communication signals."

So, biophotons are photons (light particles) that are generated within the body, and these can also be measured as they emanate from the skin. The subtle, scientific instruments used to measure these light particles were first developed by German researchers. Today, the Chiren is, perhaps, the most sophisticated instrument for assessment and treatment with biophotons. http://www.biophotonsessions.com/Biophoton_Sessions_Chiren.aspx

It uses fiber-optic technology to conduct biophotons to and from the body and it was developed by Johan Boswinkel. This instrument is also being used to treat patients with chronic health conditions. This approach is part of an emerging science known as cellular medicine.

With the biofeedback system of the Chiren, the quality of the light in the body is continually improved. A visual display allows patients to see the immediate effects during treatment and adjust their state of relaxation at the same time. In the 1970s, pioneering German physicist Fritz-Albert Popp developed a method to observe biophotons and began systematic experiments on a fundamental level, which inspired Boswinkel's research on the practical applications of this discovery beginning in the 1980s. Boswinkel made the critical observation that the patterns of coherent and chaotic biophotons displayed by individual cells matched the patterns of electrical resistance at acupuncture points, as described by Dr. Reinhard Voll, the German founder of electroacupuncture in the 1940s.

By way of instruments designed to test the hypotheses set forth by Oriental Medicine on which acupuncture is founded, Voll proved a foundational premise of Oriental Medicine (which has its basis in directing energy to improve cellular respiration); that each acupuncture point corresponds to a different organ. Therefore, Boswinkel developed a device that determines where biophotons in the body are disturbed, based on the electrical response at acupuncture points on the hands and feet. Since that time, other photomultiplier devices and ultra low noise CCD cameras have been developed to measure and replicate biophoton activity. A photomultiplier is a device that converts incident photons into an electrical signal.

The Circadian Output

The human body's metabolism changes in a circadian fashion, in what is likened to a rhythmic cycle occurring every 24 hours. Circadian rhythm is defined as a biological process recurring naturally on a twenty-four-hour cycle, even in the absence of light fluctuations. When measuring these rhythms, it is observed that they are beat patterns that correspond to fluctuations in biophoton emissions. For example, research has mapped out distinct anatomical locations within the body where biophoton emissions are stronger and weaker, depending on the time of the day within this circadian output. So, biophoton emissions are transmitted in a rhythm, like a pulse or beat pattern!

Researchers have concluded that "The spectral data suggest that [biophoton] measurements might well provide quantitative data on the individual pattern of peroxidative and anti-oxidative processes in vivo." These processes are part of cellular respiration in the Mitochondria (see Chapter 2) and cell methylation involved in DNA repair.

The Affect of Meditation and Food On Biophoton Output

According to Greenmedinfo.com, two areas of biophoton research focus on methods that lower the level of free radical reactions occurring in the body, in order to prevent free radical damage. Research has found an oxidative stress-mediated difference in biophoton emission among meditators versus non-meditators. *Those who meditate regularly tend to have lower ultra-weak photon emission (UPE, biophoton emission), resulting in a lower level of free radical reactions.* In one clinical study involving practitioners of transcendental meditation (TM) researchers found: The lowest UPE intensities were observed in two subjects who regularly meditate. Spectral analysis of human UPE has suggested that ultra-weak emission is probably, at least in part, a reflection of free radical reactions in a living system. It has been documented that various physiologic and biochemical shifts follow the long-term practice of meditation and it is inferred that meditation may impact free radical activity. (Eduard P A Van Wijk, Heike Koch, Saskia Bosman, Roeland Van Wijk., 2006, (19)).

Another example involving food are tests done on herbs like rhodiola and other foods high in anti-oxidants that are also known to reduce stress. These foods have been tested clinically and shown to reduce the level of biophotons emitted in human beings. In research conducted on rhodiola, for example, a study published in 2009 in the journal Phytotherapeutic Research found that those who took the herb for 1 week had a significant decrease in photon emission in comparison with the placebo group. (F W G Schutgens, P Neogi, E P A van Wijk, R van Wijk, G Wikman, F A C Wiegant., 2009, (20)).

BIG TAKE AWAY POINT: Modern science, particularly the science aimed at measuring energy transmission inside and outside of cells, continues to substantiate what the Sages of steady wisdom of spiritual lineages have been stating for millennia; We are all energetic beings with the same energy substratum I speak about in Chapters 1 and 2 as the core, the foundation of life and well-being – The Spiritual Power. The science engaged in the study of biophotons is yet another means to substantiate this fact.

ANOTHER BIG TAKE AWAY POINT: No person or entity on this Earth plane has the power to create the air we breathe, without which our cells cannot function. Further, there is a power behind that light that emanates from the Sun, that causes the photosynthesis in plants to occur, thereby providing our cells with the power they need to initiate and maintain their optimal function.

This is a Spiritual Power, part of that energy substratum I spoke of earlier that sets the stage for a sacred law here. Again, we don't need to argue over labels. Whether we call it Nature, a Higher Power or Sacred Law, it is an *energy,* an *independent force* that is a *supreme intelligence* that we cannot change but *can* harness for our well-being – what I refer to as our first Pillar of Total Well-Being – *The Spiritual Power.*

So, even our human cells need a Power source *and the energy substratum, that Highest Power, is that source.* Having stated a little of the widely-accepted biological science that clearly hinges upon *the unseen* (the air we breathe), now I will share additional support of my hypothesis, from the perspective of the spiritual leaders of my lineage.

Ancient Wisdom For Vibrant Health

We are, even at the core of our physical bodies, energetic beings. Everything we rely on for life has an energetic substratum and we all need *power* to function here. It is said in Science that a good hypothesis is one that can explain most of the observations associated with any phenomenon. If the hypothesis cannot be rejected or disproved, and is supported by a broad range of experimental and experiential observations, then it becomes a theory and even a guiding principle.

So, the Sages of steady wisdom who have led so many spiritually have also spoken at great length about the energy substratum that supports all of life in form here. For example, in the Shaiva Agamas (sacred texts of my spiritual heritage) there are many utterances of the Sages of my lineage, referencing this energy substratum. One of them is taken from the Spanda Karikas and states the following:

Yataḥ karaṇâ-vargo 'yaṁ vimūḍho 'mūḍhavat svayam/
Sahāntareṇa cakreṇa pravṛtti-sthiti-saṁhṛtīḥ// 6

Labhate tatprayatnena parīkṣyaṁ tattvam ādarāt/
Yataḥ svatantratā tasya sarvatreyam akṛtrimā// 7

"The Spanda Principle prevails everywhere with total freedom and independence. This total freedom and independence causes the group of senses, though insentient and without power, to act as a sentient force by merging with objects, taking pleasure in their sustenance, and by withdrawing those very objects. For this reason, Spanda (the energy substratum of all things) should be examined with great care and reverence." (Ksemaraja/Singh, et al., 2001, 16).

And from the commentary on the opening invocation that defines *Spanda*; "Spanda, Vibration of Divine Consciousness or the ceaseless pulse of Divine Consciousness; the slight or subtle movement of Divine Consciousness that is the foundation for the gross manifestation of the elements inside and out; the Wheel of Energies that ceaselessly manifests, sustains and withdraws (recycles) this entire Universe." (Ksemaraja/Singh, et al., 2001, 17)

In Shaivism (not the Shaivism as defined by Google and Wikipedia, but the Shaivism handed down in the oral tradition of the enlightened Masters), which is a very exact spiritual science based on a centuries-old examination of the energy substratum, there are many references to this Spanda as being a Highest Power. These references include that this power emanates first as *Light* and then as sound, to then manifest, for example, the sensory function of inhalation by which our cells are powered – a *light-dependent* process, as I stated above from biology 101!

In so many of these same Shaiva Agamas, there are utterances about Prakasha, the *Light* of Divine Consciousness or Shakti (the energy substratum), and how this light then produces sound, connected to the two aspects of this energy substratum discussed earlier in this section. So, this Light that we know is the power source for the Calvin Cycle (photosynthesis in plants) that provides us with the oxygen (air) that we inhale to produce the power our cells need to function, *is an important, scientific recognition to be aware of*. It is the foundation for the hypothesis I present here regarding the first pillar of The Spiritual Power being completely active and applicable at the cellular level.

Indeed, proponents of Western/American Science will find (and have found) that their treatises are not unlike the Yoga Science of my spiritual lineage. I think you will see that the two are also in support of each other *where vibrant health is concerned.*

Modern Wisdom For Vibrant Health

The dawn of Quantum Physics, and its branch of science known as Quantum Mechanics, has gone a very long way to debunking the old Newtonian theory of matter and life, on which until fairly recently, even medical science in the West has been based. In my view, this began with the theories put forth by Albert Einstein that are now widely accepted as underlying, guiding principles of all of science, along with the philosophy of science. Quantum Physics actually 'fills in the blanks' of what science misses *when only focusing on the material and ignoring the unseen, energy substratum that produces the material manifestation.*

It all began with Einstein's theory of relativity and his hypothesis, based on E=MC squared (matter multiplied by the speed of light, squared). This hypothesis, coupled with his theory of relativity, is now the basis for Quantum Physics, and its branch of Quantum Mechanics that is charged with analyzing the physics at the level of specific phenomenon.

To simplify, over a period of many years, the Science of Quantum Physics has presented some startling discoveries that set in motion other now widely accepted sciences such as *Epigenetics* (it means 'control above genetics'), the growing body of work coming out of the *Human Genome Project*, the ENCODE Project (Encyclopedia of DNA Elements), among others. And don't forget that the application of Quantum Mechanics is directly responsible for the development of computers, TVs, CAT scans, cell phones, laser technology and rocket ships. Most importantly, in the context of the activity of our cells, Quantum Physics offers us the following, valuable principles (now proved, in my view):

- The notion of atoms being the smallest particle in the Universe (Newtonian theory on which standard science and medicine is based) has been scientifically debunked by the discovery that the atom itself is made up of even smaller, subatomic elements.
- Atoms emit various energies such as x-rays and radioactivity.
- Atoms and their respective molecules are actually made up of vortices of energy. This fact has caused physicists to

- abandon the Newtonian theory of a Universe that is only material, because they have come to realize matter as an illusion, now recognizing that everything in the Universe is made out of energy.
- These atoms (molecules), when observed closely with today's subtler, scientific instruments, are seen to be like spinning tops that *radiate* their own identifying energy patterns.
- Every material structure has an *energy* that is the *substratum* of its compound makeup.
- These energy vortices are known as Quarks and Photons and they comprise *the energy substratum*, the *energy signature* of all atoms. In other words, they are the very structure of all atoms (molecules).
- Matter can, simultaneously, be defined as a solid particle and an immaterial, force field wave.
- Atoms and their subatomic particles are made out of invisible energy.
- Therefore, Quantum Physics puts forth the very viable premise that, as physicists focus on the structure of atoms, as the surface of that structure comes nearer (under a microscope, for example), what is observed is a physical void. *The atom has no physical structure*.
- Atoms are the building blocks of everything in our material existence, including our bodies.
- The movement of protein molecules at the cellular level comprises how the body is sustained. The laws of Quantum Physics, not Newtonian law, explain a molecule's life-generating movements.
- These material substances appear 'out of thin air,' a way of saying that they appear out of the energy vortices, knowledge of which is supported by Quantum Physics and Quantum Mechanics. (Lipton, 2015, (18), Pagels, 1982, (19), Hackermueller, 2003, (20), Chapman, 1995, (21) Henry, 2005 (22))

All of the above applies to every cell in the human body, as all our cells are comprised of atoms. So, we have to start here in coming to a basic understanding of our cells. Because, with respect to vibrant health, **the cell is the single most important 'player' in**

the phenomenon known as the human body. And, if you don't fix the cell, you'll never get well and stay well. For these reasons, it's important to have a basic understanding of the energy substratum of our cells.

The Sages of my spiritual lineage all speak of a highest power or energy, sometimes referred to as Shakti or Spanda or Divine Conscious Energy or energy substratum of everything. In their utterances, *they refer to this energy as being the power beyond all other powers*, on which our perception and experience of power (energy) in the mundane sense is based (Ksemaraja/Vasuguptacharya/Singh et al., 2001, (23)). Further, they state that this power or highest energy is both the cause and the effect, being the substratum of all mundane life in this place.

This is not unlike the theories, principles and evidence-based research coming out of the cutting edge sciences I have mentioned above. Even the newer sciences connected to cellular and molecular biology, stem cell research and the holistic treatment of cancer, heart disease, diabetes and obesity, *using food as medicine,* are in alignment with the principle of an energy substratum, as stated above. My own spiritual leader once said that modern science would, one day, catch up to and support the findings of ancient Sages of Siddha Science. I see this manifesting in so many ways today.

What About Improved Mental State and Our Cells?

All living organisms must receive and interpret environmental signals to stay alive. In this regard, the survival and health of our cells is directly related to the speed and efficiency of signaling or signal transfer. This signaling involves foundational, biological processes that must take place efficiently at the cellular level. These processes include things like the exchange of electrons and protons (ETC – electron transport chain), synthesis of proteins, production of sufficient ATP (see earlier in this section), optimal mitochondrial respiration, apoptosis (cell death of unhealthy cells), autophagy (the recycling of cells scheduled for apoptosis for reusable parts of the cell and to release the rest as waste) and a host of other functions to build healthy molecules within the body.

As mentioned earlier, in the dark matter of our DNA (the non-encoding RNA) there is also signaling taking place between Integral Membrane Proteins (effector and receptor proteins), the cytosol and organelles in the cytoplasm of the cell. As we know from the science of Epigenetics, this signaling is impacted by the environmental signaling mentioned above. This environmental signaling includes:

- Stress.
- A restless mind.
- Emotional imbalances connected to stress and other factors, due to lack of Emotional Resilience.
- Environmental toxins that we inseminate such as industrial cleaning chemicals, home cleaning solvents, EMF or electro-magnetic radiation in our environment, etc.
- Food toxins (of which there are many in the standard American diet).
- Exposure to GMO foods and GE (genetically engineered) organisms in foods and the environment.
- Lack of restful sleep.
- Extended use of over-the-counter medications.
- The side-effects and carcinogenic components of many pharmaceutical drugs.

This is a partial list and anyone one of these or combination of these impacts signaling at the cellular level, to degrade that signaling. You'll notice that a restless mind is on the above list, as well as, stress. A restless mind breeds stress and things connected to stress like anxiety, doubt, fear (the foundation for stress), frustration, worry, cynicism, sarcasm, anger and depression. So, without an improved mental state that first arrests the restless mind, cell signaling is degraded and important cellular functions like cellular respiration and apoptosis are downregulated. There is, in fact, a delicate ecology to cell signaling that can be nurtured, by way of optimal signaling both inside and outside the cell.

What About Emotional Resilience and Our Cells?

When we ride the emotional roller coaster, we increase stress exponentially. Today, medical science has placed stress very high up on the list of causes of chronic health conditions and disease. It is also a major factor in upregulating oncogenes and tumors. This is due to the direct impact lack of Emotional Resilience has on cell signaling. For example, in Oriental

Medicine, Ayurveda, Eastern and Asian Medicine, anger has been recognized for centuries as having the ability to cause cancer. Again, this is due to the direct impact that stress has on cell signaling *when you lack Emotional Resilience.*

So, what has been stated in the previous section also applies here. For these reasons, Nityananda Shaktipat Yoga integrates that aspect of our Siddha Science that directly addresses well-being, by way of our Total Well-Being approach.

REFERENCES

1. Lipton, B. H, 2015, The Biology of Belief, Hay House
2. Howell, E., 2017, Einstein's Theory of Special Relativity, https://www.space.com/36273-theory-special-relativity.html
3. Kedarji, Shenoy G. 2007, The Chidakasha Gita with commentary by Kedarji, The Endless One, Supreme Meditation
4. Lamb, R., 2013, What does Einstein's famous equation really mean?, https://science.howstuffworks.com/science-vs-myth/everyday-myths/einstein-formula.htm
5. Lipton, B. H, 2015, The Biology of Belief, Hay House
6. Lipton, B. H, 2015, The Biology of Belief, Hay House
7. Sheldrake, R., 2009, Morphic Resonance, Park Street Press
8. Lipton, B. H, 2015, The Biology of Belief, Hay House
9. Sayer Ji, 2013, Biophotons: The Human Body Emits, Communicates with, and is Made from Light, GreenMedInfo.com
10. B T Dotta, K S Saroka, M A Persinger. Increased photon emission from the head while imagining light in the dark is correlated with changes in electroencephalographic power: support for Bókkon's biophoton hypothesis. Neurosci Lett. 2012 Apr 4 ;513(2):151-4. Epub 2012 Feb 17. PMID: 22343311
11. I Bókkon, V Salari, J A Tuszynski, I Antal. Estimation of the number of biophotons involved in the visual perception of a single-object image: biophoton intensity can be considerably higher inside cells than outside. J Photochem Photobiol B. 2010 Sep 2 ;100(3):160-6. Epub 2010 Jun 10. PMID: 20584615
12. Seyfried, T., 2012, Cancer As A Metabolic Disease, A John Wiley & Sons, Inc.
13. Doerr A., 2014, The Citric Acid Cycle, khanacademy.org
14. Krulwich R., 2011, Lord, Save Me From The Krebs Cycle,

https://www.npr.org/sections/krulwich/2011/09/14/140428189/lord
-save-me-from-the-krebs-cycle?sc=fb&cc=fp

15. Koning R. E., Openstax College, 1994, The Calvin Cycle,
https://www.khanacademy.org/science/biology/photosynthesis-in-
plants/the-calvin-cycle-reactions/a/calvin-cycle

16. Herbert Schwabl, Herbert Klima. Spontaneous ultraweak
photon emission from biological systems and the endogenous light
field. Forsch Komplementarmed Klass Naturheilkd. 2005
Apr;12(2):84-9. PMID: 15947466

17. Hugo J Niggli, Salvatore Tudisco, Giuseppe Privitera, Lee Ann
Applegate, Agata Scordino, Franco Musumeci. Laser-ultraviolet-
A-induced ultraweak photon emission in mammalian cells. J
Biomed Opt. 2005 Mar-Apr;10(2):024006. PMID: 15910080

18. Masaki Kobayashi, Daisuke Kikuchi, Hitoshi Okamura.
Imaging of ultraweak spontaneous photon emission from human
body displaying diurnal rhythm. PLoS One. 2009;4(7):e6256.
Epub 2009 Jul 16. PMID: 19606225

19. Eduard P A Van Wijk, Heike Koch, Saskia Bosman, Roeland
Van Wijk. Anatomic characterization of human ultra-weak photon
emission in practitioners of transcendental meditation(TM) and
control subjects. J Altern Complement Med. 2006 Jan-
Feb;12(1):31-8. PMID: 16494566

20. F W G Schutgens, P Neogi, E P A van Wijk, R van Wijk, G
Wikman, F A C Wiegant. The influence of adaptogens on
ultraweak biophoton emission: a pilot-experiment. Phytother Res.
2009 Aug;23(8):1103-8. PMID: 19170145

21. Ksemaraja/Singh, et al., 2001, Spanda Karikas. The Divine
Creative Pulsation, Motilal Banarsidass Pvt. Ltd.

22. Ksemaraja/Singh, et al., 2001, Spanda Karikas. The Divine
Creative Pulsation, Motilal Banarsidass Pvt. Ltd.

23. Lipton, B. H, 2015, The Biology of Belief, Hay House

24. Pagels, H.R., 1982, The Cosmic Code: Quantum Physics As
The Language of Nature. Simon and Schuster

25. Hackermueller, L.S., 2003, Wave Nature of Biomolecules and
Fluorofullerenes, Physical Review Letters 91(9): 090408-1

26. Chapman, M.S., 1995, Optics and Interferometry With Na2
Molecules, Physical Review Letters 74(24): 4783-4786

27. Henry, R.C., 2005, The Mental Universe. Nature, 436:29

28. Ksemaraja/Singh, et al., 2001, Spanda Karikas. The Divine
Creative Pulsation, Motilal Banarsidass Pvt. Ltd.

Glossary

Simple Pronunciation Table

Below we have selected common transliteration from Sanskrit vowels and consonants and given you an English word that will aid you in its proper pronunciation. Please see the glossary for further information.

a	as in cup.
ā	as in father.
i	as in fill or lily.
ī	as in seen.
u	as in full.
ū	as in rude.
ṛi	as in written.
ṛī	as in marine.
e	as in cave.
c	as in church.
ai	as in aisle.
o	as in stone.
au	as in house.
ś	as in sure.
ṣ	as in shun or bush
s	as in saint.
d	as in the th in gather.

The following is a glossary of Sanskrit terms most frequently used in this book, as they appear in Roman type: śaktipāta, for example, appears as shaktipat; sādhana is written as sadhana, etc. Due to challenges with special character printing when going to press, we were not able to use the standard international transliteration scheme for the transliteration from the Sanskrit language throughout the book. Romanized vowels and consonants have been substituted instead. The pronunciation table above will help with the correct pronunciation for some of the words and terms in this book that appear below with their correct pronunciation.

Ābhāsa
a manifestation of God; an appearance tied to something greater.

Adityas
the 12 suns representing the Perfect "I" Consciousness of God; the vision of prakasa, Shiva's light, bestowed in the state of Purnaham Vimarsha.

Āgama
a scripture; a sacred text.

Āstra
a specific power taking the form of a weapon or symbol for protection, healing and the destruction of evil and ignorance.

Āsāna
seat; a specific yoga posture; a common seated posture for meditation with legs crossed.

Bābā
an affectionate term given a Sadguru or spiritual Master: literally means father.

Bhāvana
emotion; a feeling of absorption; identification with an aspect of divine consciousness; a spiritual attitude.

Bhairavī Mudrā
Shiva mudra; a specific mudra expressing the state of Liberation contained in Shiva where everything and everyone is seen as that same light of Consciousness that is God; see "mudra" below.

Bindi
point; a representation of the transcendental and immanent aspects of Divine Consciousness; an expression of Shiva's Vimarsha aspect.

Brahmarandra
the subtle spiritual energy center at the top of the head; see "sahasrar" below.

Cakra (pronounced Chakra)
a subtle spiritual energy center.

Dhārāna
a contemplation; a specific focus designed to experience the Self.

Dharma
righteousness; essential duty; the act of supporting and following the Truth.

Darshan
a vision of the Absolute; a vision of God or a saint or siddha; being in the

presence a Siddha or a holy person in a way that causes you to experience your own Divinity.

Dikśa (pronounced Diksha)
the spiritual awakening that occurs upon receipt of Shaktipat; spiritual or religious initiation imparted by a Shakta Adept or Sadguru.

Guru
literally, from darkness to light; a spiritually-perfected Master or Shakta Adept who leads you from the darkness of spiritual ignorance to the light of God; a spiritual companion and mentor.

Guru Gītā
a morning chant, comprised of passages from the Sri Guru Charitra, the Puranas and other scriptures.

Hṛidaya
(pronounced "ridaya") heart; the heart of God; the heart chakra; sahasrar.

Iccā (pronounced Icchaa)
(pronounced "itchaa") divine will; the immanent aspect of divine will at work in humankind; the first of Shiva's three divine powers.

Iśā (pronounced Ishaa)
another name for Shiva.

Jīvanmukta
one who is completely liberated while still in the body; a Self-realized being; the state of Purnaham Vimarsha.

Jñāna
(pronounced "gynaana") knowledge of the inner Self; direct knowledge that rises spontaneously from within when one becomes Self-realized.

Jñānī
(pronounced "gynaanee") one who has direct knowledge of the Supreme Principle or the Self; a jivanmukta.

Kashmir
(pronounced "cashmere") a region in Northern India where many sages and saints of the Shaivite tradition have lived.

Kavacha
a piece of armor or a medallion worn around the neck or on the chest.

Kedār (Kedārji)

the name given to the author, by his Master. The name Kedār is a reference to Lord Kedār, a manifestation of Shiva in the moment that he has just risen from meditation to offer Shiva's Blessings. It is also a reference to one of the holiest and most revered shrines to Shiva on the planet, Kedārnath at Kedārā and also refers to Kedārā Ganga, a place in the Ganges river where people go to perform oblations to Lord Shiva. The word "Kedār" is divided into two syllables, "Ke" and "dār." In the first syllable, the "e" in "Ke," is pronounced just like the "a" in "cave." The "d" in the second syllable, "dar," is pronounced like the "th" in "gather" and the "a" in "dār" is pronounced like the "a" in "father."

Kumbhaka

retention of the breath at Prana or Apana. The breath stops spontaneously or is consciously stopped in order to direct Kundalini Shakti upwards into the Sahasrar at the top of the head. This is not merely holding your breath. The effect is not the same. Kumbaka should not be attempted without the instruction of a siddha. When done correctly with practice, the Bliss of the Absolute is experienced in its fullness.

Kriyā

spontaneous bodily movements (often experienced during meditation and chanting) that result from the purifying activity of Kundalini Shakti after the receipt of Shaktipat; the sudden welling-up of emotions and unrecognized leanings and tendencies that surface as a result of the purifying activity of Kundalini Shakti after the receipt of Shaktipat and during the Kriyā process.

Mahāpuruṣa

another name for Shiva.

Mahāsamādhi

the passing of a liberated, Self-realized being from the body. Such a being is not reborn again. Instead, a liberated sage takes Mahāsamādhi. In Mahāsamādhī, the subtle body (sushumna) does not leave the physical body at death to take another form. It remains in the body. The breath does not leave the body either (as is typical at death). It flows to the Sahasrār and remains there.

Mudrā

an advanced Hatha Yoga technique for retaining the Prana in the body to direct it upward into sahasrar, a symbolic gesture or movement that expresses various inner states of meditation and contemplation. Many saints and siddhas can be seen in these mudras granting benediction.

Murtī
statue; a statue of a deity, saint or siddha that has been infused with Shakti through a ceremony known as Pranaprathistha.

Pradākśina
(pronounced "pradaakshina") circumambulation of a statue of a deity, saint or siddha as part of a sacred ceremony or in a devotional gesture; inner darshan resulting from remembrance of God or the Master.

Prakāśa
(pronounced "prakaasha") the light of Shiva or God; the light of the universe from which all of creation springs; Shiva's transcendental aspect; light symbolic of the Absolute.

Prānam
to bow to a living Master, Sadguru or murti in an expression of egolessness and reverence; to have darshan of the Self by placing the head below the heart; a gesture of devotion and respect that disciples of certain traditions offer each other by bowing their heads to each other in reverence; the practice of engaging humility by bowing down to the Master.

Sādhāna
spiritual practice under the guidance of a Shakta Adept or living Master that begins after the descent of Grace through Shaktipāt.

Sahasrār
the subtle spiritual energy center at the top of the head; see "brahmarandra" above.

Śaktī
(pronounced "shaktee") the immanent or active aspect of Shiva that is responsible for the creation of the universe; spiritual energy that takes the form of the body and all objects and places; the spiritual energy inside a human being that lays dormant in three-and-a-half folds at the base of the spine until awakened by the Shakta Adept; the energy responsible for the creation, sustenance and withdrawal of the universe. This energy becomes the letters of the alphabet so that language can come into being in order for the creation to be sustained; the cause of everything that exists and everything that does not exist; the inner Guru; God.

Śāmbhu
(pronounced "shaambhoo") another name for Shiva.

279

Samādhi

a state of pure bliss in which there are no thoughts in the mind whatsoever; the nirvikalpa state arrived at in meditation; the final state of liberation in which the yogi experiences God in everything and everyone, everywhere.

Seva

Also Guruseva; selfless service to the Master and to God; service done out of love for God and humanity; any work done with the understanding that it is God who is doing the work and God who is being served as a result; work done as an offering to God, to the Master or to others, without any concern for what you will get in return; supreme dispassion while engaged in action; work done in the absence of limited desire.

Śiva

(pronounced "shiva") the absolute; divine consciousness; the supreme or perfect "I" consciousness of God; Brahman; the highest God-principle; the Guru principle; the primordial Guru or being; the first Guru; the blue being; nileshwara.

Śivārātri

(pronounced "shiva raatree") (also known as Maha Shivaratri) the celebration to Shiva that occurs each year in the dark half (waning half) of the moon cycle February to March. This is a time of great celebration and of great spiritual intensity where one repetition of the mantras Hamsa or Om Namah Shivaya is worth a thousand repetitions at any other time.

Spanda

universal creative vibration; divine energy of consciousness or the ceaseless pulse of divine consciousness; the slight or subtle movement of divine consciousness that is the foundation for the gross movement of the elements inside and out; the wheel of energies that ceaselessly creates, maintains and withdraws (recycles) this entire universe; one's own inner essence.

Suṣumṇā

(pronounced "sushumnaa") the subtle body containing the individual soul, it is this body that moves from one physical body to another at the time of death and rebirth; the central channel or nadi known as the "city of eight" because it houses the individual intellect, the mind and the ego, along with the 5 senses. It is this subtle body that contains all of the latent impressions, notions and past/present karmas. After Shaktipāt, Kundālinī Shakti goes about purifying this central channel in order to remove these vasanas entirely. The chakras are also housed in this subtle body.

Svāha
a mantra intoned during a sacrificial offering usually made during a fire ceremony; an offering made to the yajna fire.

Tandra
a state of meditation in which all body consciousness is lost and visions and premonitions are experienced; a state in which the yogi can see the past, present and future.

Trika
(pronounced "tricka") meaning three; a reference to the divine God-principle of Shiva-Shakti-Nara (the absolute, his active aspect and the individual bound soul); a reference to the Advaita (non-dualistic) branch of Shaivism; also a reference to three of Shiva's powers, Iccha (divine will), Jnana (divine knowledge), and kriya (action).

Vasana
a latent impression, notion, thought or desire that is responsible for creating present and future Karma; traces of past karmas that shape one's thinking in the present and future. One of the goals of spiritual practice is to remove these vasanas from the sushumna so that they can no longer create more Karma for the yogi.

Vedās
the four ancient Hindu scriptures that contain treatises for daily spiritual, mystical teachings of the sages, practice, codes for religious practice and proper social conduct; instructions for sacred ceremonies and sacrificial rites that include mantras, prayers and chants; the four Vedas are Rig Veda, Yajur Veda, Sama Veda and Atharva Veda.

Vikalpa
a thought, thought construct, notion or seed of thought that sets up a chain reaction of thinking; various perceptions that rise and dissolve constantly.

Vimarśa
(pronounced "vimarsha") Shiva's active aspect; Spanda Shakti; the force or energy responsible for the creation, sustenance and withdrawal of all forms of existence; God's divine power.

Yajña

(pronounced "ya-gyna") a sacred fire ceremony conducted to make offerings to God and to change the vibration of energies on the planet

Yogī

a spiritual aspirant who engages in spiritual practice for the purpose of having a direct and personal experience of God; a liberated or God-realized being; a siddha.

Bibliography

Maharaj, Jnaneshwar. Amritanubhava. Wisconsin: Lotus Light Publications, 1997

Maharaj, Jnaneshwar. Jnaneshwari. Volume 1. Bangalore, India: Blackie & Son Publishers, 1969

Maharaj, Jnaneshwar. Jnaneshwari. Volume 2. Bangalore, India: Blackie & Son Publishers, 1969

Singh, Jaideva. VijnanaBhairava. Delhi, India: Motilal Banarsidass, 1979

Prabhavananda, Swami and Fredercik Manchester. The Upanishads. Madras, India: Sri Ramakrishna Math

Vidyaratna, Taranatha, and M.P. Pandit. Kularnava Tantra. Delhi, India: Motilal Banarsidass, 1965

Vasuguptacharya, and Ksemaraja and Jaideva Singh. Spanda-Karikas. Delhi, India: Motilal Banarsidass, 1980

Vasuguptacharya, and Ksemaraja and Jaideva Singh. Siva Sutras. Delhi, India: Motilal Banarsidass, 1979

Ksemaraja and Jaideva Singh. Pratyabhijnahrdayam. Delhi, India: Motilal Banarsidass, 1987

Venkatesananda, Swami. The Concise Yoga Vasistha. New York: State University of New York Press, 1984

Utpaladevacharya. Meditations On Shiva, The Shivastotravali of Utpaladeva. New York: State University of New York Press, 1995

Prabhavananda, Swami. Narada's Way of Divine Love. The Bhakti Sutras. California: Vedanta Press, 1971

Shankara and Swami Prabhavananda. Shankara's Crest Jewel of Discrimination (Viveka-Chudamani). California: Vedanta Press, 1975

Kabir and Rabindranath Tagore. Songs of Kabir. New York: Samuel Weiser, Inc., 1915

Foster, Titus. Agaram Bagaram Baba. Life, Teachings and Parables – A Spiritual Biography of Baba Prakashananda. California: North Atlantic Books, 1999

Abhinavagupta and Jaideva Singh. Paratrisika-Vivarana. The Secret of Tantric Mysticism. Delhi, India: Motilal Banarsidass, 1988

www.ingramcontent.com/pod-product-compliance
Lightning Source LLC
Chambersburg PA
CBHW060902120626
46553CB00001B/173